This book is dedicated to our communities and ancestors
who gave us such a rich and diversified heritage.

Miles of Mules, History with a Colorful Kick
ISBN 0.9742944.0.3

Written by: Rayne R. Schnabel
              Elisabeth Flynn, Carole Hurst, Amy Lent
              Amy Ambler, Mark Demko, Norman Girardot and Laurie Stoudt
              Bob Curry, Donna M. Wench
              Elizabeth Orlemann
              K. Bailey Fucanan

Edited, Designed and Produced by: Oxford Communications team members K. Bailey Fucanan, Heather R. Kolesa
                            and Heather L. Roche
Photography by: Ryan Hulvat

First Edition: October 2003
Printed by: Progress Printing
Copyrighted 2003 by The Delaware & Lehigh National Heritage Corridor

Miles of Mules

2003

HISTORY WITH A COLORFUL KICK

C★NTENTS

INTRODUCTION

THE MULES

ARTISTS AT W★RK

...mastering
the art of visual
storytelling...

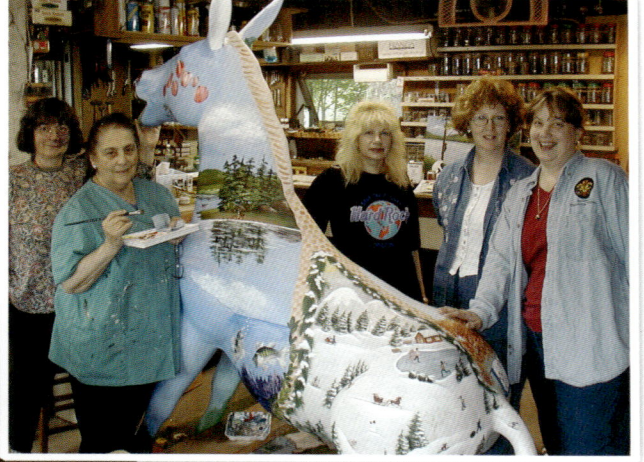

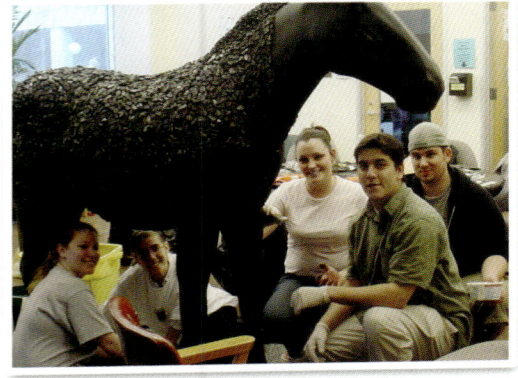

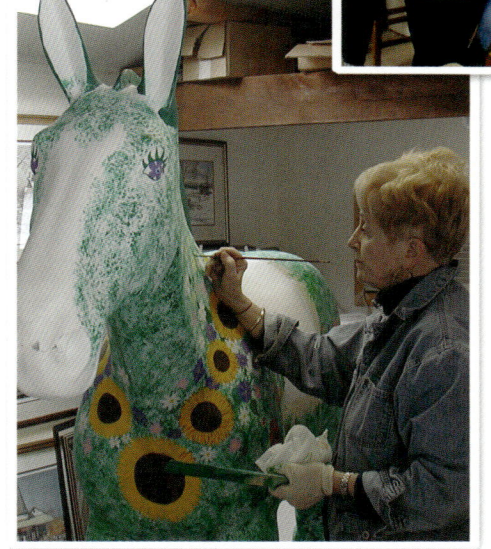

...bringing out
the creativity in
everyone...

...a learning experience
for artists of all ages...

…twenty-mule
teamwork…

…a vibrant
celebration of
history…

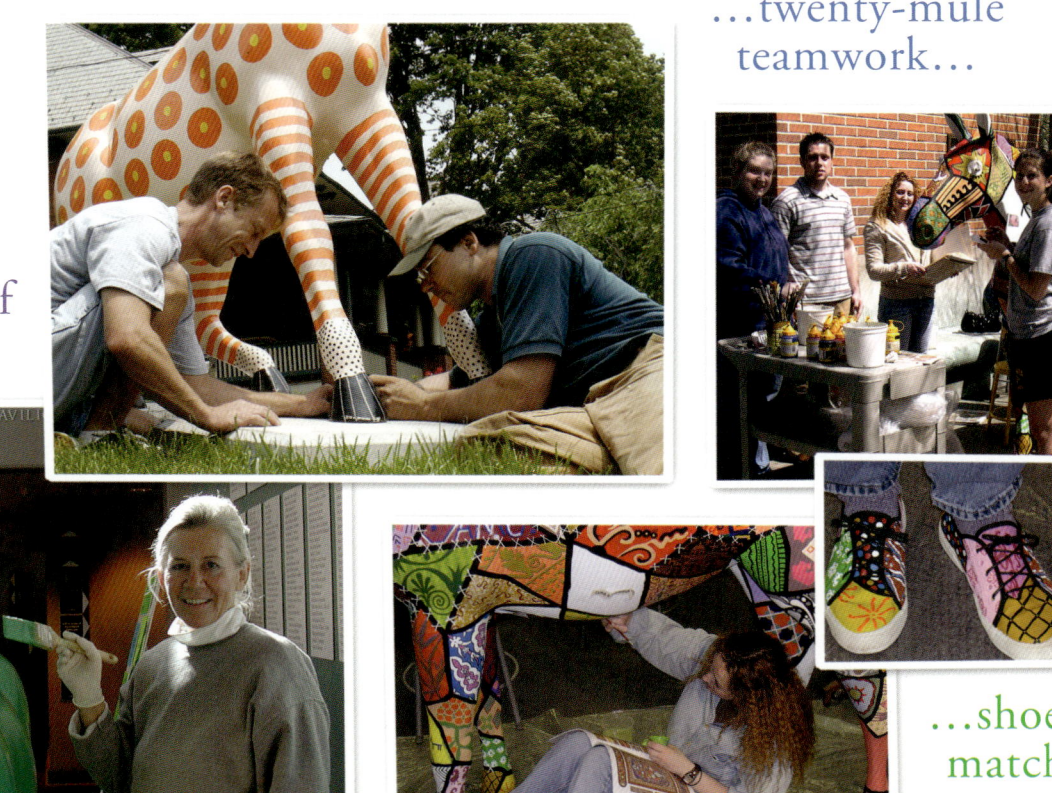

…shoes to
match…

…a technicolor labor of love…

ABOUT THE PH★TOGRAPHER

Coffee cups and candy wrappers littered photographer Ryan Hulvat's car in the aftermath of his trek along the Delaware & Lehigh National Heritage Corridor to shoot the 175 mules of this project. Based in Allentown, Hulvat drove more than 1,000 miles to digitally capture these dazzling creatures, completing the two-month mission just in time for the birth of his son, Ryan Walker.

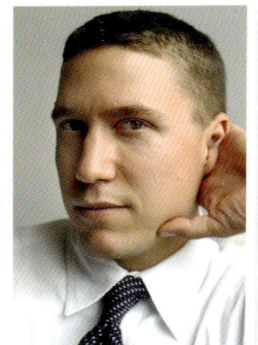

Ryan Hulvat

"I shot dozens of different angles and perspectives of the mules, trying to really capture their sense of place," he said. "I wanted to approach this unique art form with a fresh eye, so whenever possible I incorporated the grandeur of the local architecture or the greenery that surrounded each mule."

Hulvat said he met interesting locals and tourists in the towns and rural areas along the corridor. "It was so interesting to hear how the mules affected these people. And all so uniquely. I met retired couples and moms and their children who were traveling to see every one of them."

Images of Pennsylvania and its people have been Hulvat's bailiwick for the past decade, working with a variety of corporate and advertising clients. His photos have been featured in Lehigh Valley Magazine,

"I wanted to approach this unique art form with a fresh eye…"

Chesapeake Life and NJ Monthly. Last year, Hulvat was named the official photographer for Musikfest, a renowned international festival of music and culture held annually in Bethlehem.

Hulvat's studio is located at 930 North 4th St. in Allentown. His website is www.ryanhulvat.com.

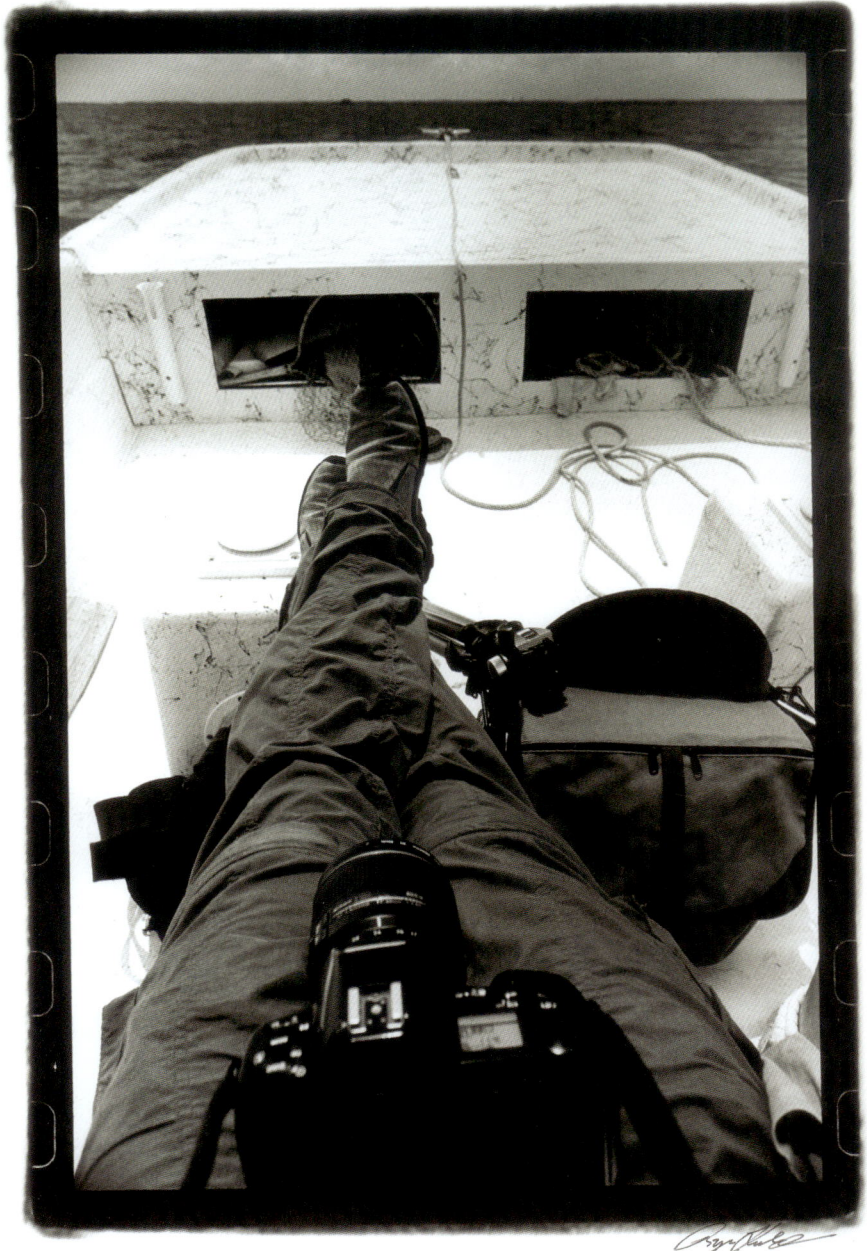

A B O U T   T H E   P R★J E C T

Miles of Mules is a public art project modeled after the successful **Cows on Parade** exhibit introduced in Zurich, Switzerland, several years ago. Since then, the idea has been replicated in many cities throughout the world with a wide variety of animals, including dogs, horses, and even fish.

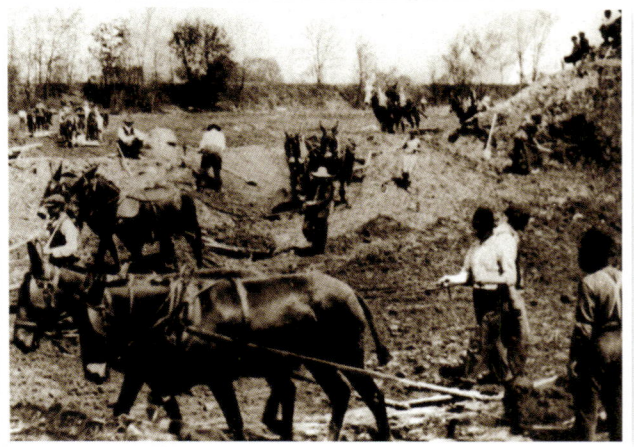

Miles of Mules expanded the idea to bring together the expressive power of art and the richness of history. The mule, a lively hybrid created by mating a horse with a donkey, was chosen to stand as a symbol of eastern Pennsylvania's heritage and thus the figurehead for this project.

The 19th century witnessed coal mines, canals and farms flourishing in Bucks, Northampton, Lehigh, Carbon, Luzerne, and Lackawanna Counties in Pennsylvania and New Jersey towns along the Delaware River. Mules were right there alongside the workers from day one. It was primarily anthracite coal that fueled industry in the area and it was the coal business that capitalized upon the strengths of the mule.

Mules pulled the mine cars and towed the canal boats, bringing coal from the ground to the surface and from the surface to the markets of Philadelphia and New York. Before the advent of mechanized trains and coal cars, mules provided all the power.

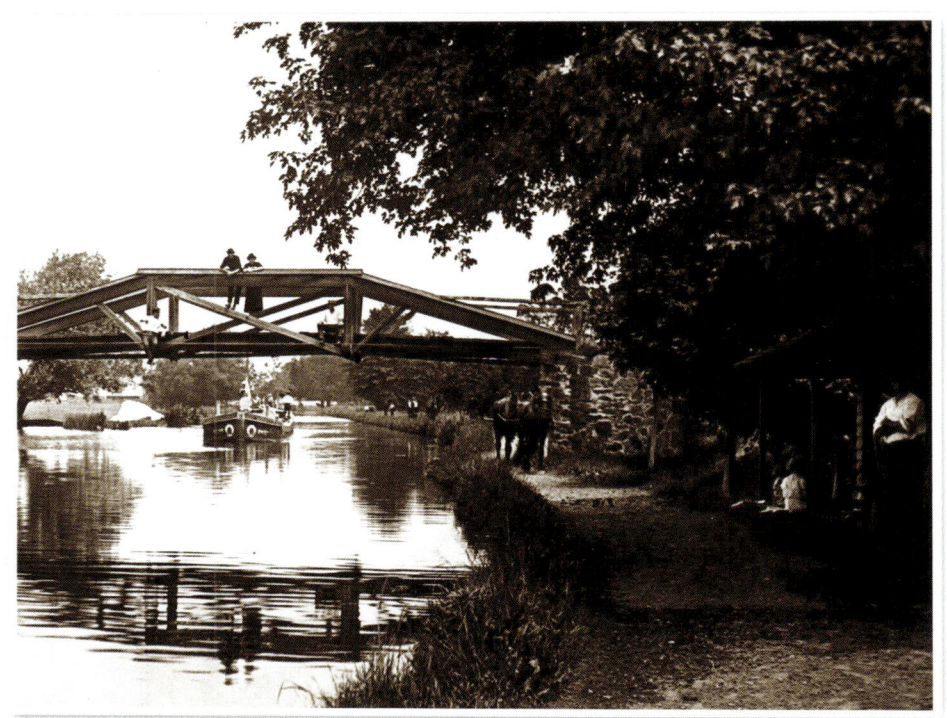

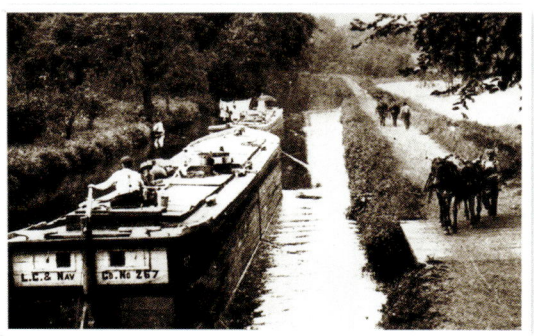

"Mules were right there alongside the workers from day one."

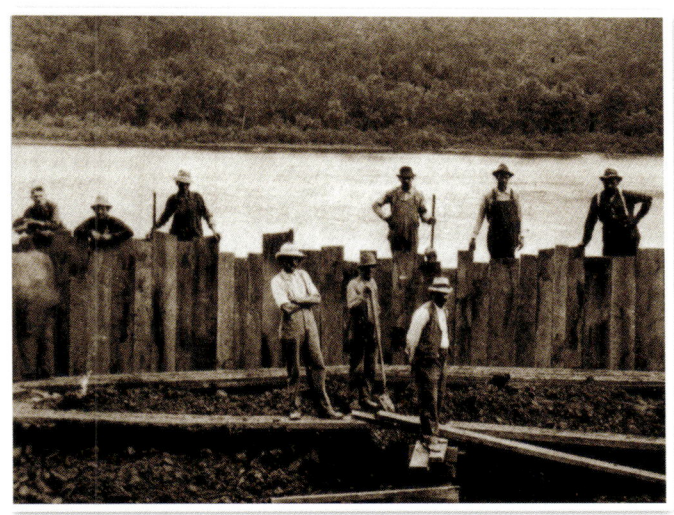

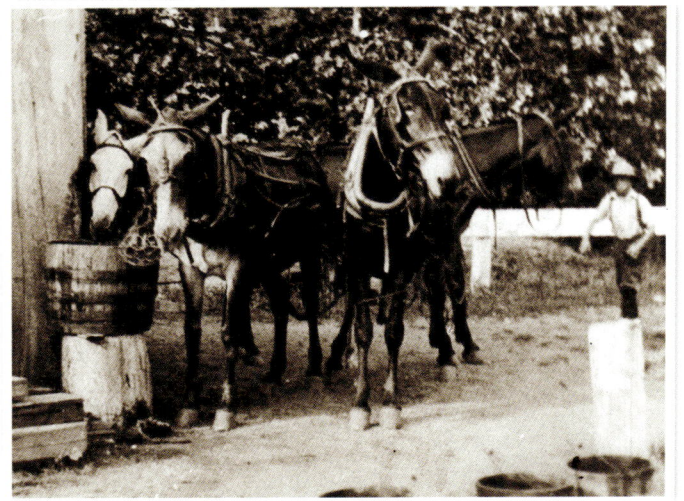

Miles of Mules linked the present to the past. The project generated excitement along the 165 miles of the Delaware & Lehigh National Heritage Corridor throughout its five counties, to the north in the Lackawanna Heritage Valley and to the east in New Jersey, where the decorated mules were corralled. Many were purchased for private collections, and the remainder were auctioned with the proceeds benefiting the organizing partners and other area nonprofit groups.

"Miles of Mules linked the present to the past…"

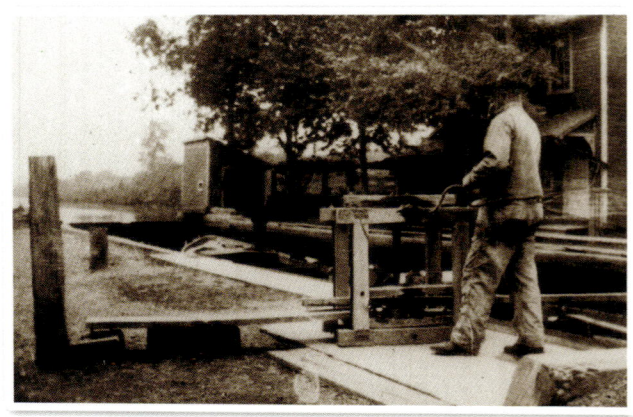

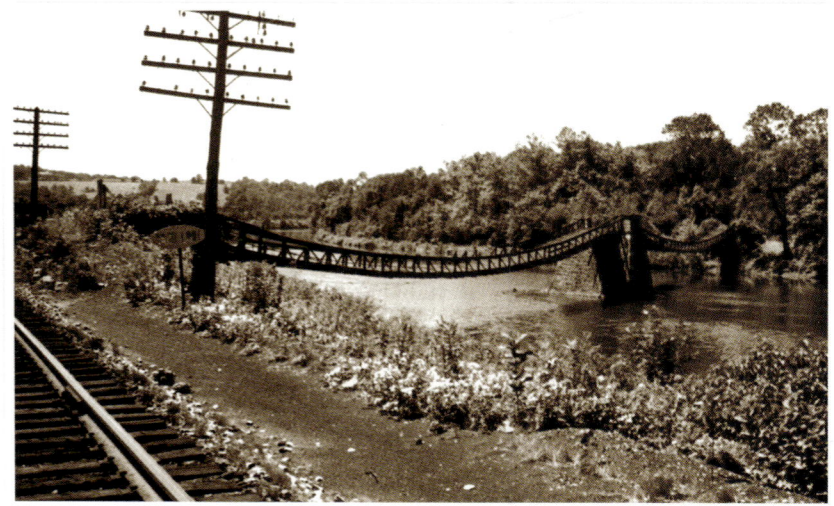

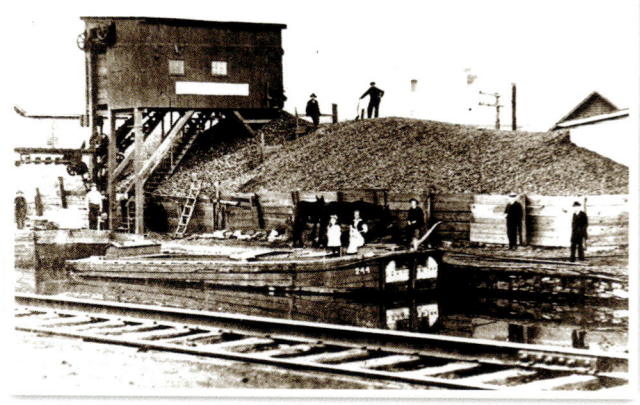

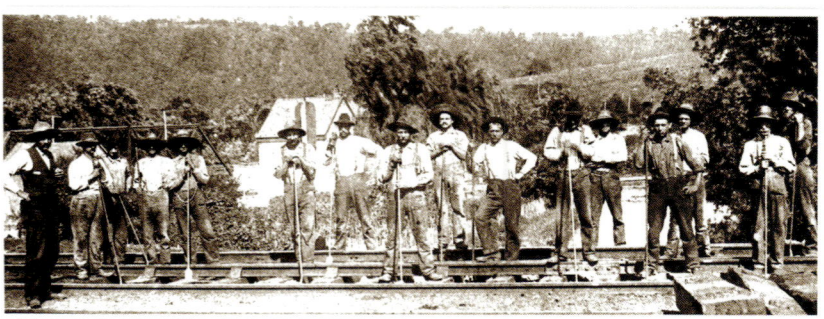

ABOUT THE D&L NATIONAL HERITAGE CORRIDOR

The Corridor is a living landscape of great historical significance. Early visionaries established a society which was unusually open and prosperous – a land of great opportunity. Beginning in the late 17th century, eastern Pennsylvania was the most desirable destination in North America.

Congress recognized the 165-mile Delaware & Lehigh National Heritage Corridor in 1988 for its historic importance and rich cultural and natural resources. The Corridor stretches through

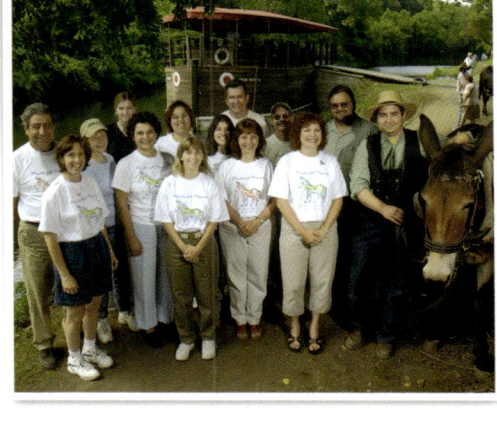

From left to right:
Bill Mineo,
Denise Holub,
Betty Orlemann,
Abby Randall,
Elissa Marsden,
Alyssa Vazquez,
Sherry Acevedo,
Julie Ziff Sint,
Allen Sachse,
Diana Rollar,
Doug Reynolds,
Rayne Schnabel,
Dale Freudenberger,
Mule Tender & Daisy

Luzerne, Carbon, Lehigh, Northampton and Bucks Counties where anthracite coal was first discovered and mined. Its unique inheritance of settlement, industrial development and recreational opportunities has earned both recognition and support from the National Park Service and Pennsylvania's State Heritage Parks Program.

With a Management Action Plan created in the 1990s, these organizations now work together to help local residents and organizations guide the Corridor's preservation and development, conserve its heritage and build its future.

When the Corridor staff began kicking around the **Miles of Mules** idea, they contacted the James A. Michener Art Museum in Doylestown (in the southern region), The Banana Factory in Bethlehem (in the central region), and the Cultural Council of Luzerne County in Wilkes-Barre (in the northern region), to create a partnership.

The four partners organized teams, assigned responsibilities, harnessed staff and recruited volunteers to help tow the load.

The Theme Factory of Philadelphia produced two fiberglass mule molds – one in a stately standing pose, the other in a stubborn sitting pose. In July of 2002 the first four prototype mules were born.

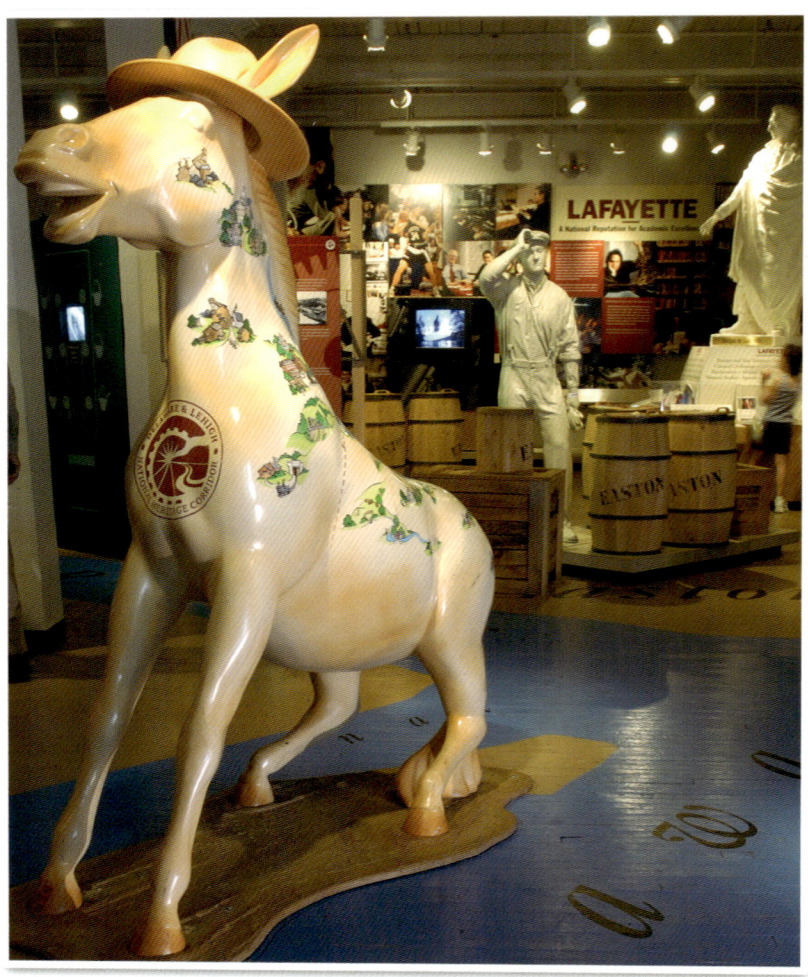

"Mule-gellan is known to some as the Navigator…"

Mule-gellan, one of the first mules created, is known to some as the Navigator, for he was the one to help guide this project. His body is a map of the Corridor highlighting cities and showcasing places of interest and recreational opportunities. His tail symbolizes the area's free-flowing rivers. A park ranger hat atop the mule's head signifies the Corridor's connection with the National Park Service.

MULE-GELLAN
MOBILE

Artist: The Theme Factory of Philadelphia
Sponsor: The D&L National Heritage Corridor, DCNR

DEPARTMENT OF CONSERVATION AND N★TURAL RESOURCES

✝he Pennsylvania Heritage Parks Program (PHPP), through the commonwealth's Department of Conservation and Natural Resources, fosters grass roots efforts that encourage heritage development and conservation of cultural resources such as history, traditions and folklore in the commonwealth's 11 State Heritage Parks.

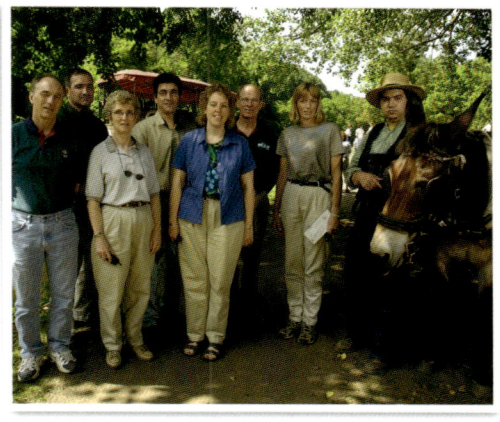

From left to right:
Larry Williamson;
Don Gephart;
Rita Calvan,
Deputy Secretary;
Michael DiBerardinis,
Secretary;
Meredith Hill;
Dick Sprenkle,
Deputy Secretary;
Cindy Dunn;
Mule Tender & Daisy

As the first Production Underwriter, PHPP provided a financial grant to the **Miles of Mules** public art project for the design and production of the first four prototype mules: *Blossom* in the northern region, *Capshaw* in the central region, *Chairman of the Barge* in the southern region and *Mule-gellan,* the navigator for the entire Delaware & Lehigh National Heritage Corridor.

These beautiful beasts were then showcased throughout the Corridor at different events and attractions to encourage artists, sponsors and the public to participate in the project.

The Delaware & Lehigh National Heritage Corridor, the Cultural Council of Luzerne County, The Banana Factory and the James A. Michener Art Museum thank the PHPP for its initial assistance in generating this spectacular public art project.

Artist: Shirley Trievel
Sponsor: Luzerne County Convention and Visitors Bureau

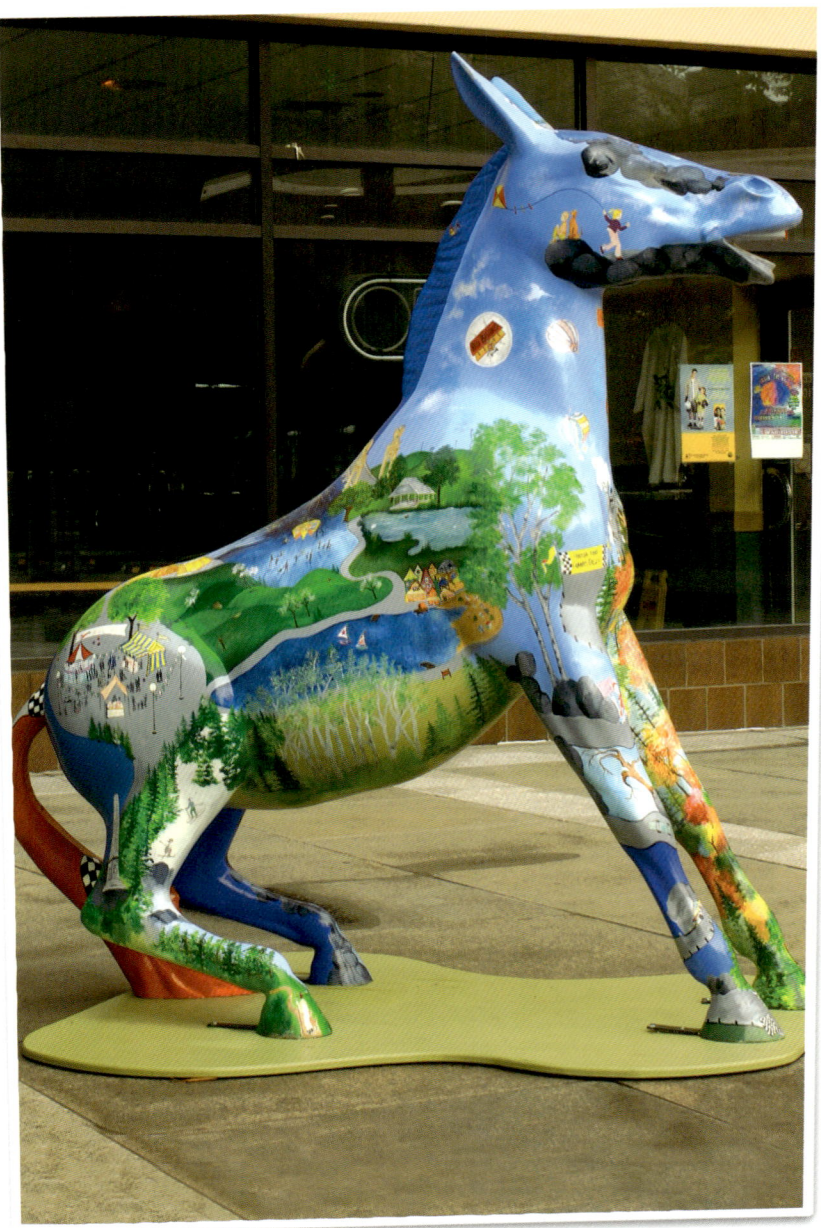

WELCOME

MOBILE

Shirley Trievel, a talented educator and award-winning artist, worked with the Luzerne County Convention and Visitors Bureau to create a vision of Luzerne County that showcased its cultural, recreational and historical assets.

Amidst the wonderful montage on *Welcome* is the rich architectural heritage of the county, with familiar landmarks like the Market Street Bridge Archway and the Wyoming Monument. Annual regional events are incorporated, including the Fourth of July fireworks at Kirby Park, the Pittston Tomato Festival and the Harvest Moon Balloon Festival. Destinations are also depicted, such as Pocono Downs, Wachovia Arena and the waterfalls of Ricketts Glen.

Four seasons of spectacular beauty, which include fall foliage, winter snowscapes, spring flowers and summer sailing on Harvey's Lake are also included. All are reminders of why Luzerne County is such a wonderful region.

The Luzerne County Convention and Visitors Bureau works to attract visitors to Luzerne County, Greater Wilkes-Barre, Hazleton and Pittston. The Bureau maintains a close relationship with the Delaware & Lehigh National Heritage Corridor and the **Miles of Mules** public art project became a great opportunity to encourage corridor-wide tours.

Artist: The Pocono Painters of Northeastern Pennsylvania
Sponsor: Pocono Mountains Vacation Bureau, Inc.

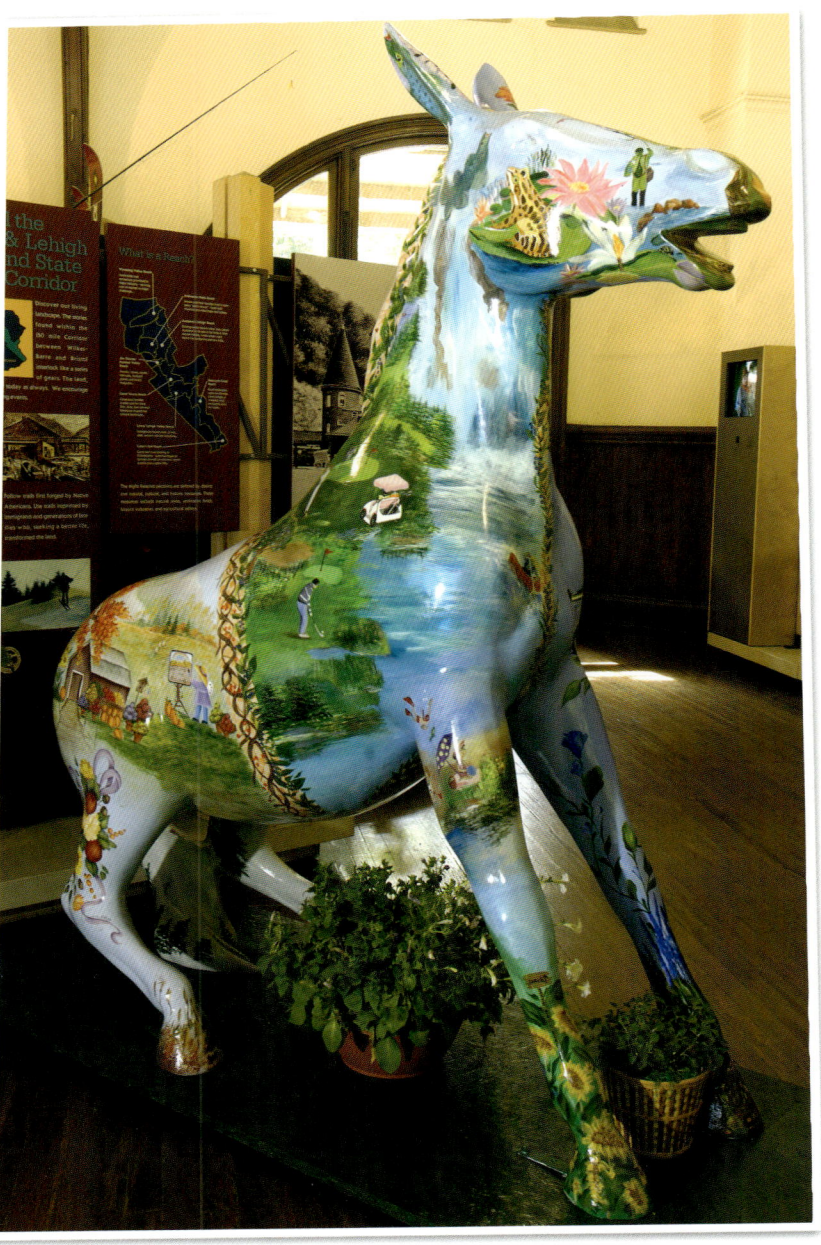

A MULE FOR ALL SEASONS
MOBILE

A Mule for All Seasons depicts the scenic beauty and abundant recreational activity available in the Pocono Mountain region throughout the four seasons of the year. From the robust colors of the fall harvest to peaceful white winters to golfing in springtime and canoeing on wondrous lakes in the summer, the design captures the treasures that have lured visitors to the Pocono Mountains for more than 175 years.

Each of the four painters from The Pocono Painters of Northeastern Pennsylvania created a personal vision of a season, reconnecting with special memories from childhood or of time spent in the area. Ten other painters from the group prepped the fiberglass mule's surface so that these key images could come to life.

The diverse personalities of the artists and the camaraderie created among them during the 180-hour project truly attested to their commitment to showcasing the best the Pocono Mountains has to offer.

The Pocono Mountains Vacation Bureau, Inc. (PMVB) is the designated tourism promotion and marketing organization for the region of Carbon, Monroe, Pike and Wayne Counties in northeastern Pennsylvania. The main goal of PMVB is to enhance the economic and environmental well-being of the Pocono Mountains and its members through the promotion of the region as a tourist destination.

Artist: Karen Dixon
Sponsor: Lehigh Valley Convention & Visitors Bureau

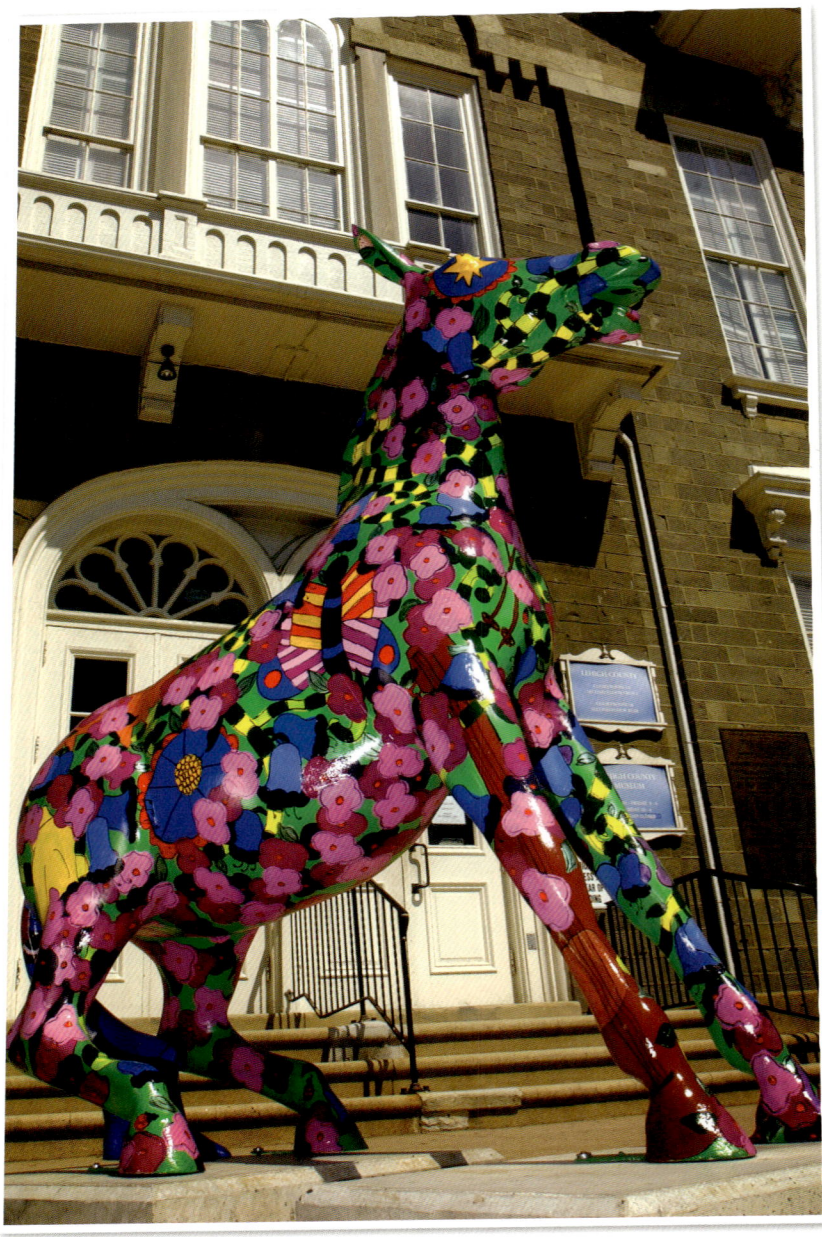

LEHIGH VALLEY MULE-O-RAMA
ALLENTOWN, PA

Lehigh Valley Mule-O-Rama, sponsored by the Lehigh Valley Convention & Visitors Bureau, showcases a stylish design bursting with color and hidden surprises. Interwoven in its pattern are 12 tourism icons representing the best of the Lehigh Valley.

Created by Bethlehem artist Karen Dixon, the design includes a Crayola crayon, symbolic of the company that has called Easton home for 100 years and its factory attraction that has welcomed families for six years. A roller coaster is reminiscent of Allentown's Dorney Park & Wildwater Kingdom, and a glistening Moravian Star pays tribute to the historic past of the city of Bethlehem. Vignettes of skis, golf clubs and a bicycle from the Lehigh Valley Velodrome are also included.

Showcasing the best of the Lehigh Valley, the mule is also a reminder of the major impact tourism has on the local economy – the source of thousands of jobs and millions of dollars in revenue!

The Lehigh Valley Convention & Visitors Bureau is the designated tourism promotion agency of Lehigh and Northampton Counties. It played an integral role in the **Miles of Mules** project and continues to promote the scenic and exciting Delaware & Lehigh National Heritage Corridor.

Artist: Michael Pantuso
Sponsor: Bucks County Conference & Visitors Bureau

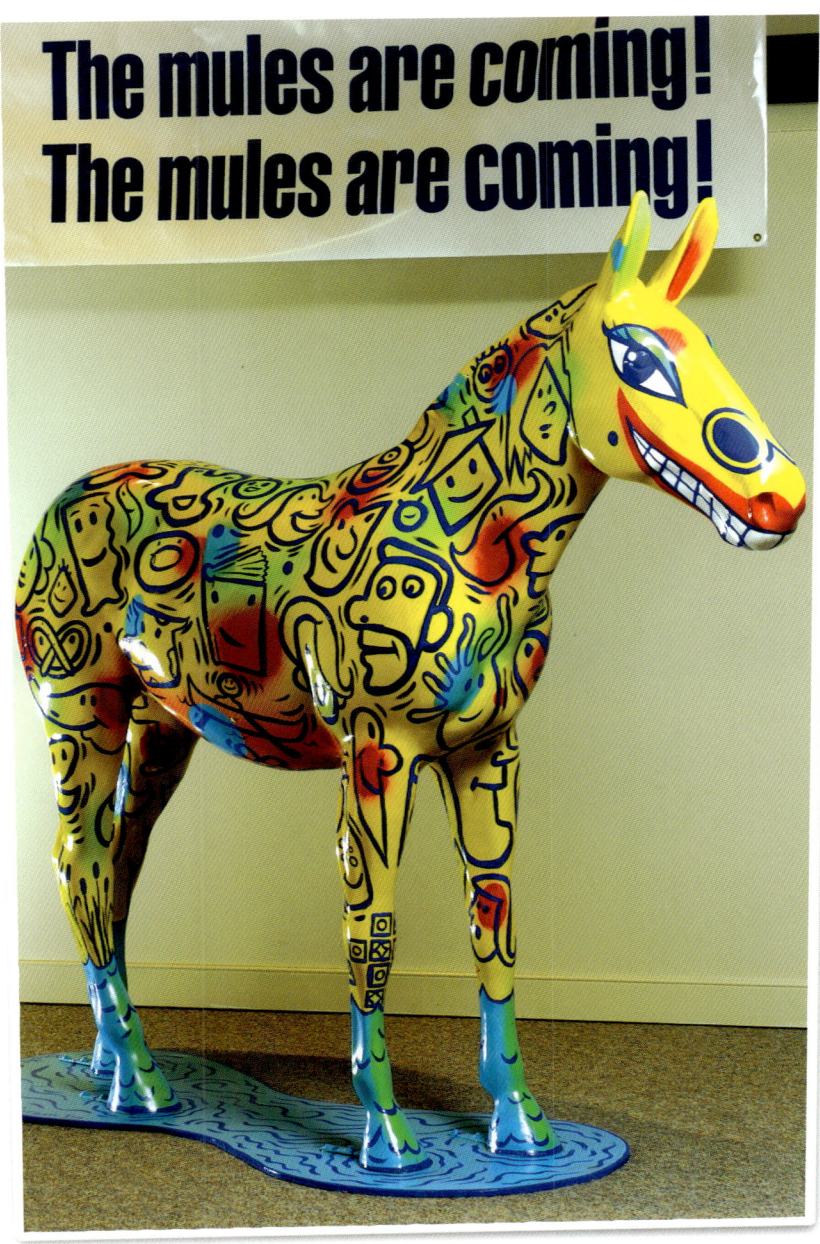

BUCKS

Bucks County is well known for arts, culture and beautiful countryside. It was a natural decision for the Bucks County Conference & Visitors Bureau to participate in the **Miles of Mules** public art project to showcase these strengths.

In Bucks County, the Delaware Canal runs through the towns of Riegelsville, Upper Black Eddy, Uhlerstown, Point Pleasant, Lumberville, Centre Bridge, New Hope, Washington Crossing, Yardley, Morrisville and Bristol. These towns and villages exhibit the charm and history of the region's early technological advances.

Michael Pantuso, a three-time Emmy Award-winning graphic designer from the Children's Theater Workshop production, "Sesame Street," painted the Bureau's mule. Pantuso chose bold, vibrant colors to depict Bucks County's most important assets: its people, historic sites, institutions and landscapes. On his broad shoulders, *Bucks* carries many images, including those of children and adults, food and wine, the arts, farmland, waterways, historic properties and Native Americans.

The mule greets visitors at the Bureau's offices on 3207 Street Road in Bensalem. His larger-than-life smile shows how happy he is to help promote the wealth of Bucks County to visitors from all over the world. The Bucks County Conference & Visitors Bureau was founded in 1961 as the official tourist promotion agency for Bucks County, which markets the county's heritage, diverse sites and attractions.

N ⭐ RTHERN CORRAL

*M*ules..? Not exactly the most whimsical creatures in the animal kingdom, are they? Sure, they have historical significance; pulling barges along the canals in the Lehigh Valley and working side-by-side with the coal miners in the anthracite industry. But, aren't mules a bit somber, sort of... joyless? How will the artists add pizzazz to this stoic creature and energize this project?

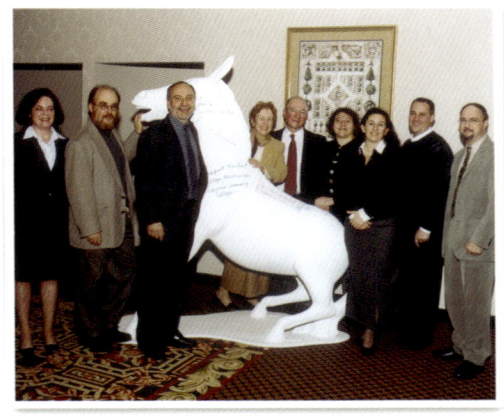

From left to right:
Enid Harris,
CCLC Treasurer;
Sam Cramer;
Bob Curry,
CCLC Chairperson;
Judy Plummer;
Tom Durkin;
Donna Wench,
Project Coordinator;
Cheryl Lynn Murnin;
Michael Thomas;
Jim Rogowski

We certainly had our doubts. That is, until the Cultural Council's prototype mule, *Blossom,* was born. The wonderfully rendered flower-child mule was conceived in the imagination of Kingston artist Nina Davidowitz and captured perfectly Pennsylvania's natural beauty. *Blossom*'s uncommon grace and stately presence provided the impetus for recruiting many area artists and sponsors. In the weeks following *Blossom*'s debut, a veritable flood of design submissions and sponsors' inquiries reached our office. Before *Blossom,* we at the Cultural Council were trying to sell an elaborate concept; afterwards we were part of the largest public art project in the history of northeast Pennsylvania.

Ultimately, the success of the project belongs to two groups. We are indebted to the many individuals and organizations who sponsored this project simply because of the delight it would bring to the people in our area. Mission accomplished. Most importantly, we need to thank the artists who worked on the project and proved to the world that mules could indeed be fantastic whimsical creatures. What the artists have done is to take a simple idea and turn it into magic. And for that we are all sincerely grateful.

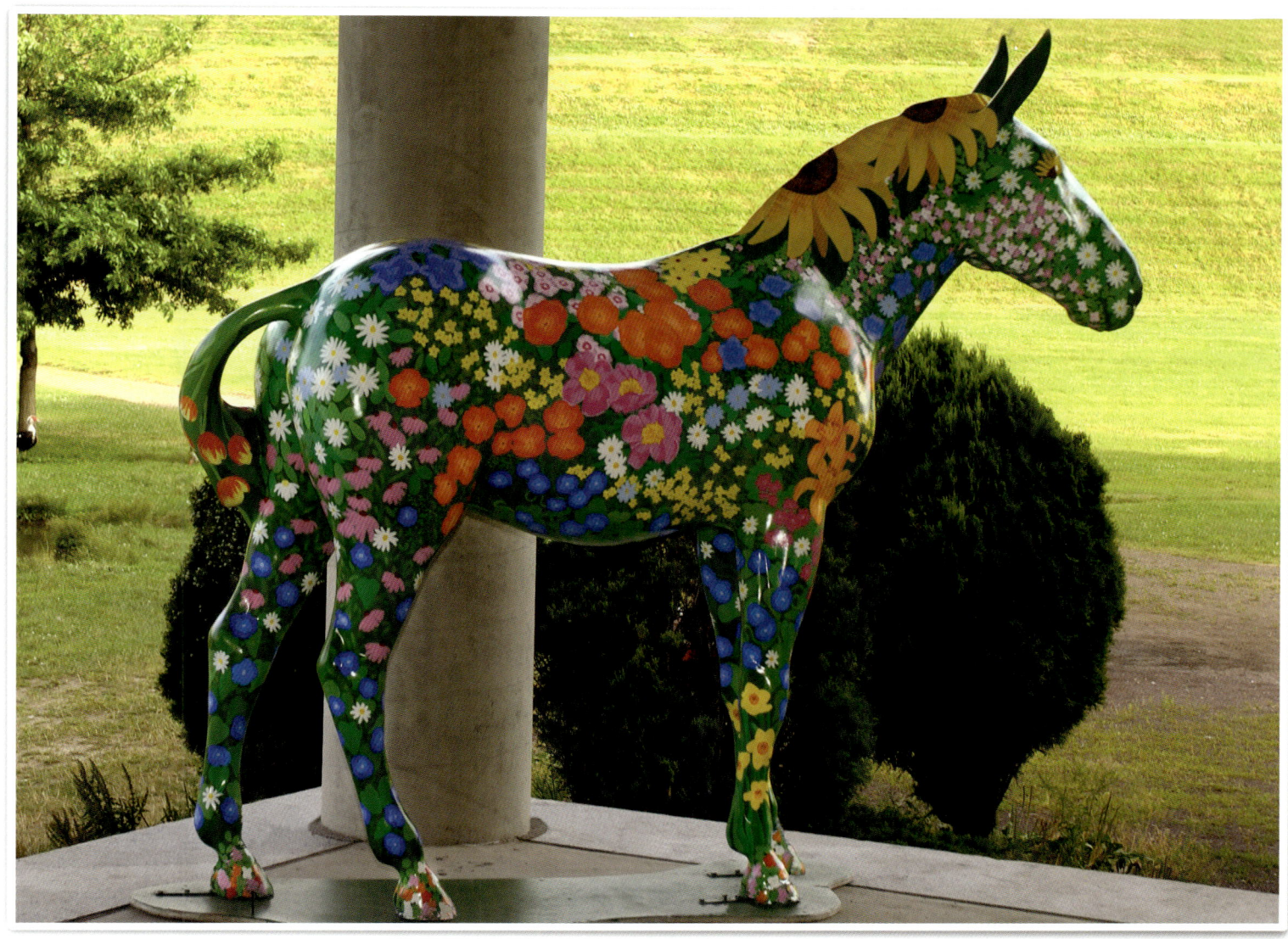

BLOSSOM

MOBILE

Artist: Nina Davidowitz
Sponsor: Cultural Council of Luzerne County, The D&L National Heritage Corridor, DCNR

"The wonderfully rendered flower-child mule…
captured perfectly Pennsylvania's natural beauty."

Artist: Jill Elizabeth
Sponsor: Debby and Allen Sachse

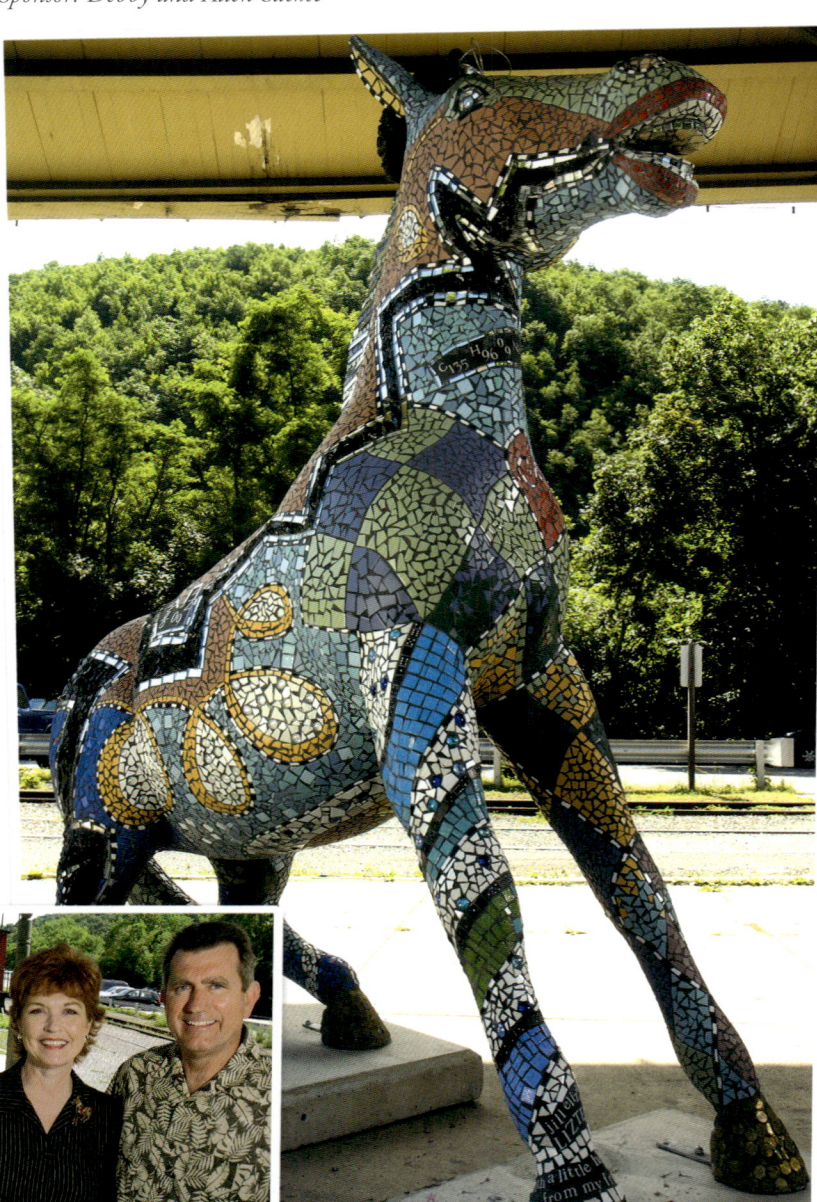

Debby and Allen Sachse

POP JONES
JIM THORPE, PA

On the front hoof of *Pop Jones* is the inscription "with a little help from my friends." And that is exactly how this mule was created.

Allen and Debby Sachse of Moscow sponsored it and contacted their friend Elissa Marsden for a suggestion on an artist. She recommended her friend Jill Elizabeth, who creates handmade jewelry at her own store in East Stroudsburg. It seems that Elizabeth's grandfather was a mule tender, who worked the mines in northeastern Pennsylvania. For her this project was personal – a venue to combine her artistry with a permanent tribute to her grandfather.

The first task was to break thousands of tiles into tiny pieces. Volunteer George Riggin did just that and then numerous other friends came by to affix them to the mule's fiberglass body. Jill applied the first tiles to give *Pop* his heart. A line of coal and a river of mirror tiles were applied from his back to his leg, with the help of Elissa's son, Jay. These depict the route of the canal where the mules pulled the barges. Toll bridge tokens adorn *Pop*'s hooves and jewels are his teeth. A miner's cap, donated by Dale Freudenberger, sits atop his head.

Pop Jones will long be remembered – especially by all those who helped create him.

"…with a little help from my friends."

Artist: Hazleton Area Career Center
Sponsor: The Luzerne Foundation

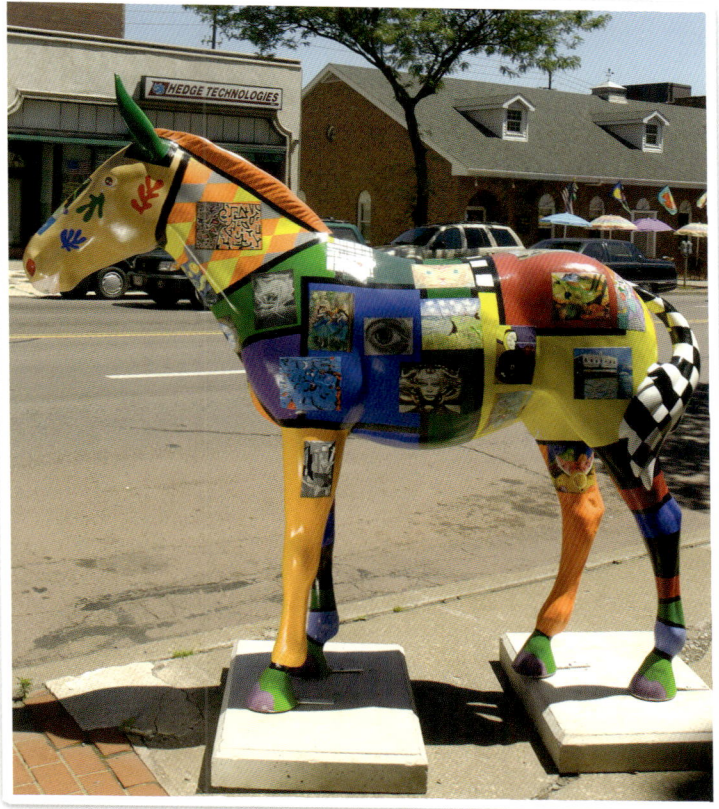

Artist: Alice Laputka
Sponsor: CAN DO, Inc.

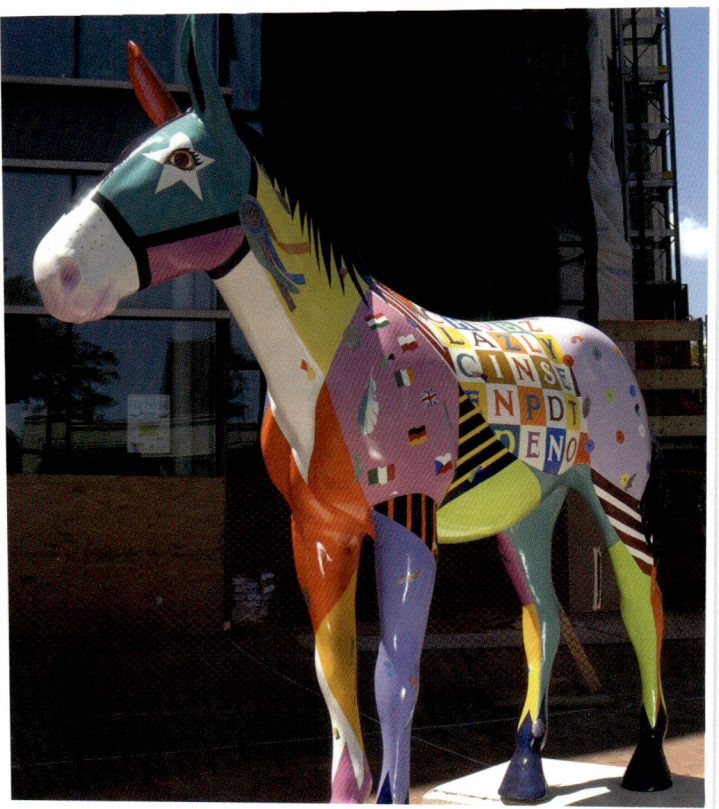

ART "Z" MULE

HAZLETON, PA

Visual arts students from Hazleton Area Career Center re-create a series of famous paintings and display them on a background inspired by Dutch artist Piet Mondrian.

BEDAZZLED

HAZLETON, PA

The design is loosely based on a crazy quilt pattern with patches that incorporate symbols significant to the history of CAN DO! and the Hazleton area.

Artist: David Watkins Price
Sponsor: Jim Thorpe Chamber of Commerce, Mauch Chunk Trust Company

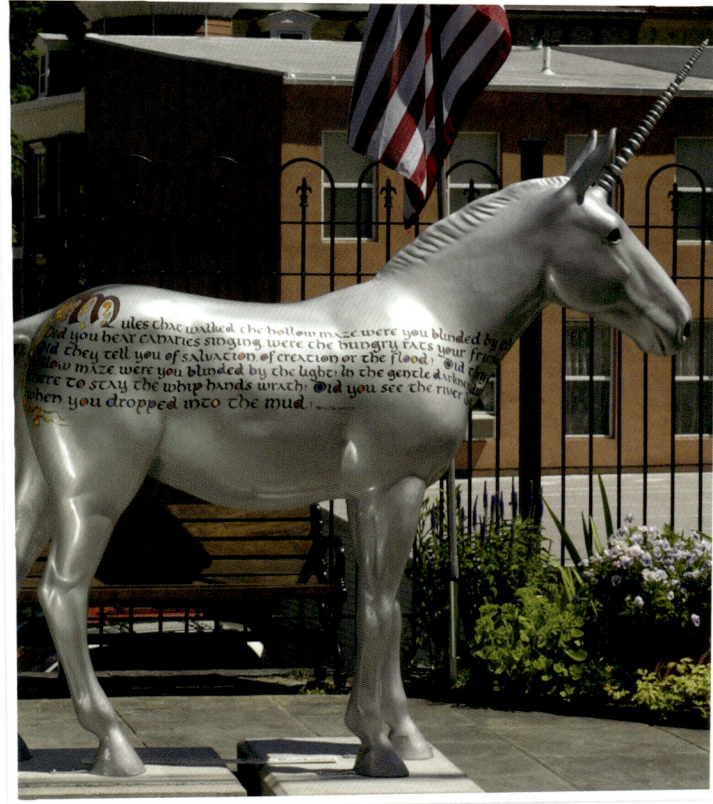

PACKER MULE

JIM THORPE, PA

Packer Mule pays tribute to this steadfast beast. The artist's poem depicts its difficult life in the mines. A spiral horn transforms the once lowly mule into a mythical unicorn.

Artist: John Pacovsky
Sponsor: The Waterfront

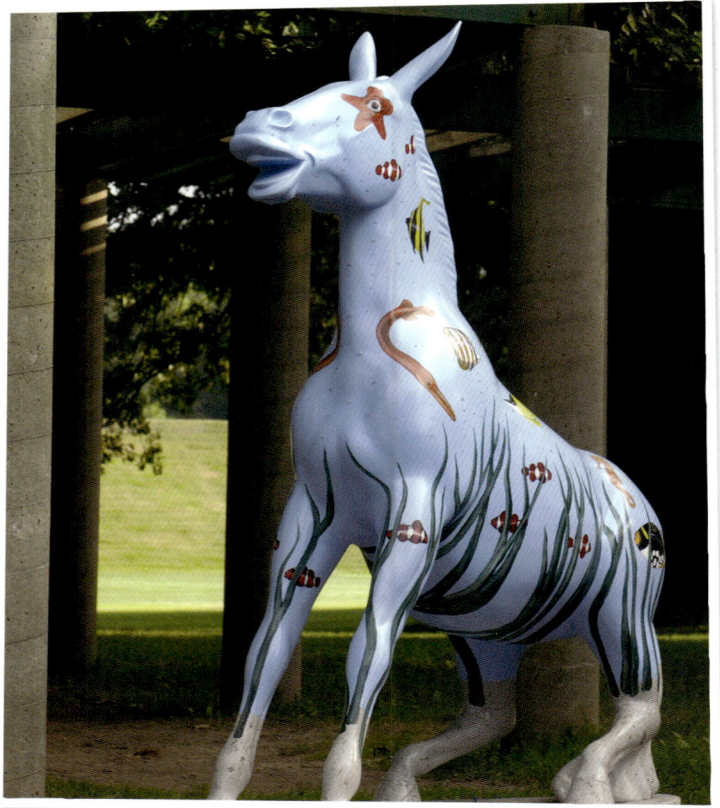

WATERFRONT

KINGSTON, PA

The view from the patio of The Waterfront is a picturesque scene of the beautiful Susquehanna River. This mule was inspired by aquatic life – right down to the delicate bubbles breaking the surface.

Artist: Patrice Cronin DeVirgilis
Sponsor: Anthracite Scenic Trails Association

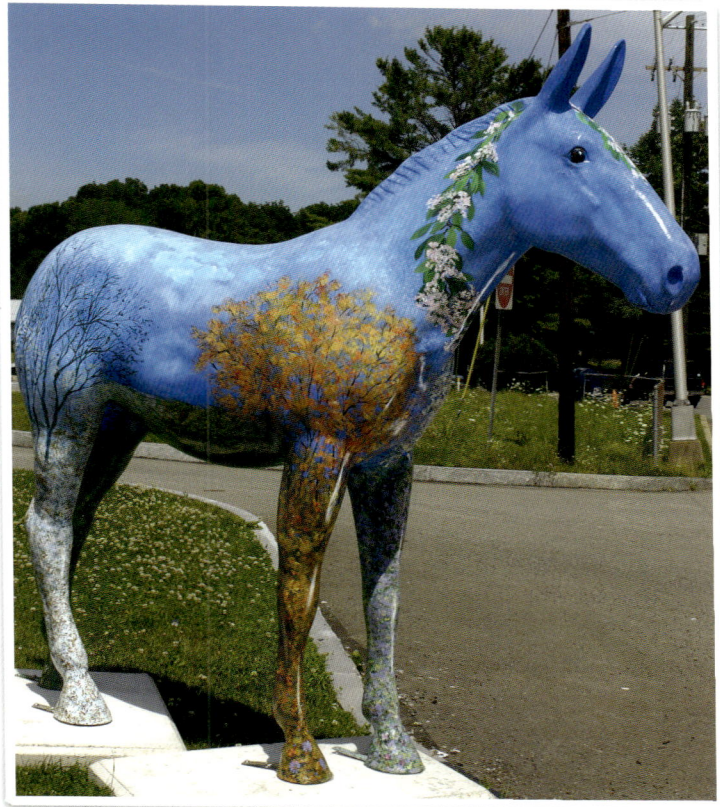

Artist: Anonymous
Sponsor: Scranton/Wilkes-Barre Red Barons

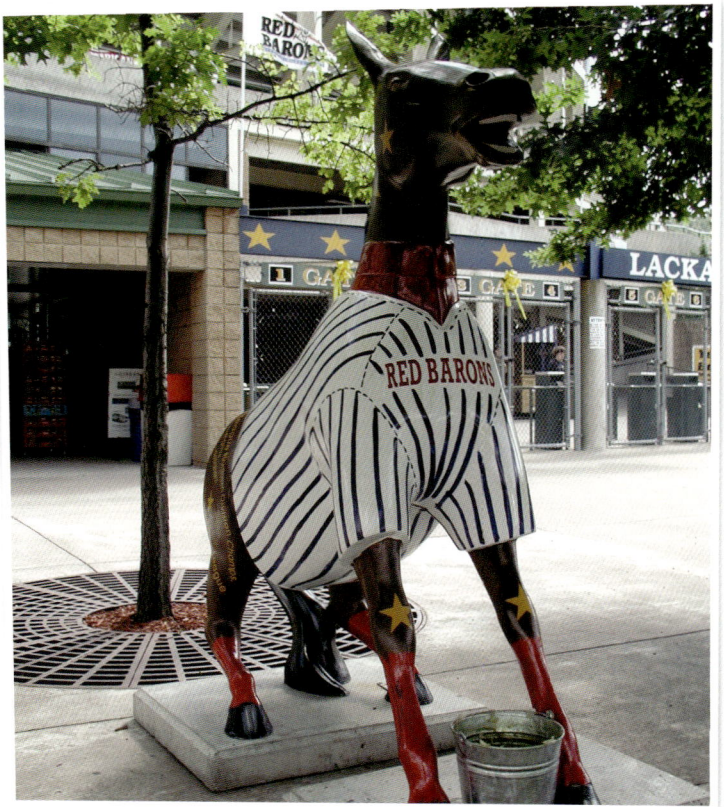

Photo by Allen Sachse

WELL-SEASONED

DALLAS, PA

In true impressionist style, *Well-Seasoned* captures the four seasons and elements of weather in layers of color. The perspective of the piece changes with the distance of the viewer.

CASEY AT THE BAT

MOOSIC, PA

Casey joins the Red Barons baseball team with bat and baseballs at the ready. Suited up in an official Red Barons uniform, *Casey* says, "Put me in, coach!"

Artist: Anonymous
Sponsor: Lackawanna County

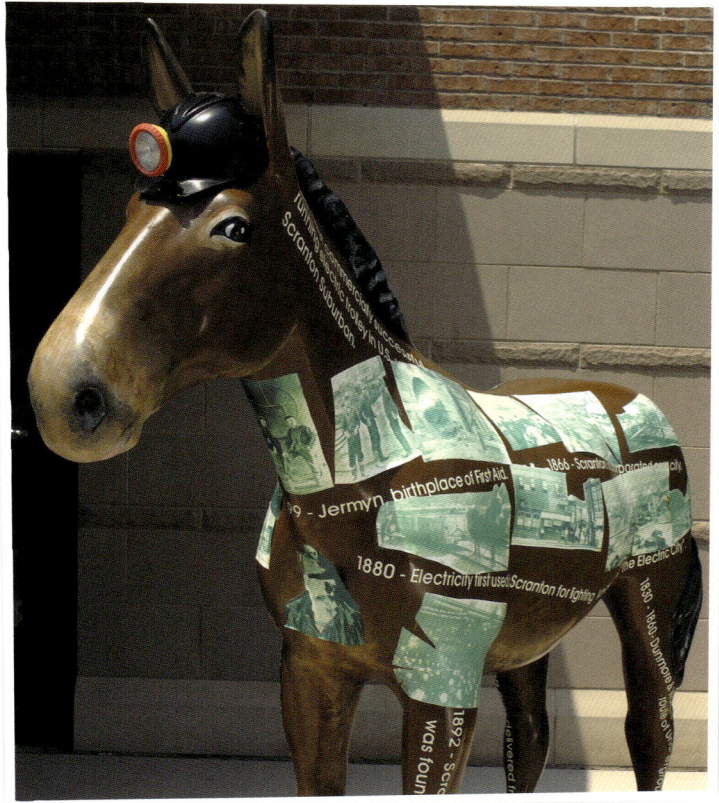

Artist: Angela DeMuro
Sponsor: City of Pittston Redevelopment Authority

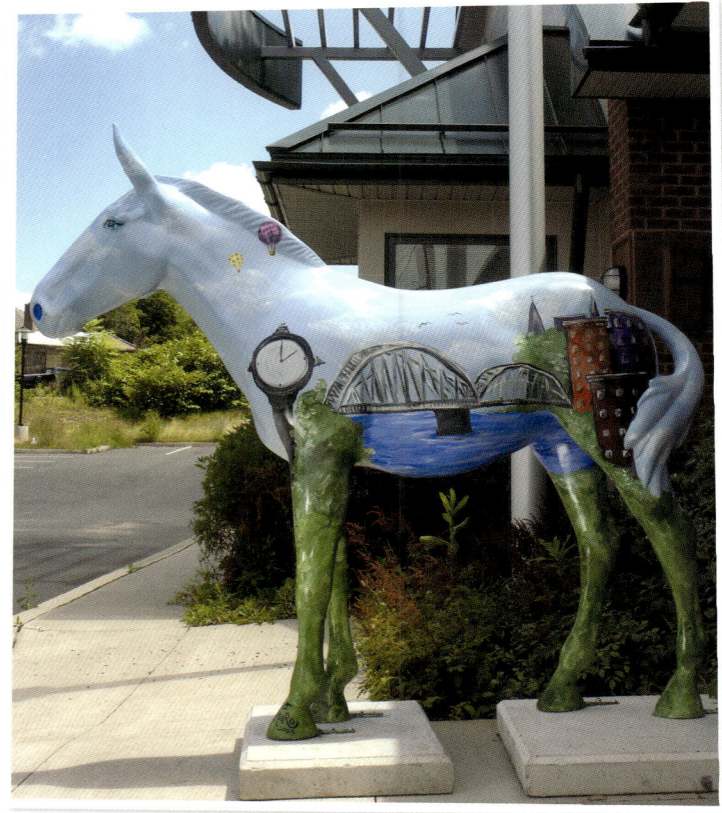

WITNESS to HISTORY
MOOSIC, PA

A tribute to Lackawanna County history: *Witness* showcases images of the county's past, including the first scheduled trolley service, the Anthracite Strike Commission, and the mighty steam engine.

PITTSTON PROGRESS
PITTSTON, PA

Evidence of Pittston's progress can be seen in the images of Riverfront Park, the landmark clock, and the beautiful bridge lights – a city with a past and a future.

Artist: Angela DeMuro
Sponsor: Pittston Tomato Festival

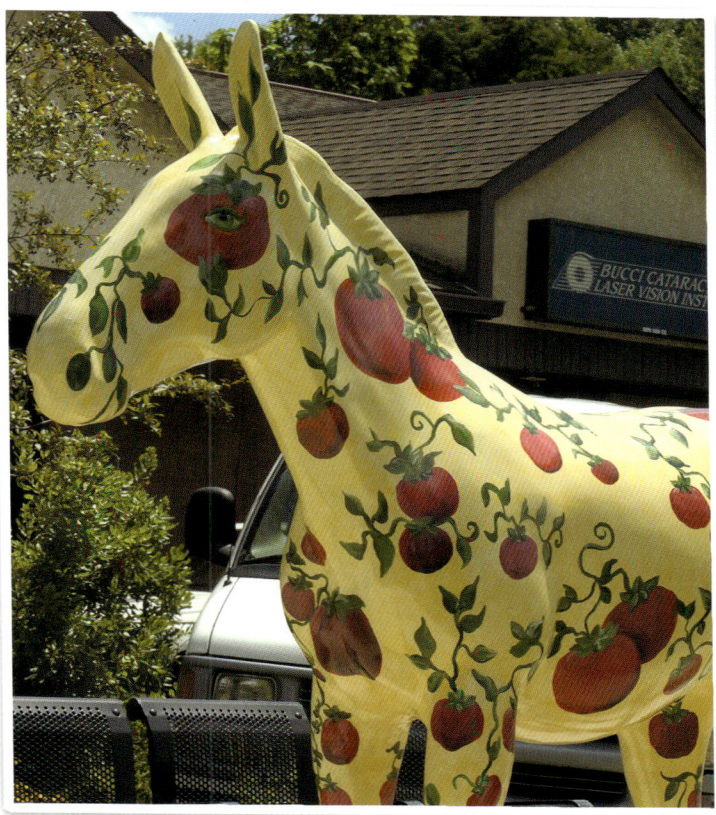

Artist: Visual Arts Students of Arts Alive NEIU
Sponsor: Arts Alive

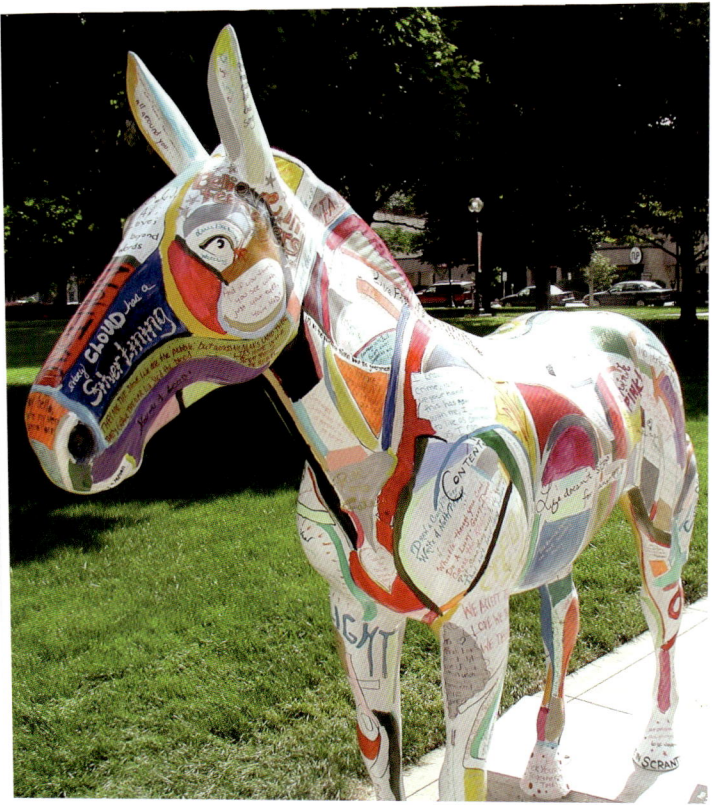

Photo by Allen Sachse

TOMATOES

PITTSTON, PA

It's been said that Pittston's tomatoes are the best in the world. Attend the annual Pittston Tomato Festival and taste for yourself. Perhaps take part in the tomato fight too!

BEYOND THE VIEW

SCRANTON, PA

Facilitated by instructor Earl Lehman, visual and performing arts students combine words, quotes, and phrases with visible muscle and tendons to design this mule with something powerful to say. Listen.

Artist: Kathleen Godwin and Eva Nicklas
Sponsor: PNC Bank

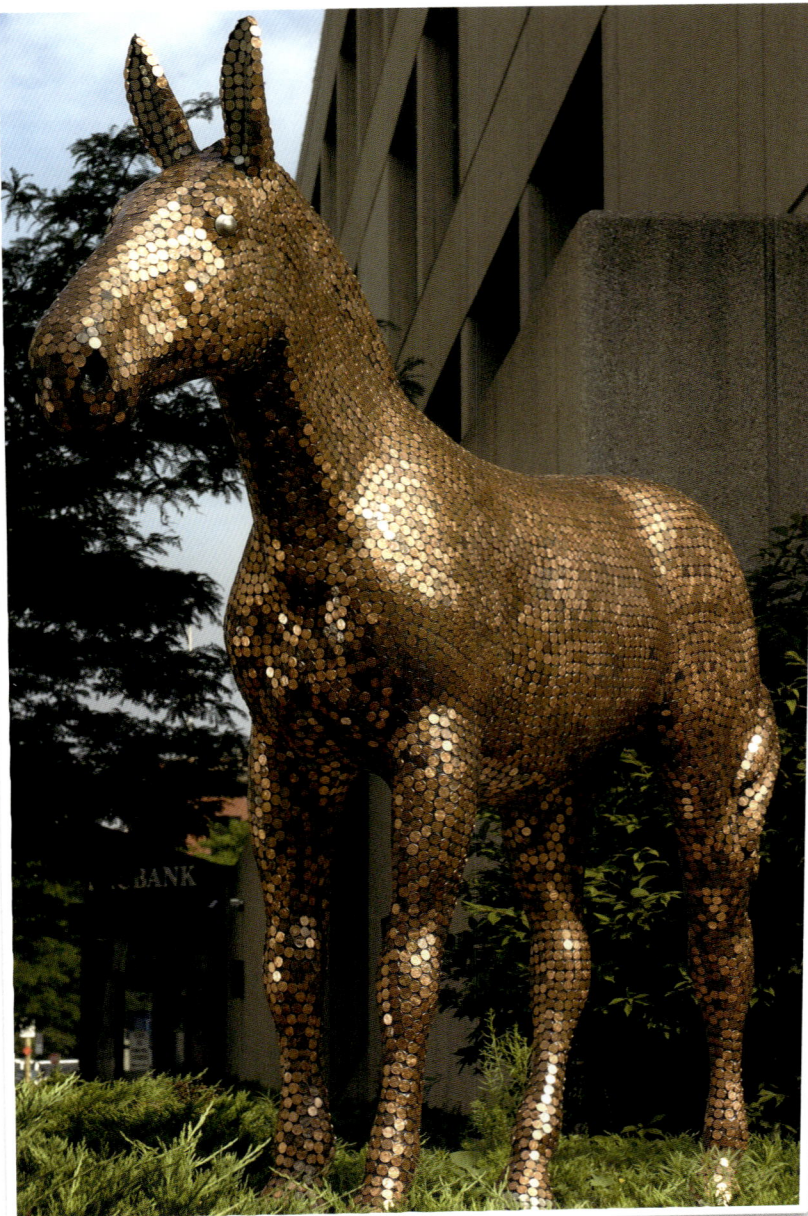

PENNY

How many pennies would it take to cover a life-size mule? That's the question PNC Bank asked its Scranton area customers in the form of a contest. The prize: 10,000 pennies in the form of a $100 U.S. Savings bond.

Sisters Kathleen Godwin and Eva Nicklas, Trucksville natives, were the artists who created the mule design, using non-toxic black silicon and sanded tile grout to adhere the currency.

To make the process of its creation even more interesting the bank let the artists decorate the mule right in the lobbies of its Wilkes-Barre and Scranton branches.

Customers were delighted and many even donated pennies to the project. Godwin said it was wonderful to watch the children close their eyes, make a wish and then affix their pennies. The interaction with the people was quite rewarding for the artist, who said it fostered an appreciation of art and encouraged the public to recall and rekindle its own artistic talents.

Godwin works with mosaic tiles, while her sister Nicklas, the artistic director of the Lewiston Council of the Arts, paints. The project was their first together and both hope it helps encourage similar art projects in the Wilkes-Barre/Scranton area.

Penny, who required 12,973 pennies, 300 dimes and two silver dollars to be completely covered, now proudly stands outside the PNC Bank administrative offices in downtown Scranton.

"How many pennies would it take to cover a life size mule?"

Artist: Shirley Trievel
Sponsor: Kane

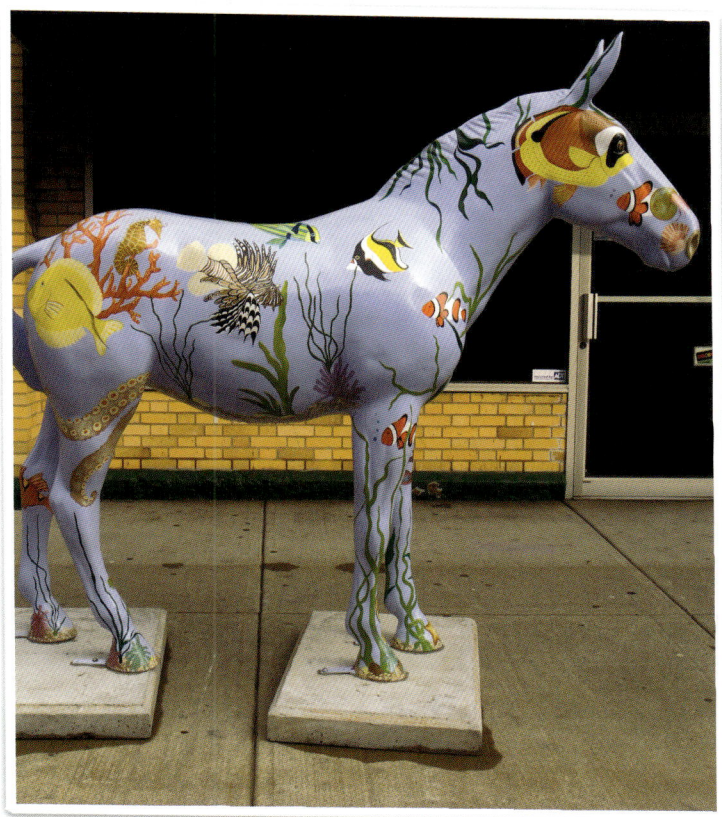

Artist: Marianne Bump Lurie
Sponsor: Diversified Information

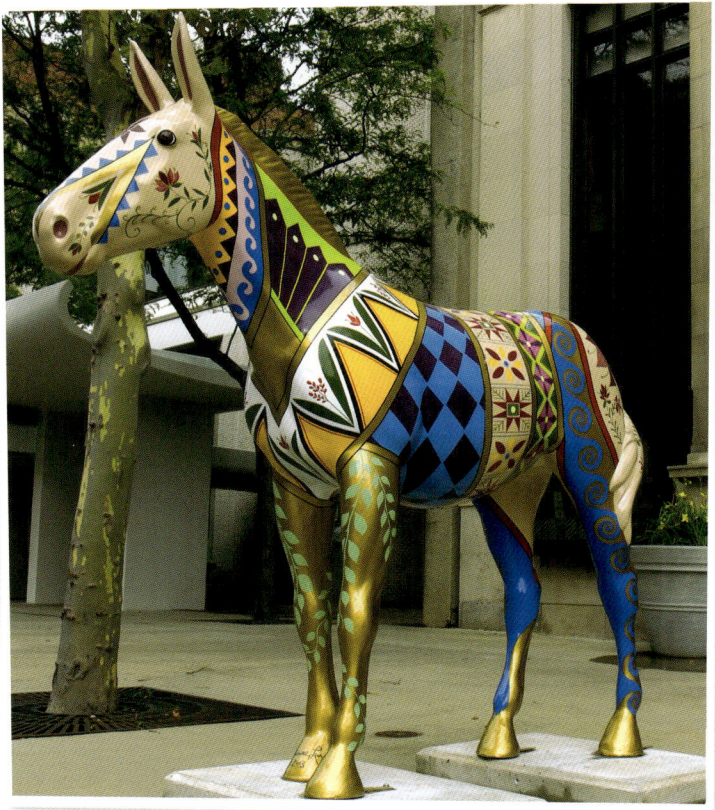

AQUARIUM

SCRANTON, PA

Something's Fishy

Whimsy and Folly
The earth's great variety
Land and sea host life

Colors and Patterns
Mother Nature's grand design
All in harmony

"PYSANKY" EGG MULE

SCRANTON, PA

Eastern European immigrants brought this tradition of egg decoration from the "Old Country." Using beeswax and dyes, the technique produces fascinating designs on an egg's surface – or even a Mule's!

Artist: Jim Rogowski
Sponsor: Patricia Atkins

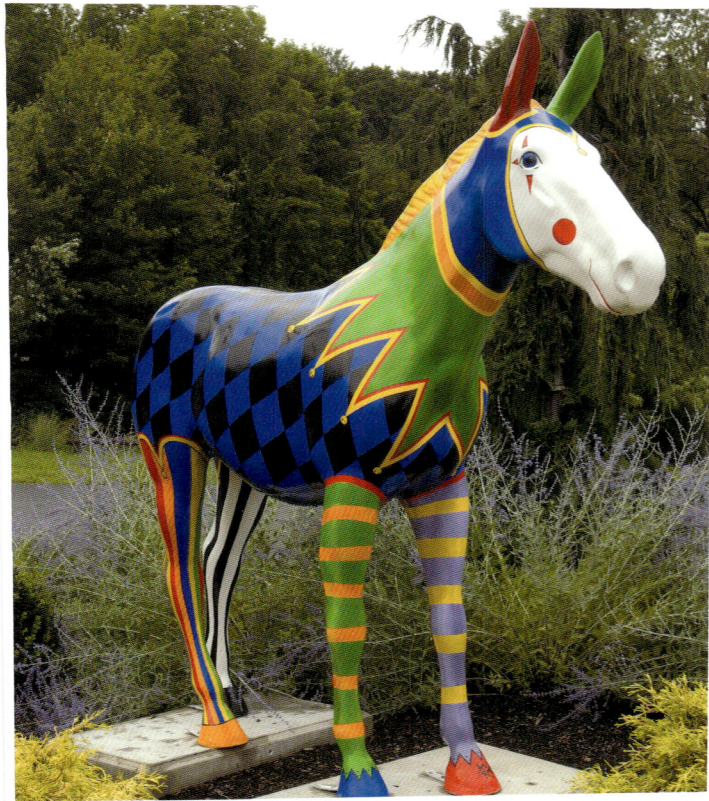

Artist: Kevin O'Neill, Megan Andrews, Adam West
Sponsor: Keystone College

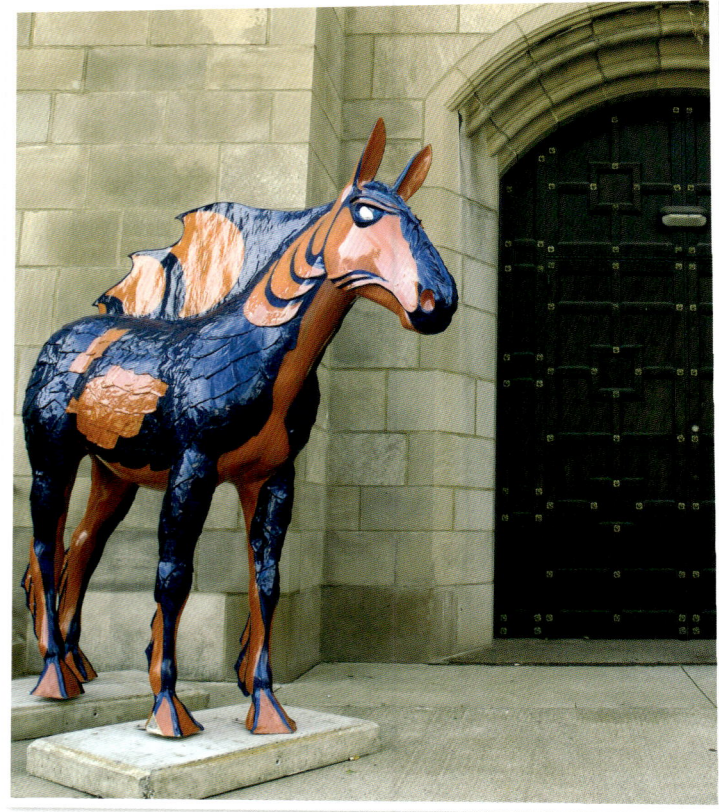

APRIL MULE

SCRANTON, PA

April is full of fun with her festive coloring and bright, happy look. In true jester form, she holds court at Patsel's, the sponsor's fine dining establishment near Scranton.

AQUAMULE

SCRANTON, PA

Part donkey, part horse, part…amphibian? *Aquamule* is rich with color and texture. There's no need for a towpath; *Aquamule* jumps right into the canal to pull the barge.

Artist: Francine Pisano Liples
Sponsor: The University of Scranton

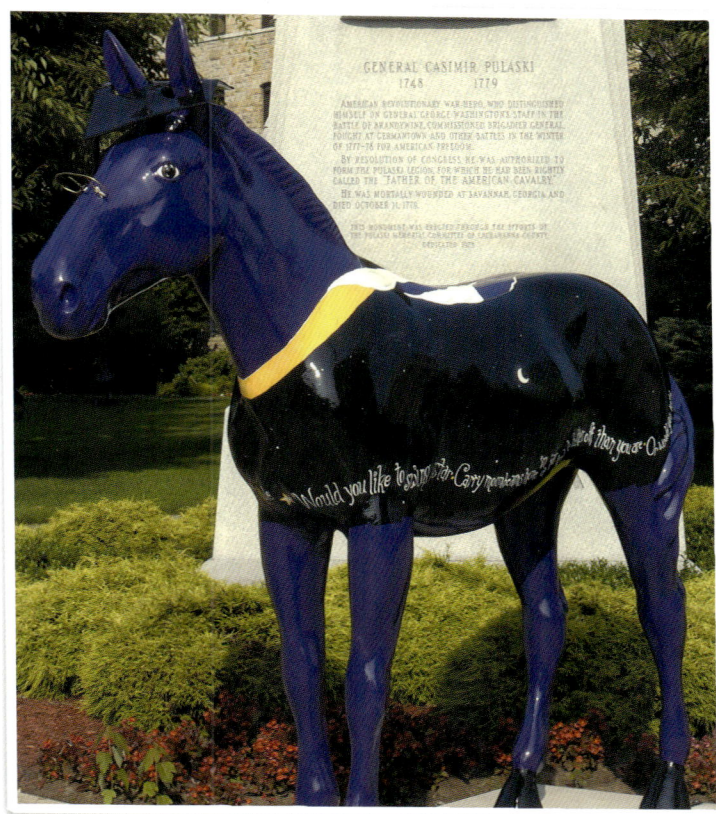

Artist: Don Rash, Fine Bookbinder
Sponsor: Scranton Public Library

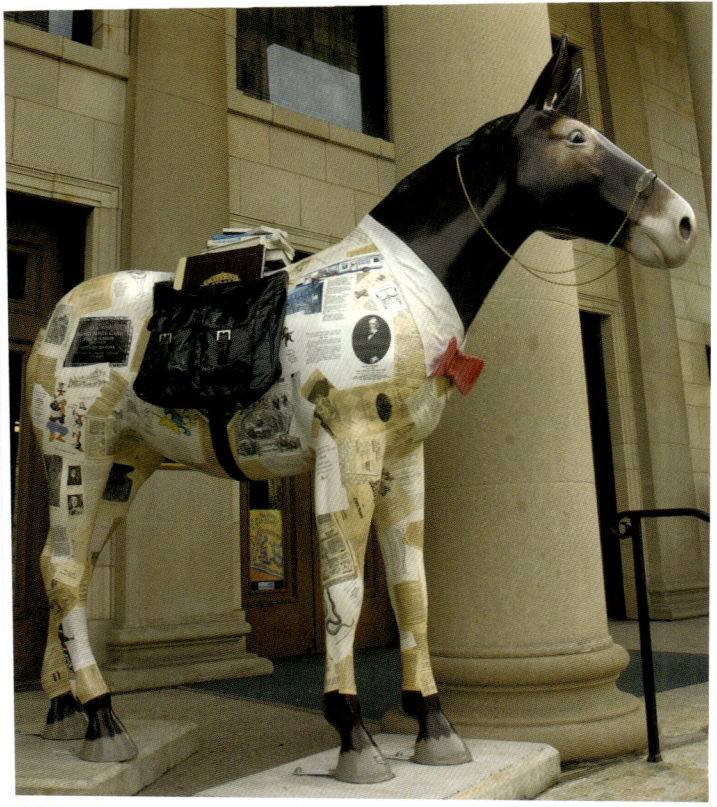

SWINGING ON A STAR

SCRANTON, PA

The Academy Award-winning tune is its inspiration. Bing Crosby performed the song, which uses animal stereotypes, including a mule, to promote education as a way to achieve your dreams.

BOOK MULE-BILE

SCRANTON, PA

The artist, who is a bookbinder, boasts a lifelong involvement with books, and based this design on a story about librarians in the Appalachian Mountains who delivered books by horseback.

Artist: N. Angeli, A. Ondush, J. DeNunzio, R. West
Sponsor: Lackawanna College

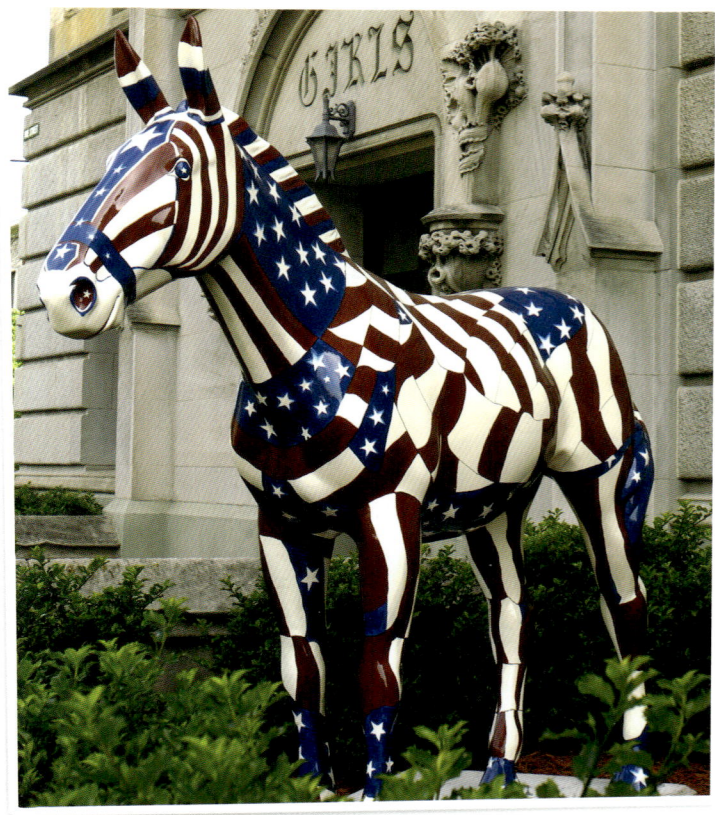

Artist: Shirley Trievel
Sponsor: First National Community Bank/Keystone Sanitary Landfill

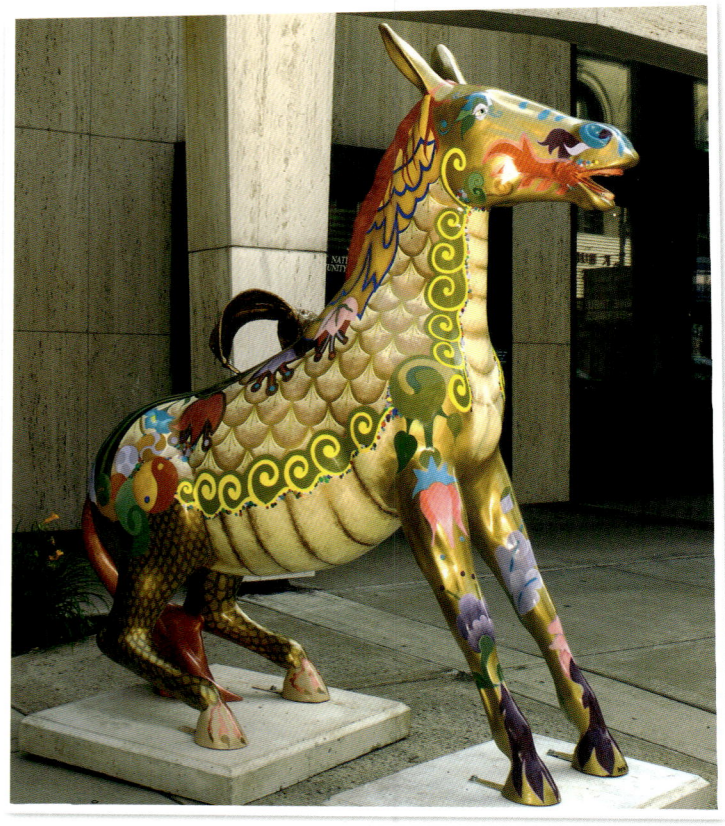

FREEDOM

SCRANTON, PA

An embodiment of the true American spirit, *Freedom* is draped in our country's beloved stars and stripes. He stands tall and strong for our area, our nation, and our people.

HEART OF A WARRIOR

SCRANTON, PA

My Heart is a Warrior

Dreamed I was a dragon
    Soared & had a ball
Roared & breathed out fire
    Put fear in hearts of all

Artist: Hank Fells
Sponsor: The Mall at Steamtown

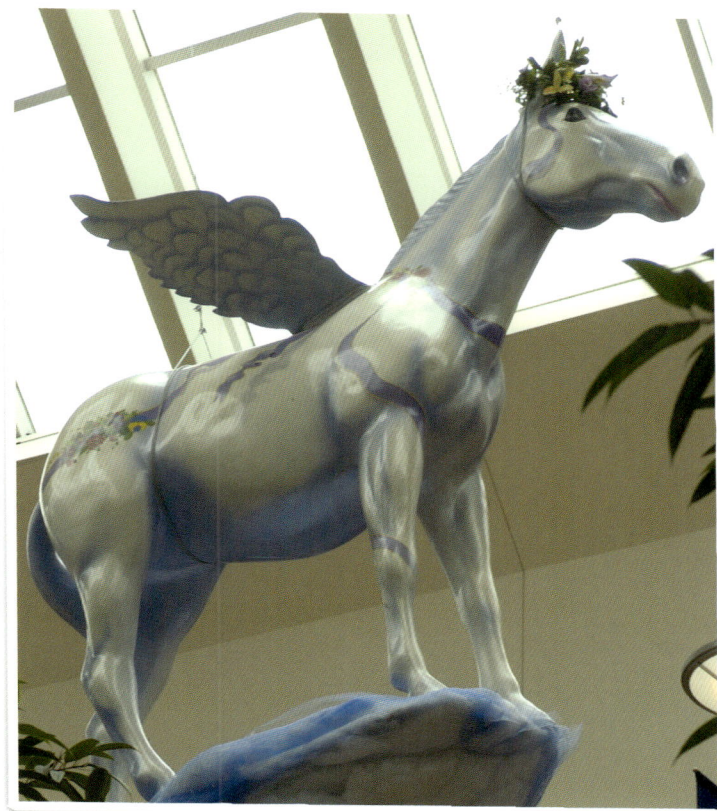

MiNE DREAMS

SCRANTON, PA

A stoic air and a proud presence symbolize the area's mining history. The mule melds aspects of the nation's heritage with that of northeastern Pennsylvania.

Artist: David Leonard
Sponsor: Scartelli Family

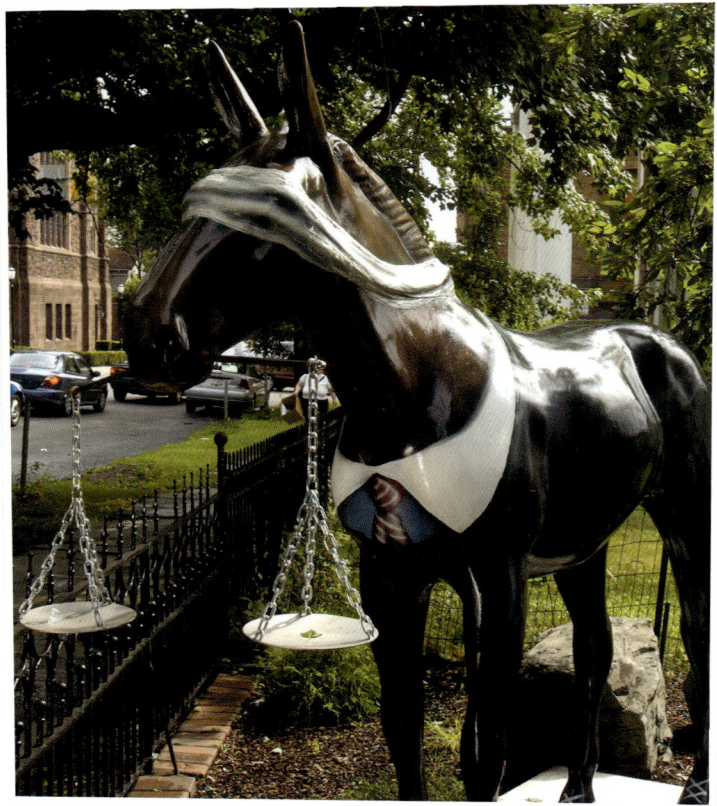

JuSTiCe

SCRANTON, PA

The artist's depiction of blind justice – draped with a blindfold and dressed in judge's robes, the mule stubbornly balances the scales of justice in his mouth.

Artist: Scranton's *BEST at West & WSIS
Sponsor: Scranton School District's *BEST Program

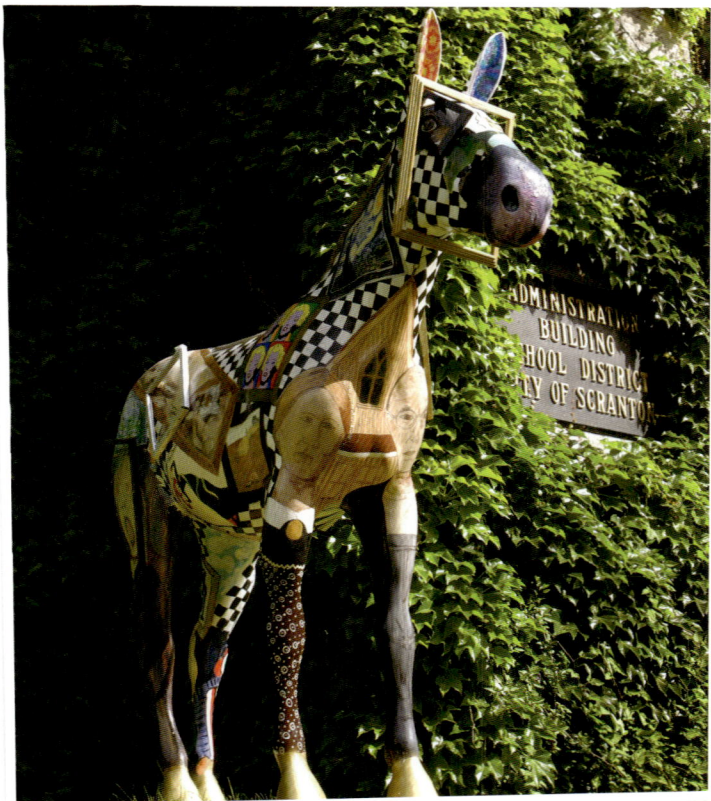

Artist: Vincent Bonavoglia Jr.
Sponsor: Louis and Pamela DeNaples

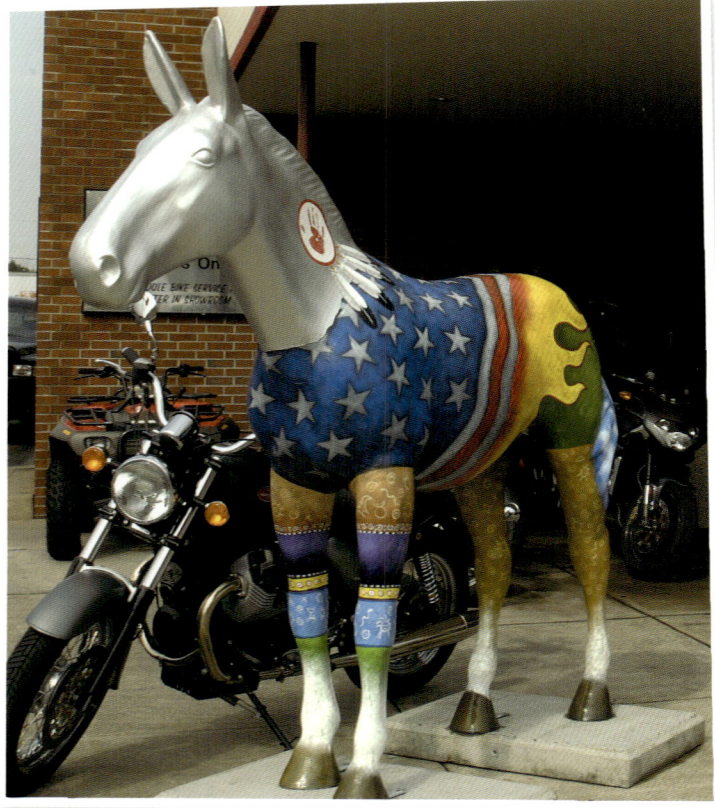

KALEIDOSCOPE

SCRANTON, PA

With talent and marvelous vision the young artists have beautifully rendered copies of famous works and framed them helter-skelter on the mule to make for a unique kaleidoscope of "Masters."

INDIAN MOTORCYCLES

SCRANTON, PA

Italian and American flags and a feathered headdress give way to racing stripes and polished chrome. Can you hear the roar of the engine?

Artist: Wilkes University Students and Friends
Sponsor: Wilkes University

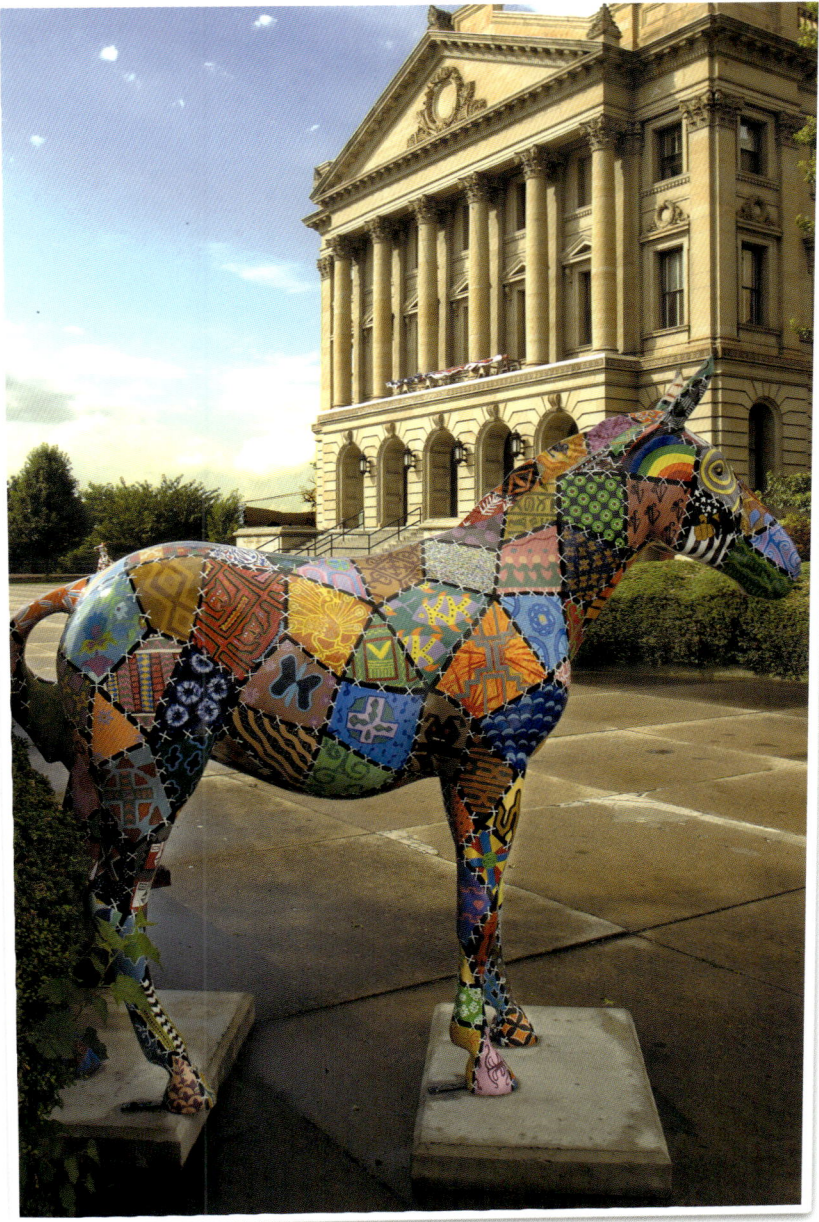

JEAN-MICHEL BASQUIAT
WILKES-BARRE, PA

Wilkes University, a private, co-ed comprehensive educational institution in Wilkes-Barre, is also a premier cultural center, enriching the lives of the students and staff on campus, as well as in the neighboring communities through music and dance performances, theatre productions, art exhibitions and lectures.

Reinforcing that commitment, Wilkes University fully embraced the **Miles of Mules** public art project. For more than a year prior to its public launch, students and faculty planned the purchase, design and painting of its mule.

Sharon Bowar, an associate professor of Art, served as faculty supervisor, and Brittany Kramer, an art minor, was the primary artist. More than 40 Wilkes students, faculty and friends transformed the fiberglass mule into a whimsical quilt adorned with 180 patterned patches. They named the mule *Jean-Michel* in honor of popular graffiti artist Jean-Michel Basquiat.

The local newspapers chronicled the mule's march to its first public display at the Fine Arts Fiesta on Wilkes-Barre's Public Square in May. For the rest of the summer *Jean-Michel* was corralled in front of the Luzerne County Courthouse. He'll soon move to his permanent home, complete with plenty of hay and light, in the Wilkes University's Henry Student Center.

"...a whimsical quilt adorned with 180 patterned patches."

Artist: Brian Keeler
Sponsor: Everhart Museum

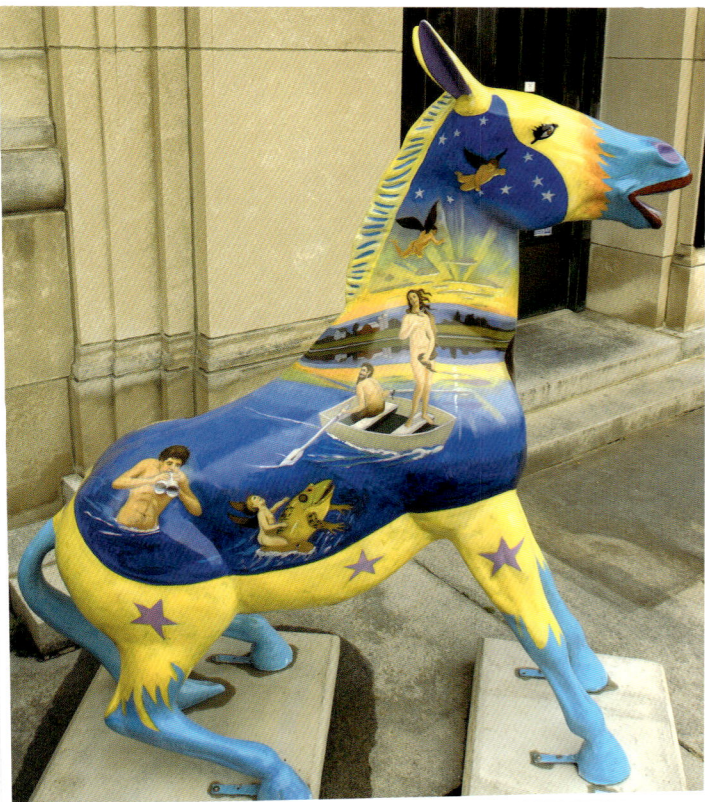

MYTHIC MULE

SCRANTON, PA

In a vision, Venus de Mulo rises. The flow of her hair in swirls of color gives this mule fluidity and motion.

Artist: Artists from "Artists For Art"
Sponsor: Scranton Tomorrow

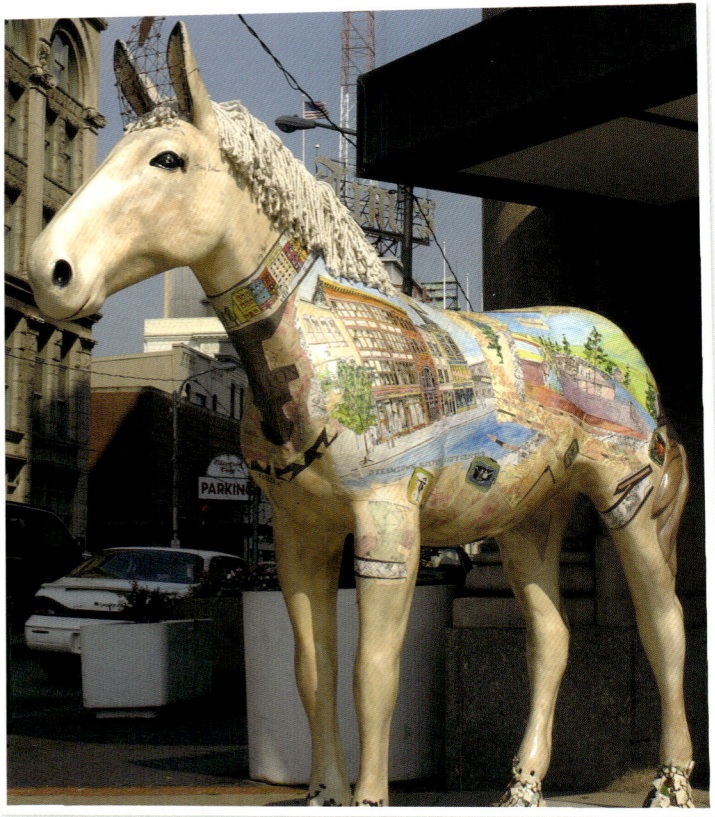

SCRANTON: A VISION OF THE FUTURE

SCRANTON, PA

Affectionately known as "Electra," this mule showcases a futuristic cityscape of a Scranton influenced by the arts. Pure brilliance, from her Electric City crown to coal, brick and slate hooves.

*Artist: Scranton School District's *BEST at South*
Sponsor: City of Scranton

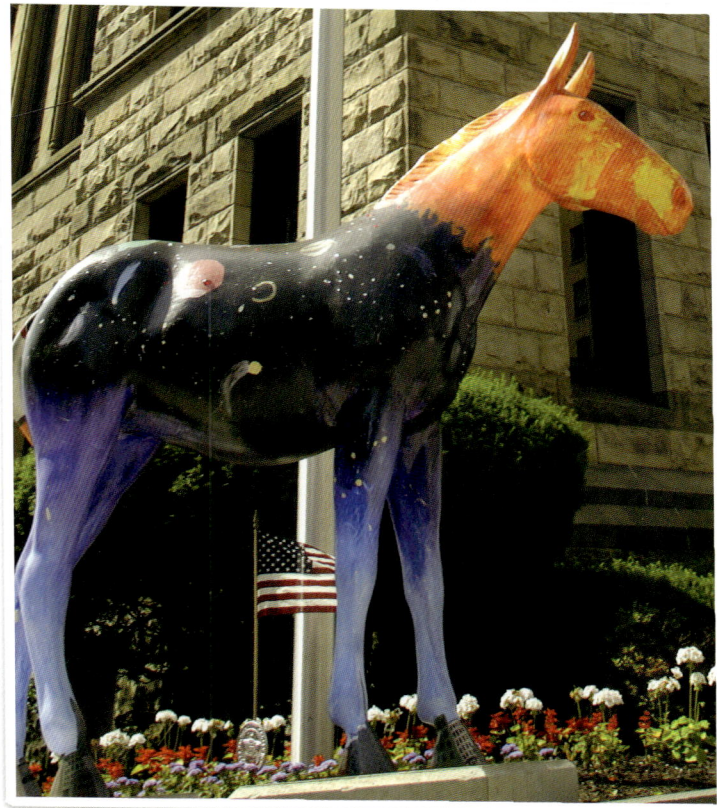

Artist: Leigh Pawling
Sponsor: Ronald McDonald House of Scranton

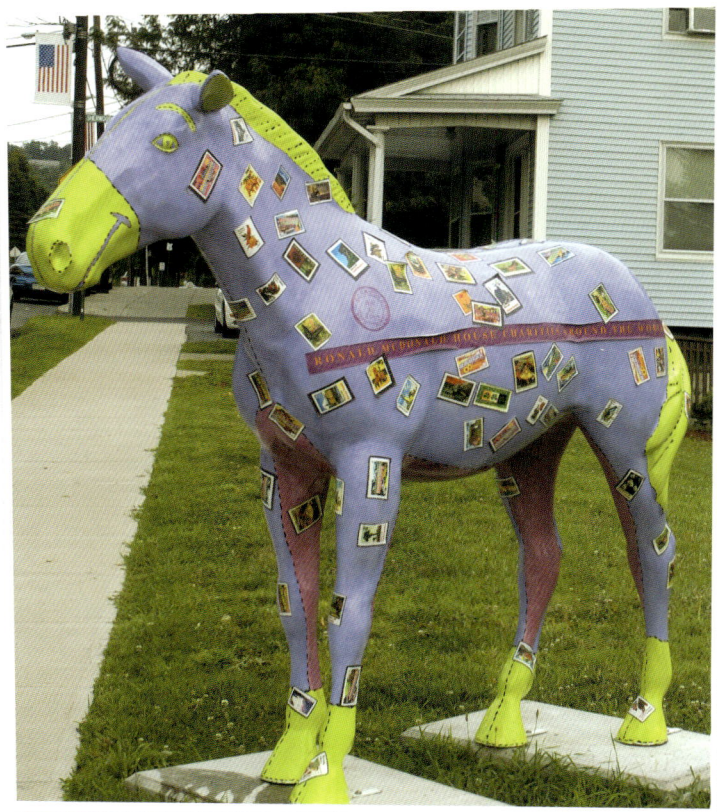

PLANETARY MULE

SCRANTON, PA

The student artists envisioned this mule as a planetarium for peace. Swirling planets forever circling in peaceful harmony with the heavens and all manner of celestial bodies.

RONALD MCDONALD HOUSES WORLDWIDE

SCRANTON, PA

Each stamp symbolizes one of the 165 Ronald McDonald Houses worldwide.

*Artist: Scranton School District's *BEST at NSIS*
Sponsor: Rural Urban Board – RUBIES

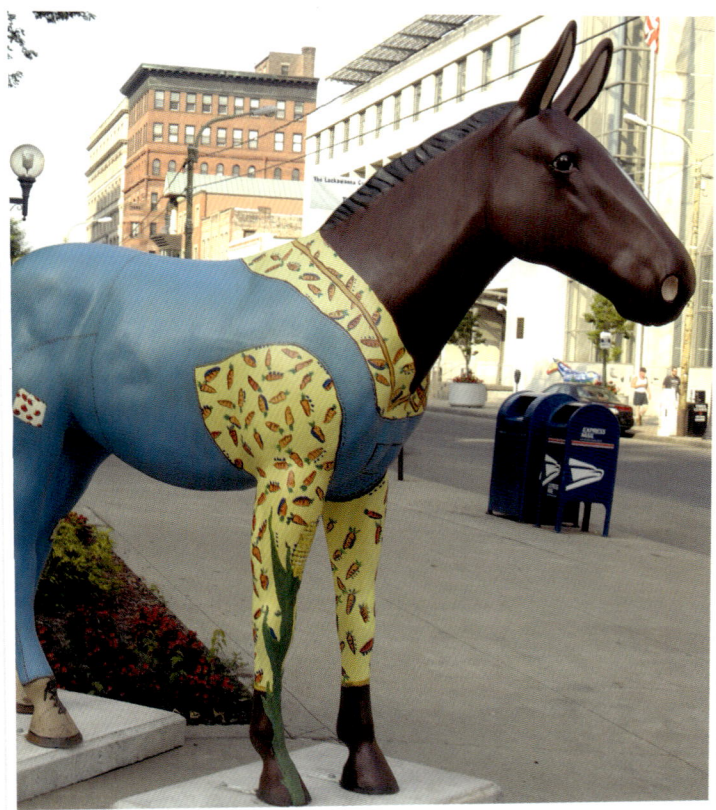

OLD MACMULE

SCRANTON, PA

Old MacMule had a farm…E-I-E-I-O! On this farm he had some…mules…E-I-E-I-O!

Artist: Peter Karis
Sponsor: The Times/Citizen's Voice/Tribune

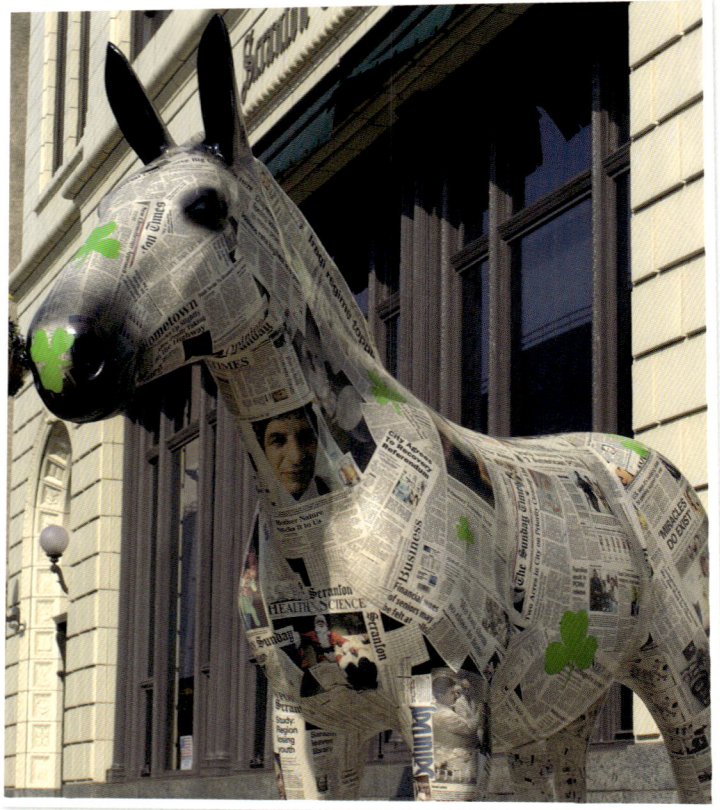

SHAMROCK

SCRANTON, PA

Extra, extra, read all about it! *Shamrock* is outfitted in all the news that's fit to print. And his cloverleaves bring him all the luck in the world!

Artist: David Klevinsky and Lance Erlick
Sponsor: Marywood University

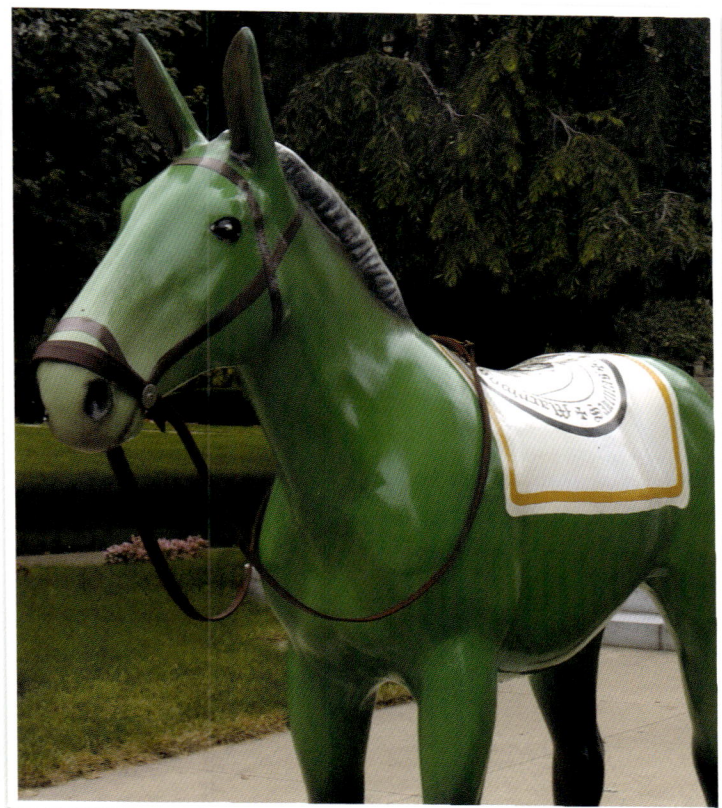

Artist: West Scranton High School Students
Sponsor: Greater Scranton Chamber of Commerce

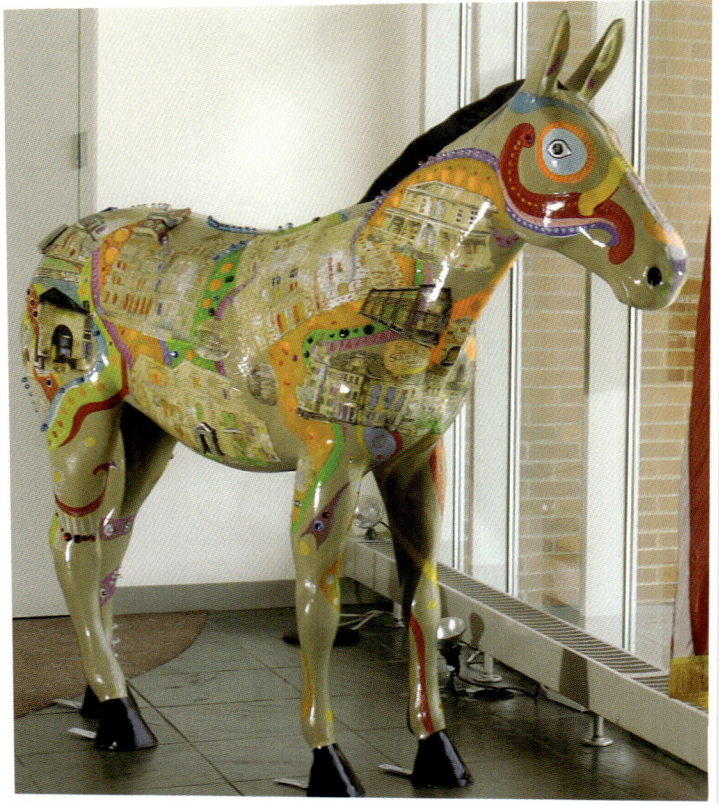

M.U.LE

SCRANTON, PA

Covered in "Marywood Green" – representative of the university's campus, a national arboretum renowned for its bucolic splendor – and emblazoned with the school seal and motto, "Sanctitas, Scientia, Sanitas."

SEEMORE OF SCRANTON

SCRANTON, PA

SeeMore features the architecture of Scranton's landmark buildings such as City Hall, Lackawanna County Courthouse, Scranton Cultural Center and other "fa-mule-iar" sites.

Artist: Cindy Trudgen
Sponsor: John and Mary Metz

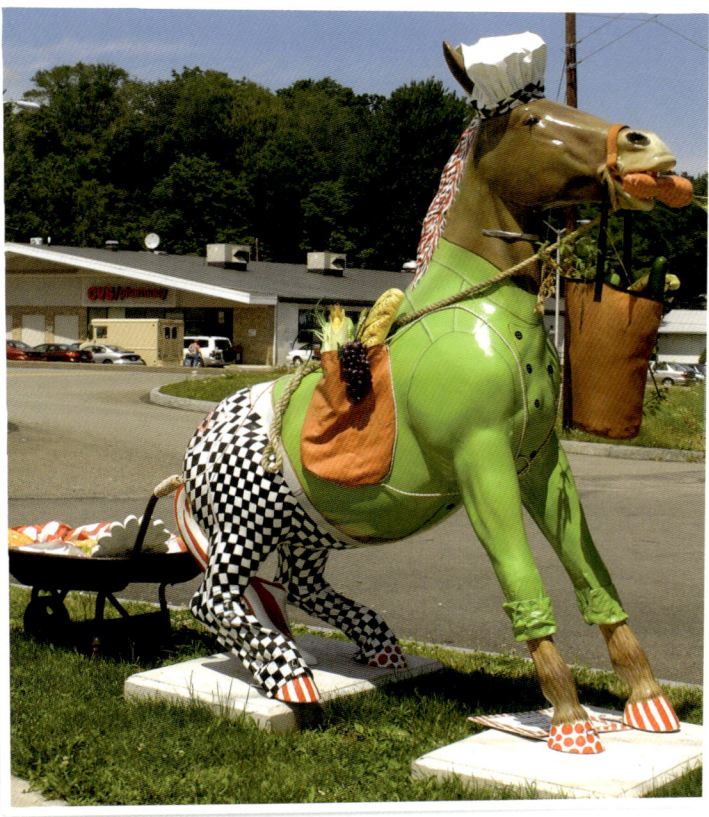

Artist: Barbara Sick and Tunkhannock Art Students
Sponsor: Johnson College

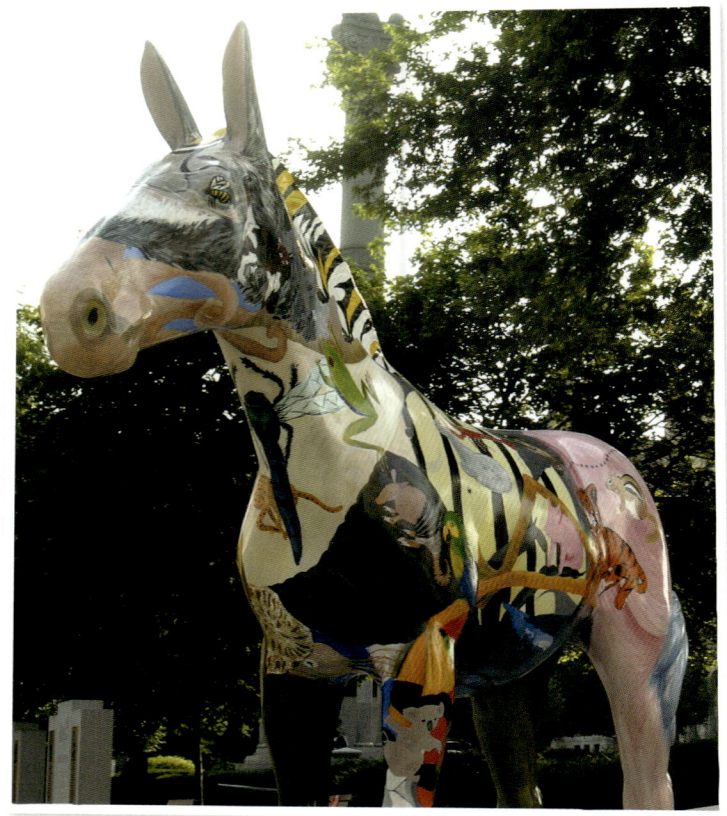

MILES OF MEALS

DALLAS, PA

This chef carries his ingredients in this mouth, in his wagon, and in his heart. He is a feast for the eyes and the mind. Bon Appétit!

NORTHEASTERN PENNSYLVANIA'S ANIMALS

SCRANTON, PA

All the region's animals, both real and imagined, cover this mule. With a lion's mane and boa snaking up one leg, one never knows what one can find with a little imagination.

Artist: MLB Advertising, Rider's World, Mark Frisco
Sponsor: Leadership Wilkes-Barre

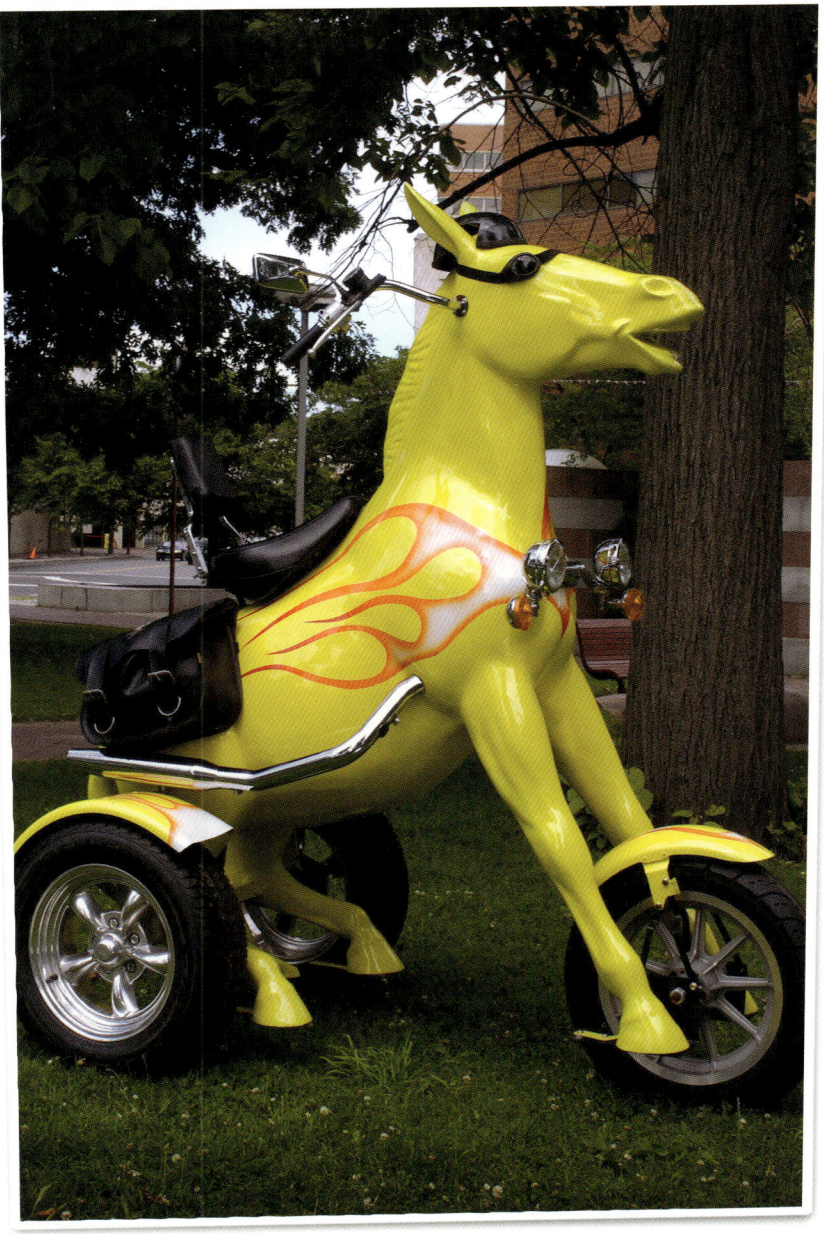

LEADER OF THE PACK
WILKES-BARRE, PA

Leadership Wilkes-Barre is a community leadership organization, which develops informed, committed leaders from all segments of northeastern Pennsylvania to serve, strengthen and improve the area. It offers programs for high school students and adults and is making an important impact throughout the region.

Miles of Mules was such an appropriate way to partner with so many others to celebrate the area's unique heritage. And with the lead mule, no less! To provide artistic vision for the daunting task of decorating this 80-pound fiberglass mule, Maslow Lumia Bartorillo Advertising was enlisted. Michael Scholl's and John Bartorillo's creation of "a mule on the move" was an instant hit!

Rider's World of Wilkes-Barre stepped into the picture to execute the design. Dr. George Volpetti, the owner, donated hardware and Steve Stahl customized the creature by installing motorcycle parts, including wheels, fenders, handlebars, a seat, headlights, a helmet, goggles, and even snazzy saddlebags.

Mark Frisco, a student at Penn College of Technology, added a shiny coat of paint and flame decals at his automotive shop. Charles Barber of Leadership Wilkes-Barre's Board of Directors assumed responsibility for transporting the mobile mule all around the Wyoming Valley. During this tour, *Leader of the Pack* attended a dinner event, made a TV appearance, and even participated in a fund-raising motorcycle ride.

"…creation of 'a mule on the move' was an instant hit!"

Artist: Fran Fasolka, IHM and Donna Korba, IHM
Sponsor: St Joseph's Center Auxiliary

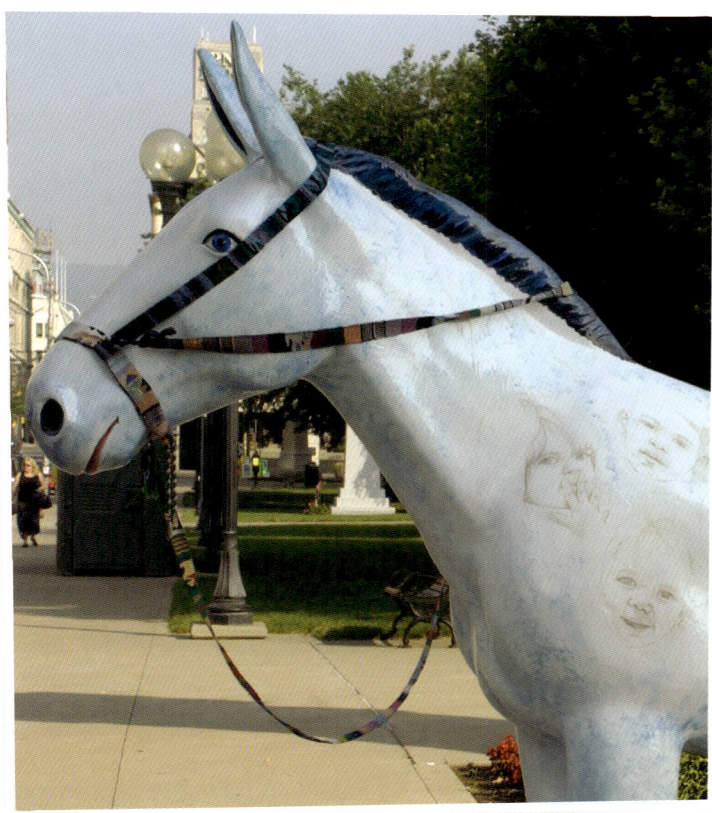

Artist: George Strasburger
Sponsor: Aventis Pasteur

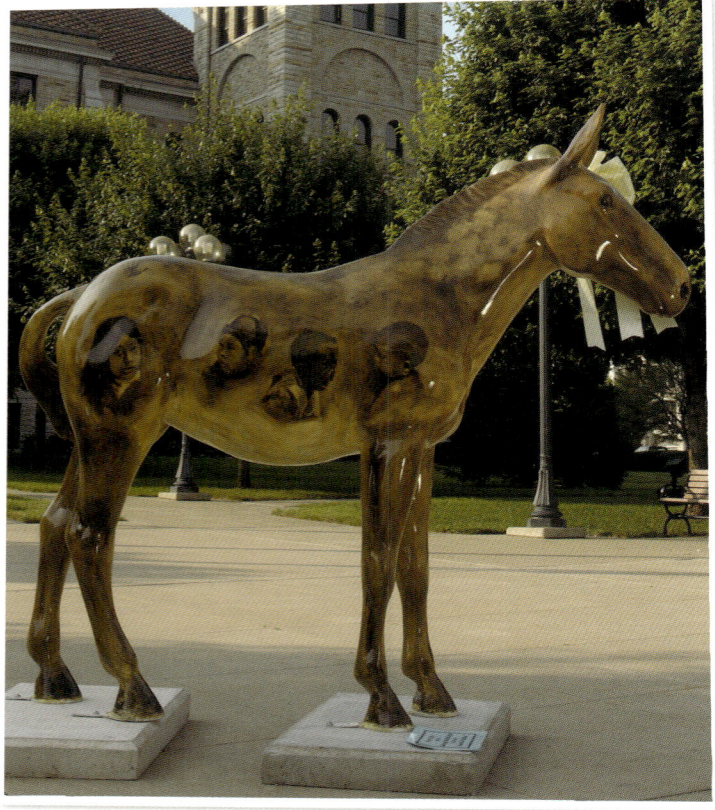

FACES OF THE FUTURE

SCRANTON, PA

St. Joe's 115-year commitment to the needs of children is reflected. The alphabet represents growth and development. Key words can be found that express the wonder of childhood.

the CHILD

SCRANTON, PA

Manufacturing life-saving vaccines brings hope to all. This design is a touching portrayal, to fuel our hearts and spirits, of children everywhere, in our mines and across the world.

Artist: Earl Lehman
Sponsor: Lackawanna Historical Society

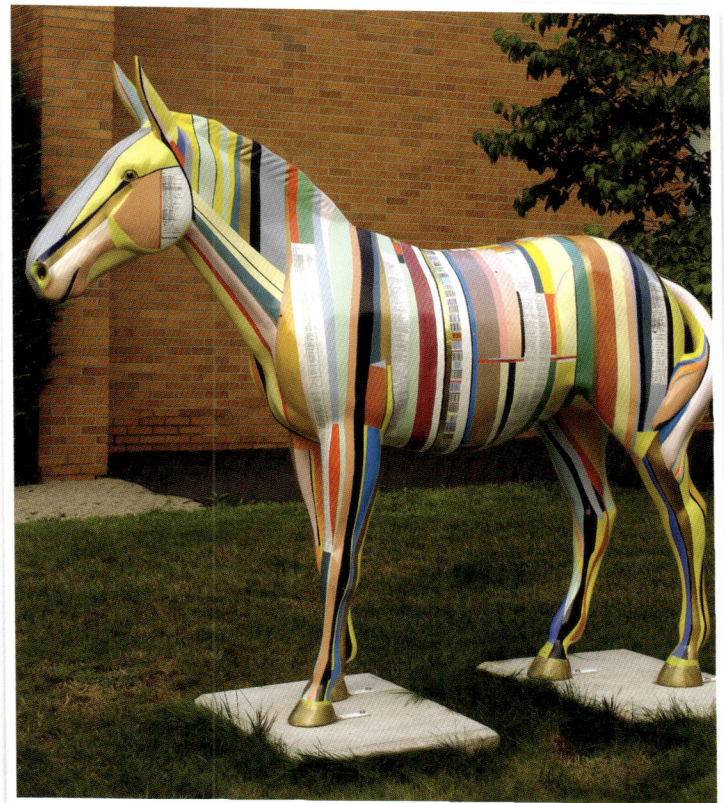

uTA NAKA 1

SCRANTON, PA

Think UPC, the universal symbol of commerce. Beautiful colors integrate the hidden components of gain and profit, greed and grandeur, with the buried stories of laborers, their resistance, persistence, and strength.

Artist: Earl Lehman
Sponsor: Southern Union Company

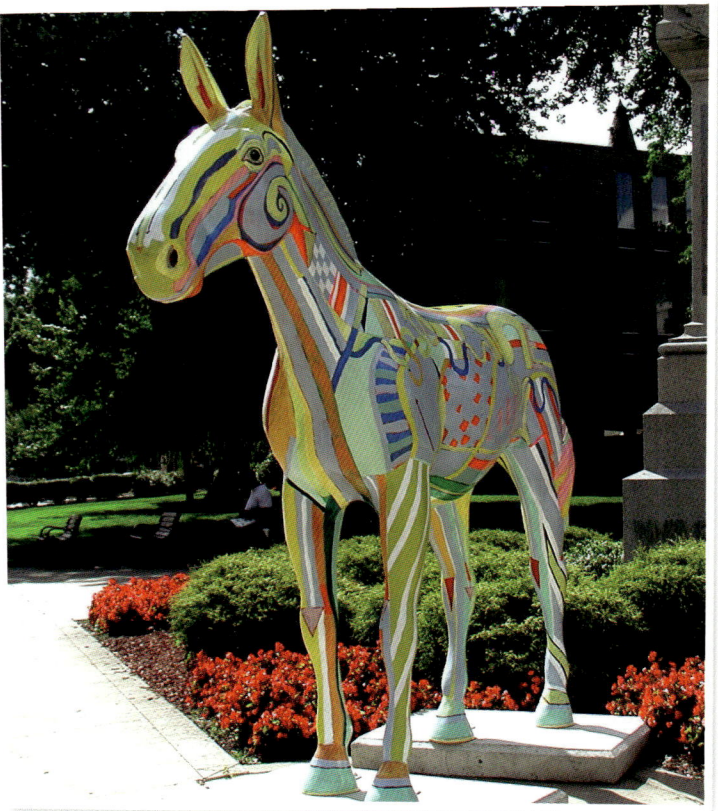

Photo by Allen Sachse

uTA NAKA 11

SCRANTON, PA

This mule brings a flag for a new tomorrow. Initially, the artist claims he was stubbornly resistant to using the mule as a canvas. Then something clicked – like hoof beats.

Artist: George Bancroft School Students
Sponsor: Lackawanna Heritage Valley

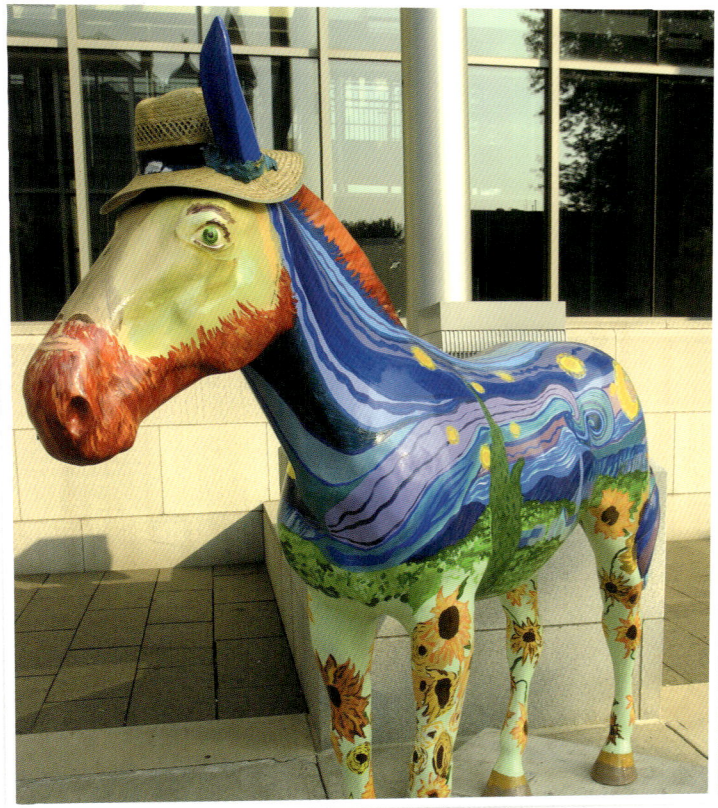

VINCENT VAN MULE

SCRANTON, PA

His realistic face gives him a quiet dignity. Does he mourn the loss of his ear?

Artist: Bill K. & LCCC/Misericordia Art Students
Sponsor: Luzerne County Community College/College Misericordia

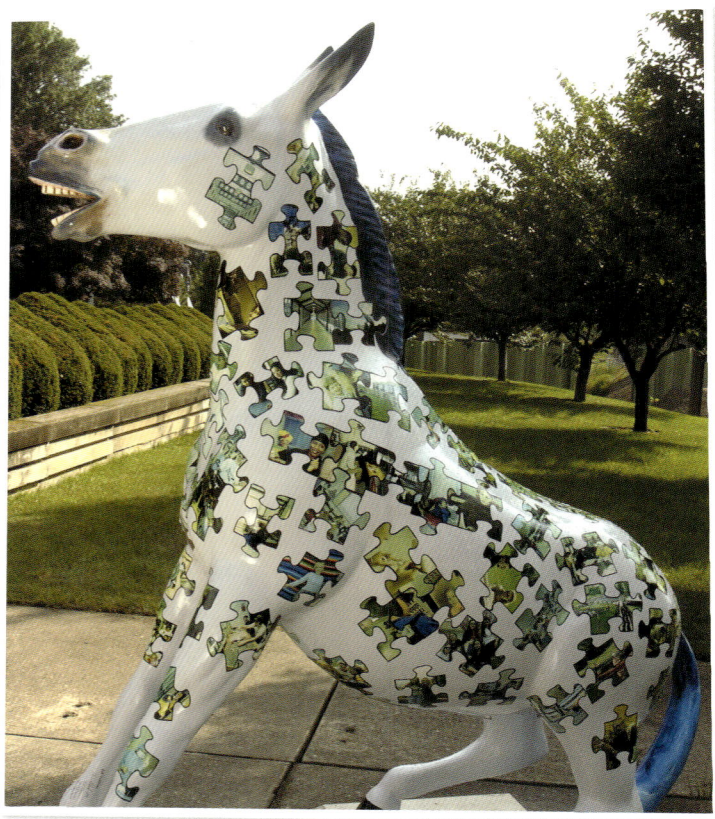

JACKSAW PUZZLE

WILKES-BARRE, PA

Like the pieces of the puzzle he sports, *Jacksaw* brings together two college communities.

Artist: Kerry Ann Vitanovec-Flaherty
Sponsor: Downtown Wilkes-Barre Business Assoc. & Diamond City Partnership

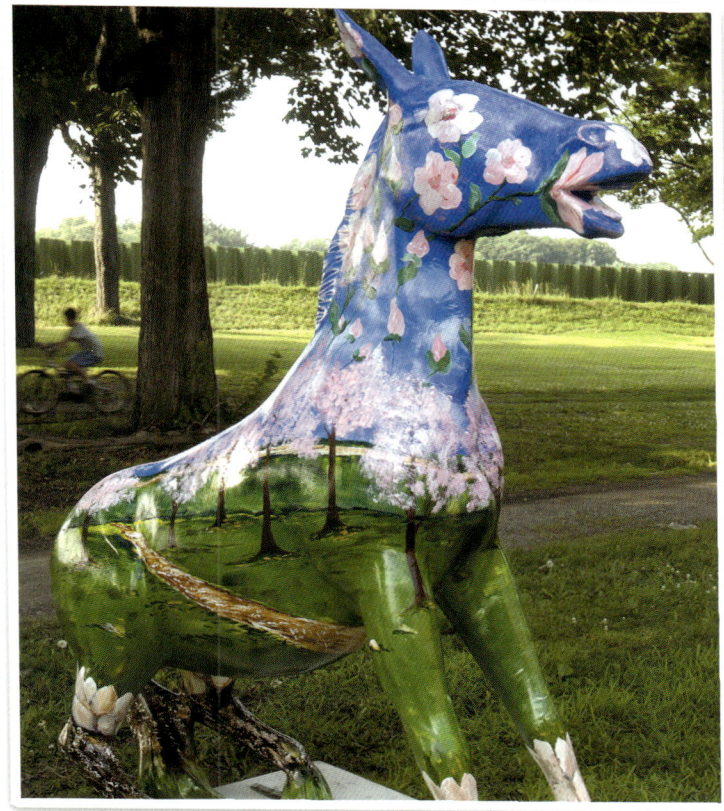

Artist: Students of King's College
Sponsor: King's College

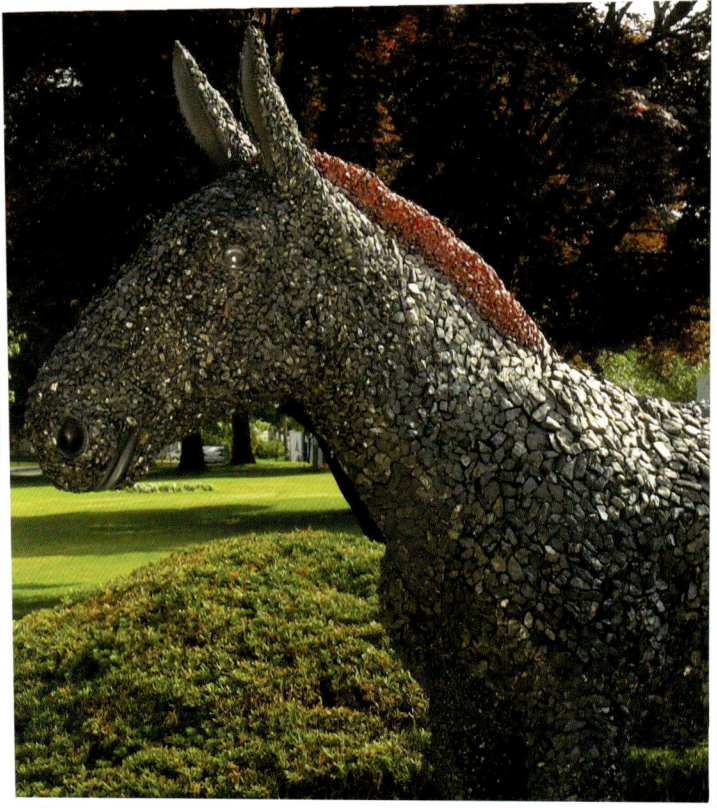

it's CHERRY BLOSSOM tiME

WILKES-BARRE, PA

In April and May, the River Commons come alive. The pink and white of the cherry blossoms are so vivid. This mule is to be enjoyed like a fine spring day on the riverbank.

HOPE

WILKES-BARRE, PA

With hope for the future, she wears her coat of coal proudly, without complaint. Just like her fellow laborers who carried coal from the mines.

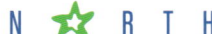

Artist: Anna Ostapiw
Sponsor: Cultural Council of Luzerne County, with thanks to the Marquis George MacDonald Foundation

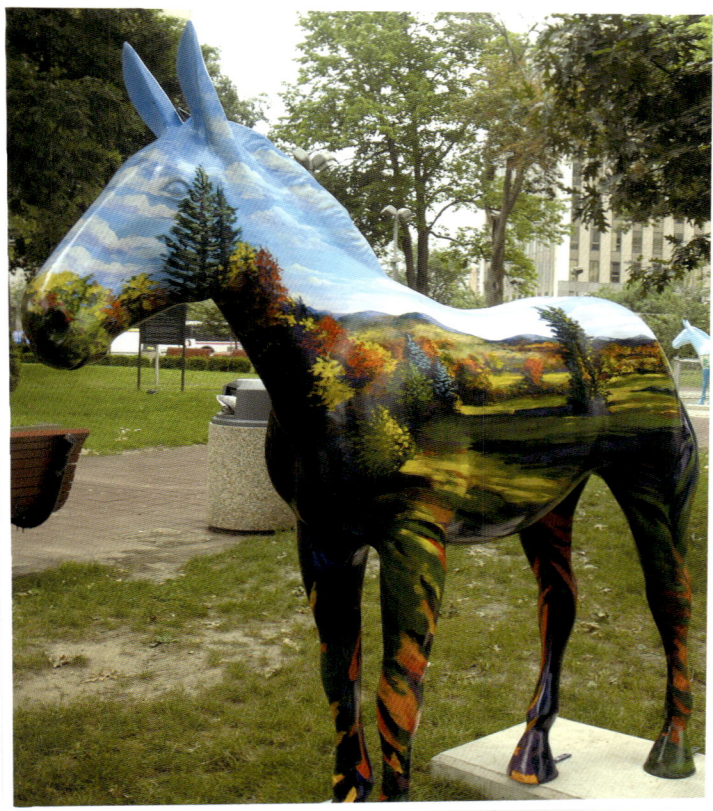

NORTHEAST
WILKES-BARRE, PA

Like autumn in northeastern Pennsylvania, here strokes of color are at first subtle hints, tentative and shy. Then Mother Nature's paintbrush becomes bold, with slashes of color, relentless and breathtaking.

Artist: Peter Karis
Sponsor: Greater Wilkes-Barre Chamber of Commerce

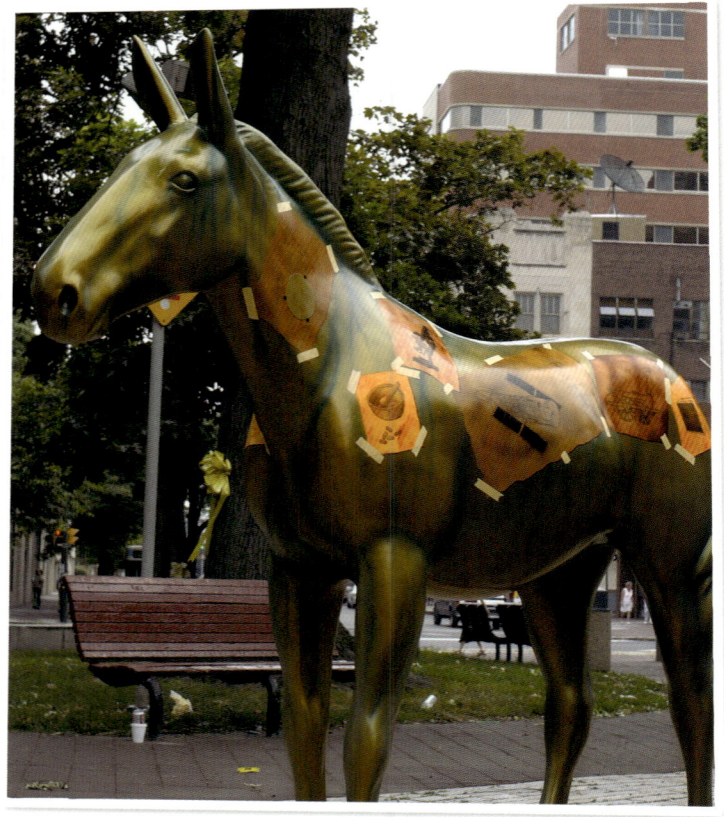

PROGRESS
WILKES-BARRE, PA

Here in Wilkes-Barre, all points lead to *Progress*. Taking steps both large and small to make the city, its people, their business and industry strong and productive.

Artist: S. Fagaly, C. Dermody, A. Koval, C. Martin
Sponsor: The Luzerne Foundation

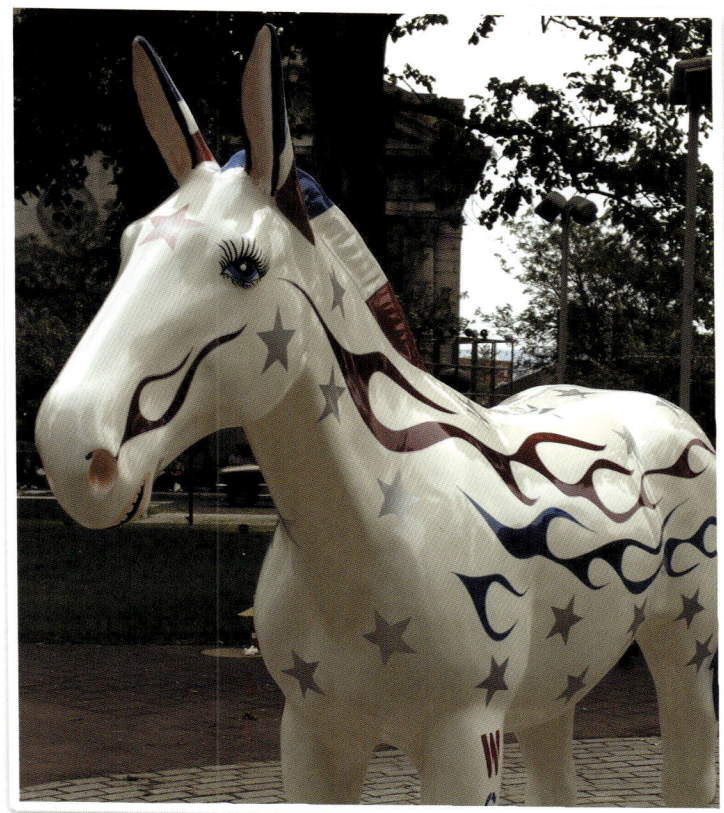

Artist: JuLiMaKaSuDi
Sponsor: F. M. Kirby Center for the Performing Arts

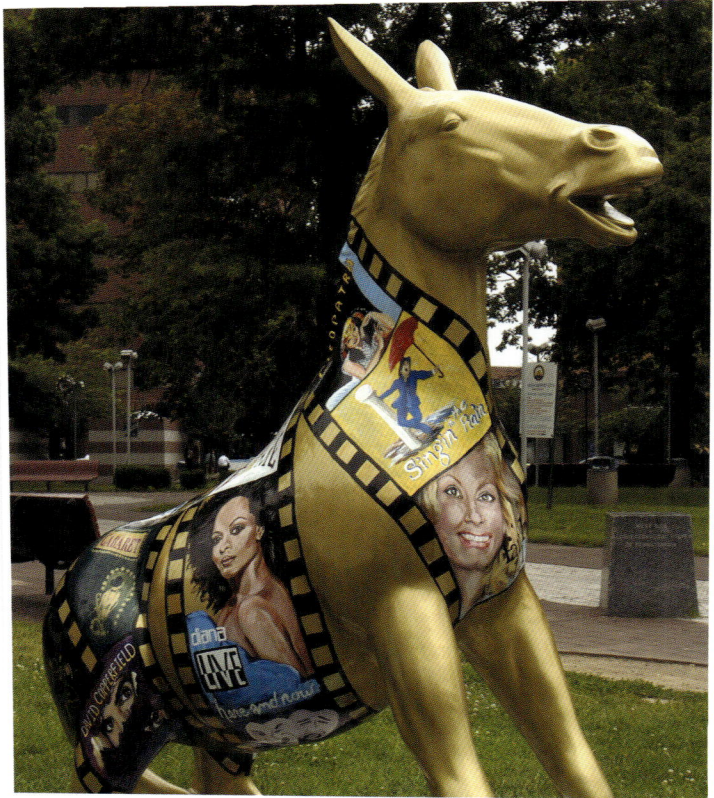

tECH StAR

WILKES-BARRE, PA

Tech Star shines with bright stars, flaming stripes, sparkles and spangles.

CECIL B. DEMULE

WILKES-BARRE, PA

Lights, camera, action! Scenes from the many events that have taken place at the historical Kirby Center. I'm ready for my close-up…

Artist: Jim Rogowski
Sponsor: Cultural Council of Luzerne County with thanks to the Wilkes-Barre/Scranton Penguins

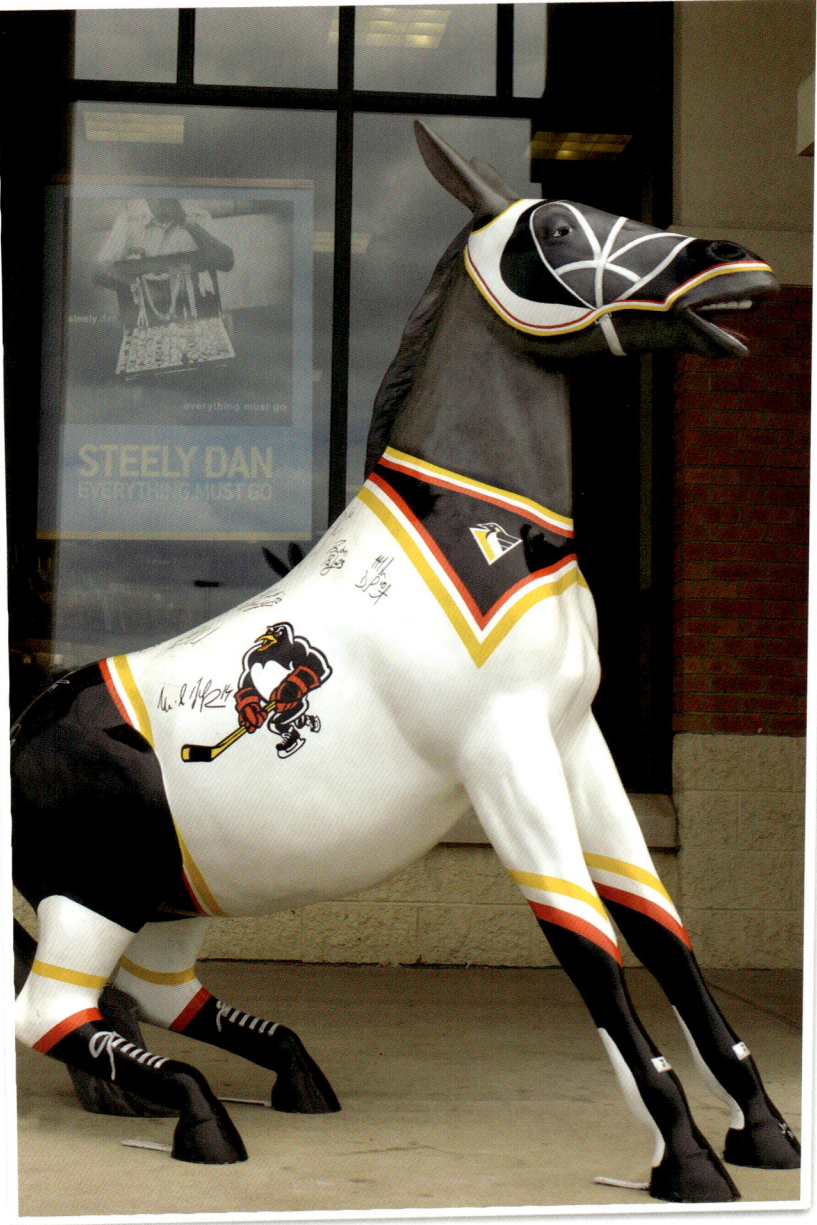

MARIO LEMULE

MOBILE

Just like his namesake Hockey Hall of Famer Mario Lemieux, *Mario LeMule* is an important team player. Artist and creator Jim Rogowski of Pikes Creek wanted *Mario* to showcase the growing sense of community unity, which develops from regional sports teams. Dressed in the colors of the Wilkes-Barre/Scranton Penguins, *Mario* is a representative of team spirit and the sportsman in all of us.

Covered in actual signatures from players on the Penguins team, *Mario* is a valuable work of art that deserves the spotlight. With a too-tight goalie mask the mule may have lost his front teeth, but not his character!

This summer *Mario* traveled to many different venues in and around Wilkes-Barre/Scranton gaining popularity and recognition. His first love is the Wachovia Center at Casey Plaza where the home games are played. However, rather than remain in one spot, *Mario* enjoyed team travel; promoting the Penguins everywhere he went. With this attitude the mule, dubbed a "Miles of Mules Ambassador," journeyed wherever his community needed him!

"...*Mario* is a representative of team spirit and the sportsman in all of us."

Artist: Michael E. Hockenbury
Sponsor: Citizen's Voice

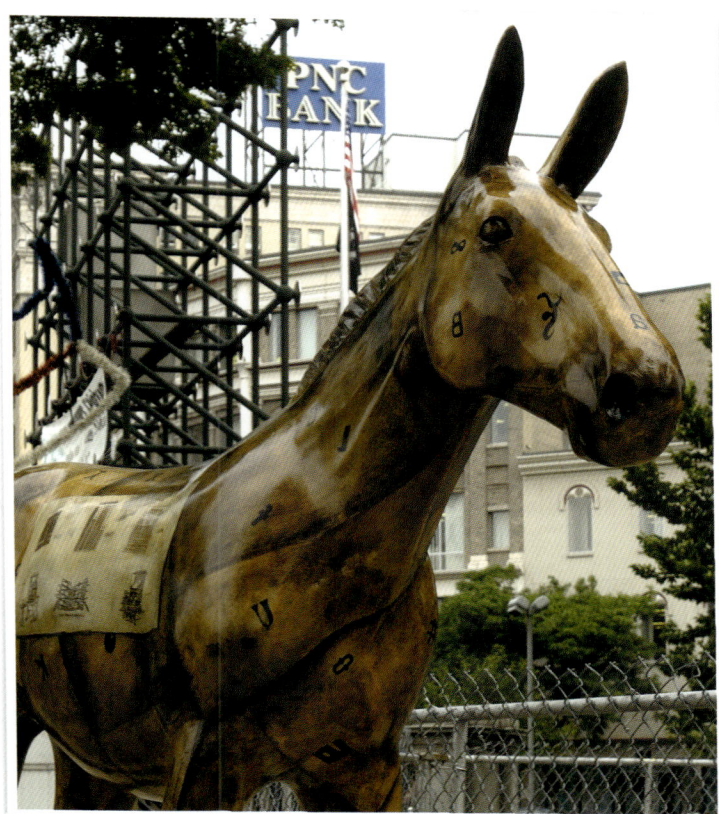

Artist: Members of Wyoming Valley Art League
Sponsor: The Luzerne Foundation

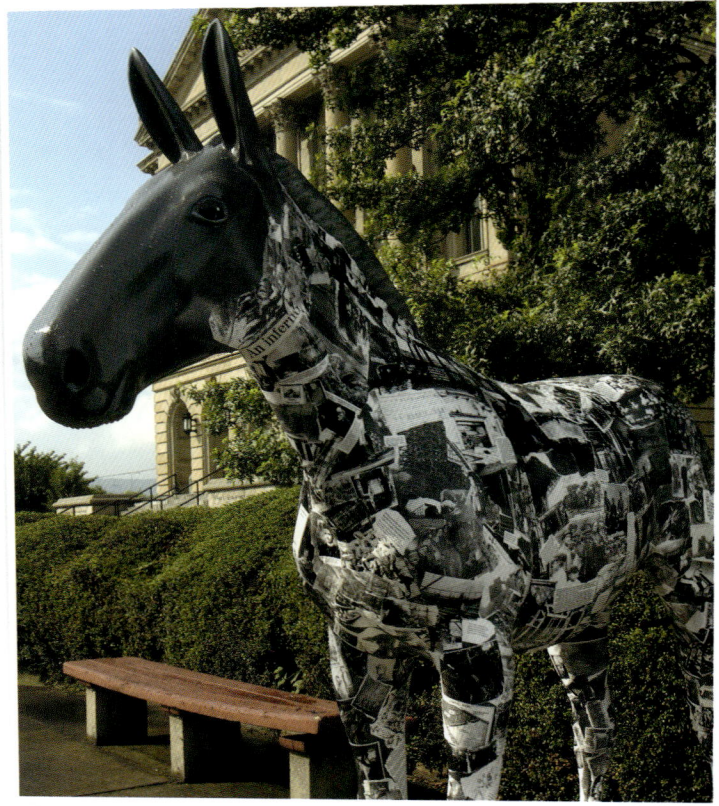

PRESSED FOR TIME

WILKES-BARRE, PA

Follow the timeline of the history of the printing press "off-set" by rich wood tones.

MOXIE THE MINER'S MULE

WILKES-BARRE, PA

The bond between miner and mule was a strong one. *Moxie* proudly carries the stories of miners, both their joys and heartaches.

Artist: Joan Schooley
Sponsor: Luzerne County Historical Society

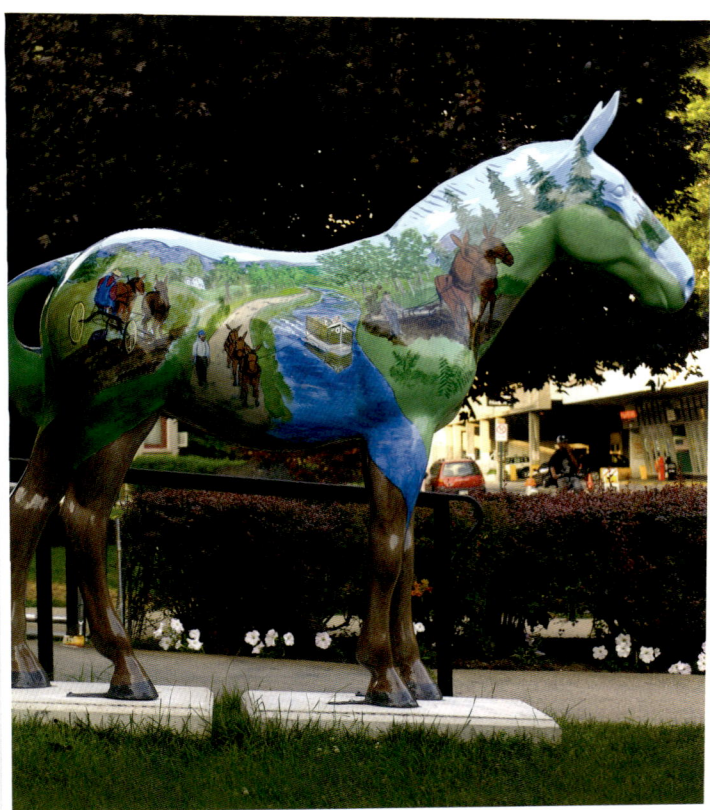

Artist: Jan Otoupalik
Sponsor: InterMetro Industries

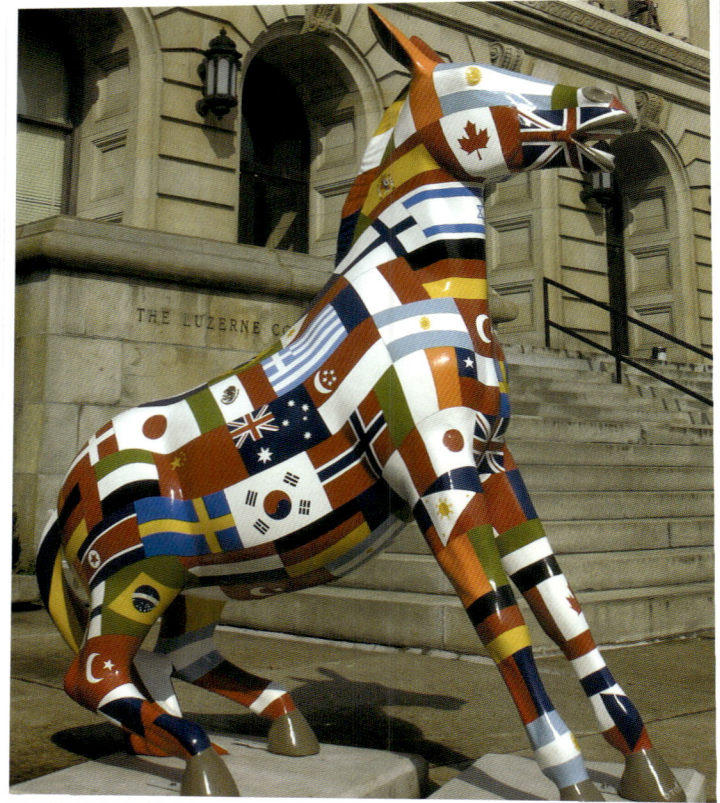

WORKING MULE

WILKES-BARRE, PA

The life of a hard-working mule includes hauling coal and timber, pulling the barge, and plowing the fields. All work and no play does not make a dull mule!

MULE-T-NATIONAL

WILKES-BARRE, PA

International flags envelop this stubborn mule to represent the many nations served by InterMetro, an international storage solutions company headquartered in Wilkes-Barre.

Artist: Marie Guglielmo
Sponsor: Times Leader

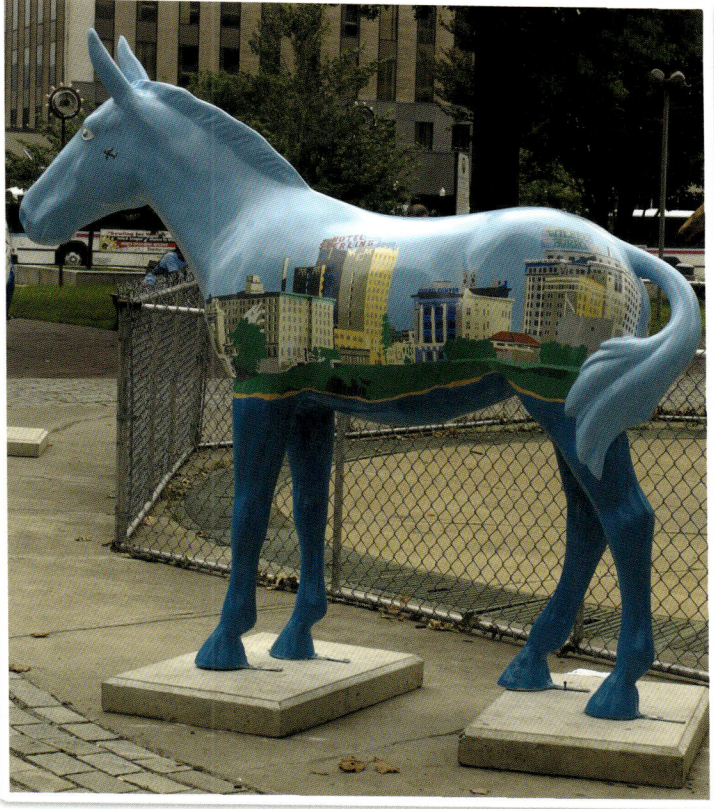

Artist: The Kid's Café Children and VidaWorks
Sponsor: Commission on Economic Opportunity

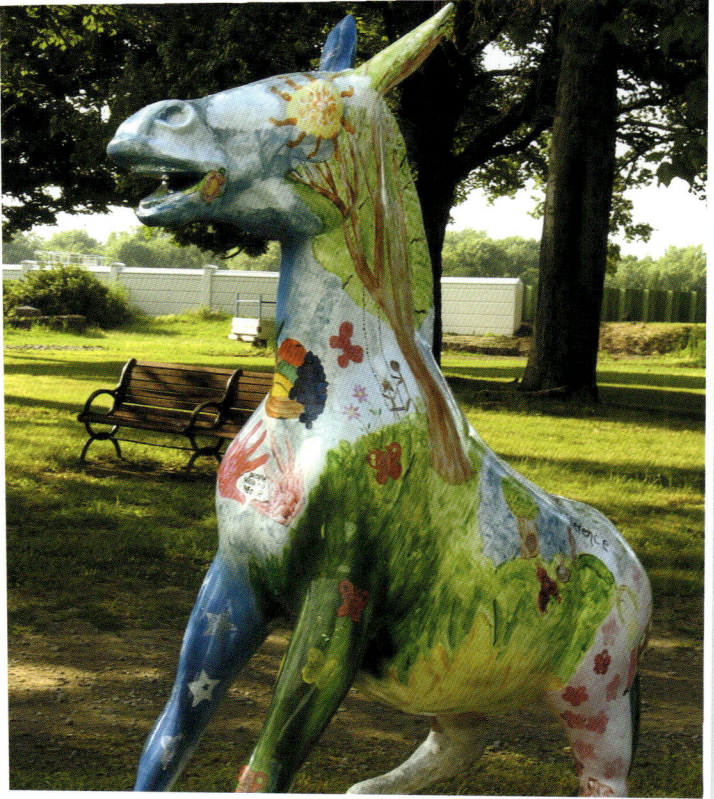

WILKES-BURRO

WILKES-BARRE, PA

Downtown Wilkes-Barre landmarks like Hotel Sterling, the Guard Center, and the Mellon Bank building can be seen. Can you find the turtle in the river?

HELPER

WILKES-BARRE, PA

You can always count on this mule to lend a helping hoof. His motto is "People Helping People."

Artist: Di Hinson
Sponsor: Donna Michak

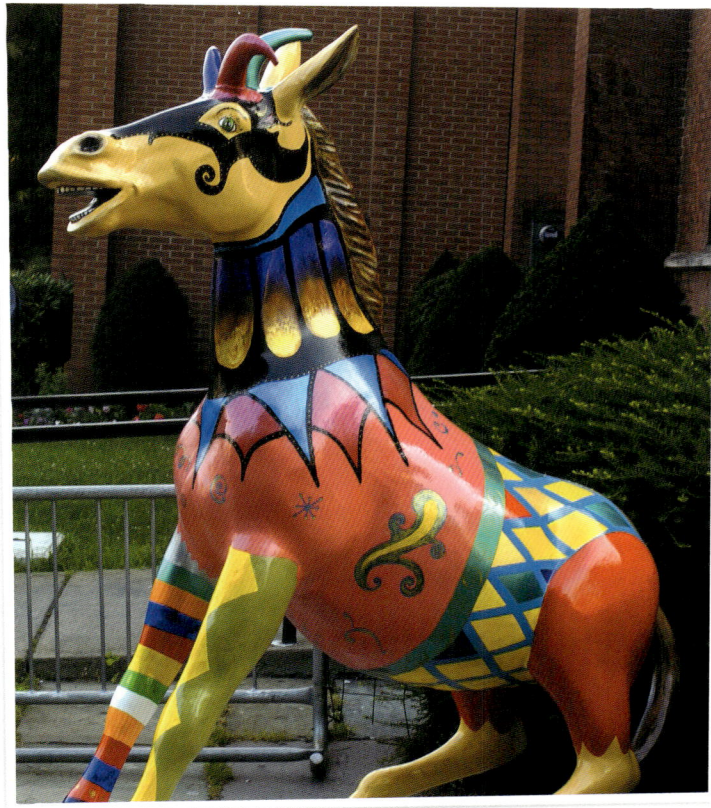

Artist: Michael Nada & Katie Gilmartin
Sponsor: Junior League of Scranton

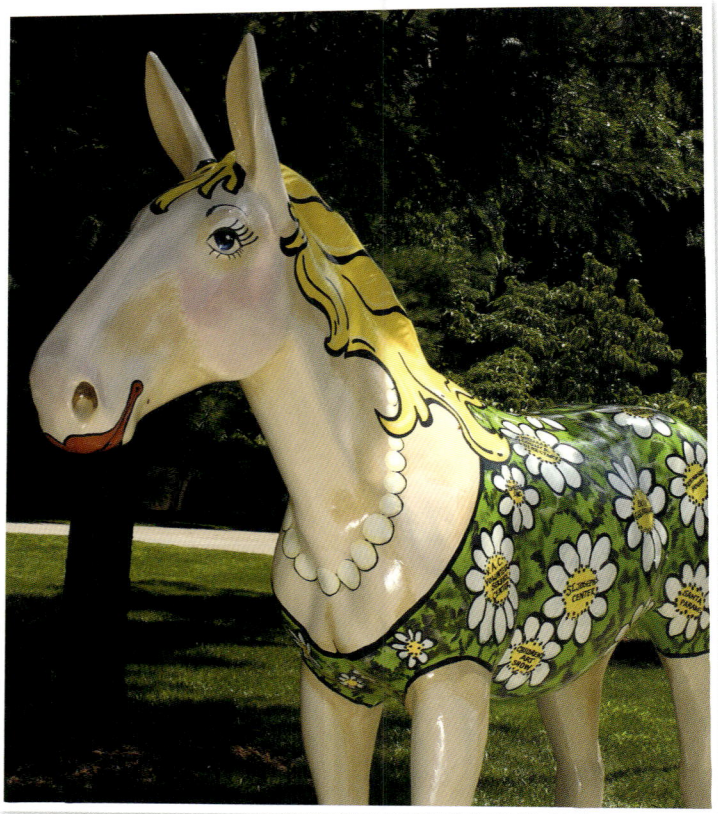

THE MOTLEY SAGE

WILKES-BARRE, PA

Inspired by Le Carnivale and Cirque du Soleil, this enchanting beast is a whimsical and glorious spectra of colors, created solely to bring merriment and celebration without reason. Imagine!

JUNIOR LEAGUE JEWEL

SCRANTON, PA

All sparkle and shimmer, *Jewel* glimmers in the sunshine. Diamonds are even a mule's best friend!

DET★ILS

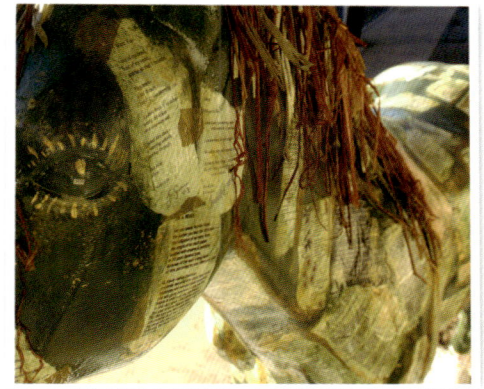
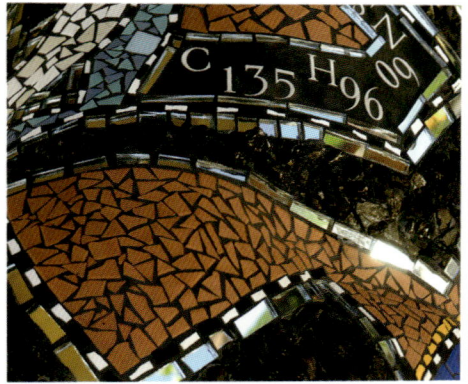
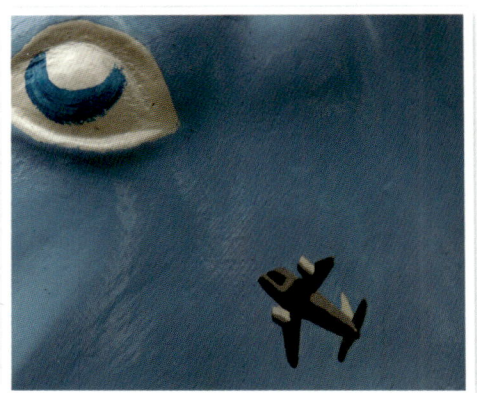
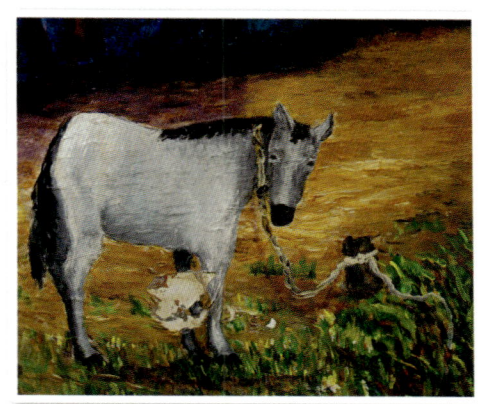
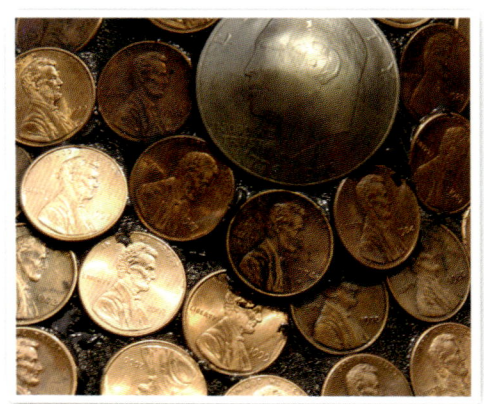
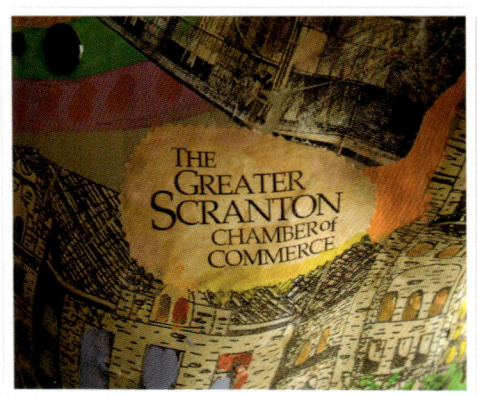
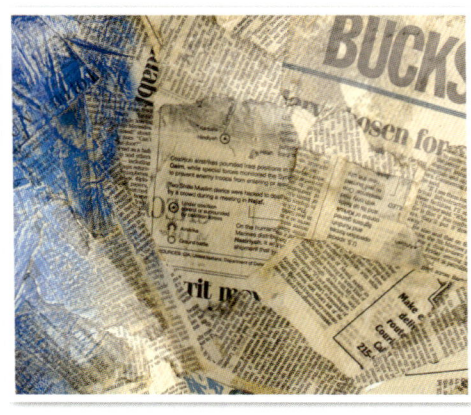
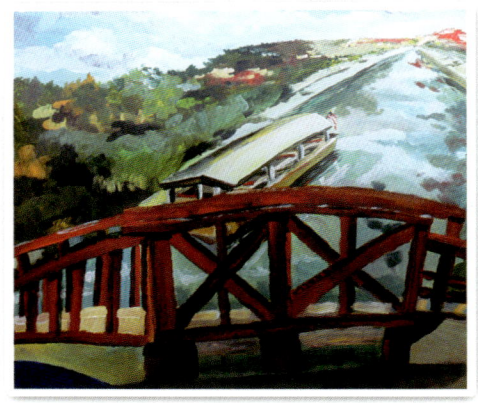
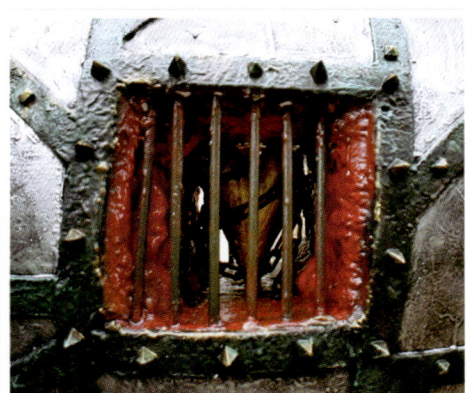

CENTR★L CORRAL

t he Banana Factory's prototype mule is an eye-catcher created by famous "Outsider Artist" Mr. Imagination. More than 25,000 different bottle caps were used to create this design, which includes strings of caps in its gorgeous mane and tail.

Each year the Bethlehem-based Banana Factory introduces the fine arts to area school children, hosts gallery exhibitions, offers educational art programs and sponsors national and international artists in residence.

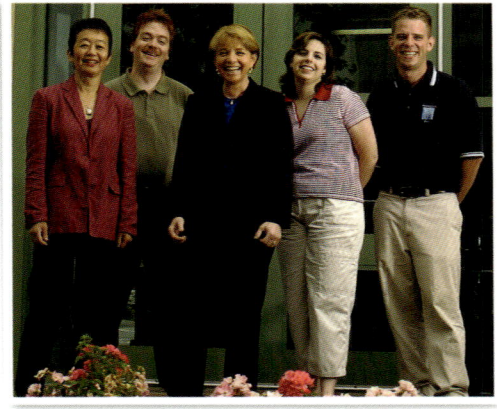

From left to right:
Michiko Okaya,
Mark Demko,
Diane LaBelle,
Laurie Stoudt,
Steven Truscott

The art center created BananaWORKS, a summer program collaboration with inner city youth who work with artists to create and implement public art projects. 2003 marks its sixth successful year.

Each year more than 50,000 people utilize the services offered through the nonprofit Banana Factory. These include tuition-based art classes available to all students regardless of ability to pay, thanks to the support of private donors.

When the arts center first opened in 1998, in a refurbished banana warehouse, it housed 24 visual artist studios, two galleries, classrooms, community space and facilities to accommodate Pennsylvania Youth Theatre and Bethlehem Area Vocational Technical School's (BAVTS) production studios. Since then, it has added a first-floor educational center with expanded visual arts classrooms, new office space and a 2,800 square foot gallery.

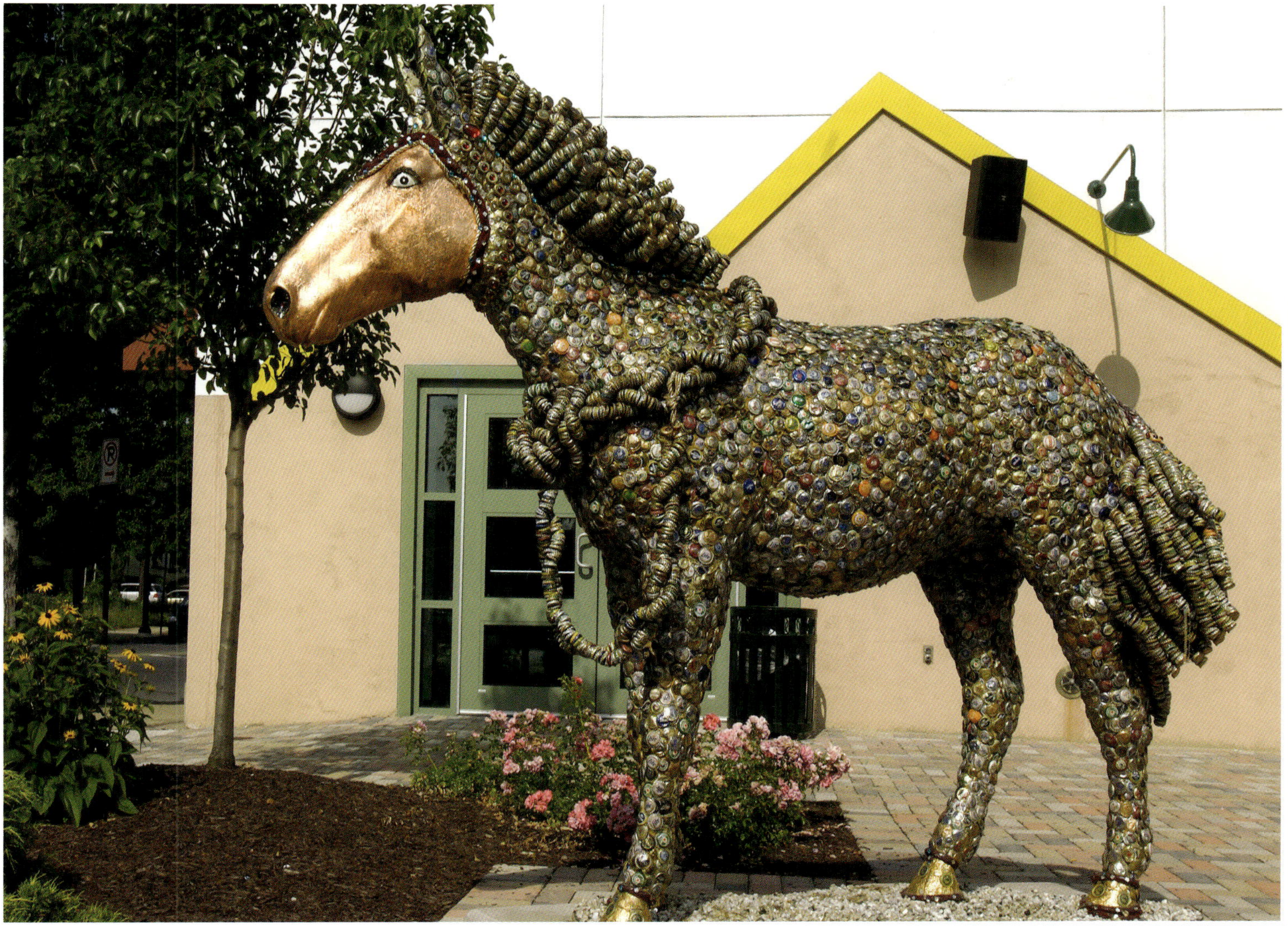

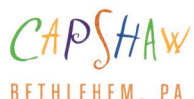

CAPSHAW
BETHLEHEM, PA

Artist: Mr. Imagination
Sponsor: The Banana Factory

"More than 25,000 different bottle caps
were used to create this design…"

Artist: Bernie Smith
Sponsor: Dan's Camera City

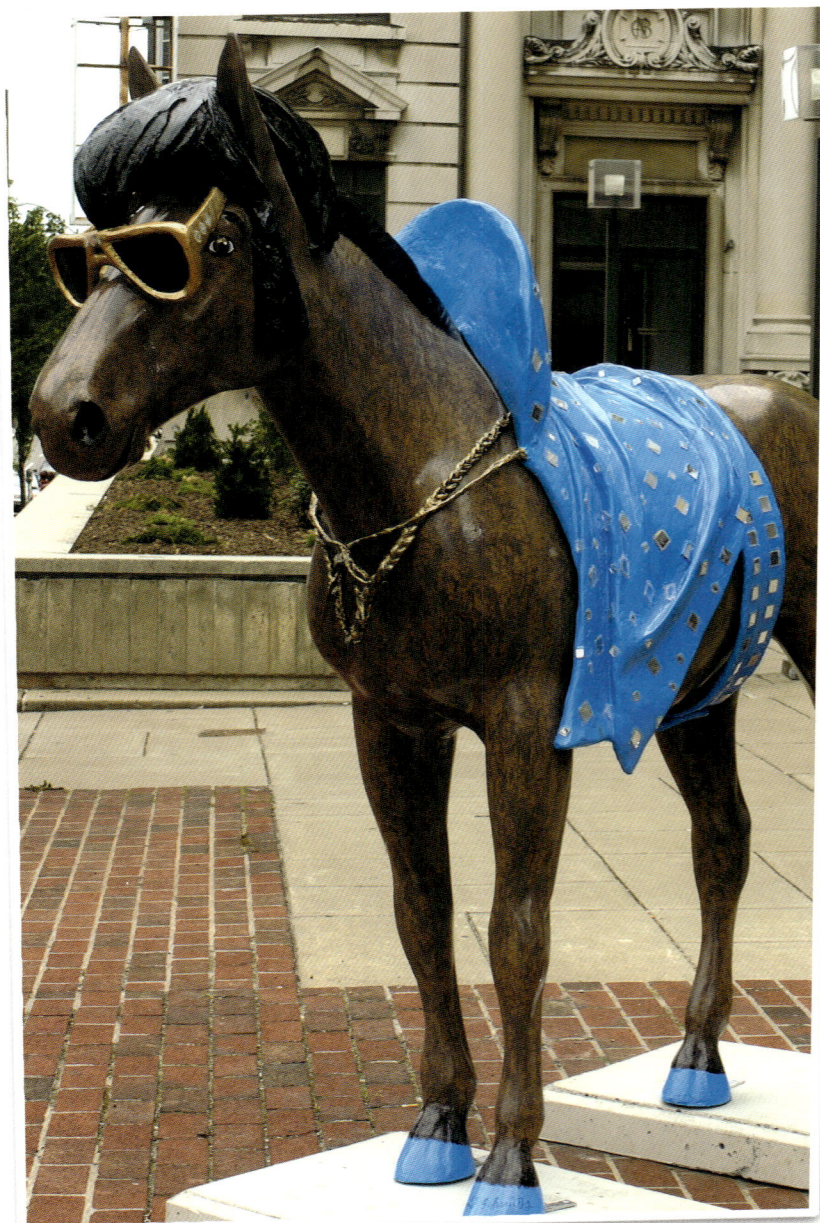

MULEVIS

Attention: The King has been spotted in Allentown.

Well, the king of the mules, that is.

Few figures in American pop culture are as recognizable and beloved as Elvis Presley. His good looks, great voice and charisma endeared him to millions throughout the world. Now, the **Miles of Mules** public art project has its very own icon – *Mulevis*.

The mule, created by Easton artist Bernie Smith, pays tribute to Presley from head to hoof with black, slicked-back hair, a rhinestone-studded cape and a pair of cool shades. Oh, yeah, and then there are the blue suede hooves… Like Elvis, *Mulevis* has attracted the attention of many. He was the first Lehigh Valley area mule to draw a sponsor, earning the support of Dan Poresky and Dan's Camera City of Allentown.

Dan's Camera City joined the **Miles of Mules** project because it supports the arts and projects that benefit the community. *Mulevis*'s design was chosen by them from more than 80 potential designs because of its simplicity, unique personality and resemblance to Elvis. The company's support got the ball rolling and prompted other area businesses, individuals, schools and nonprofits to look closely at the public art program and its benefits to the community.

Ah, Thank You, Thank You Very Much!

"Oh, yeah, and then there are the blue suede hooves…"

Artist: Rosemary Geseck
Sponsor: Mayfair Festival of the Arts

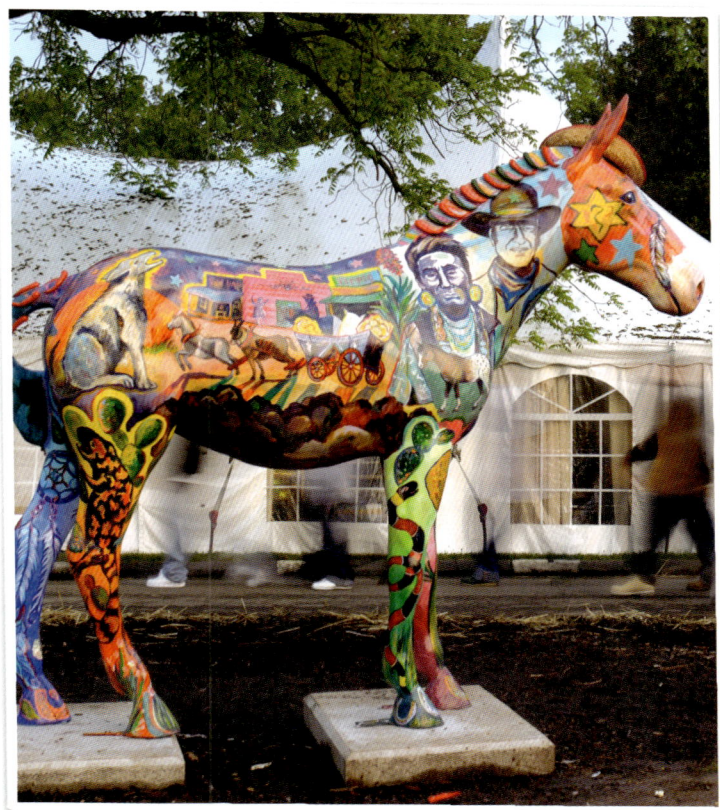

Artist: Muhlenberg College Art Association
Sponsor: Muhlenberg College

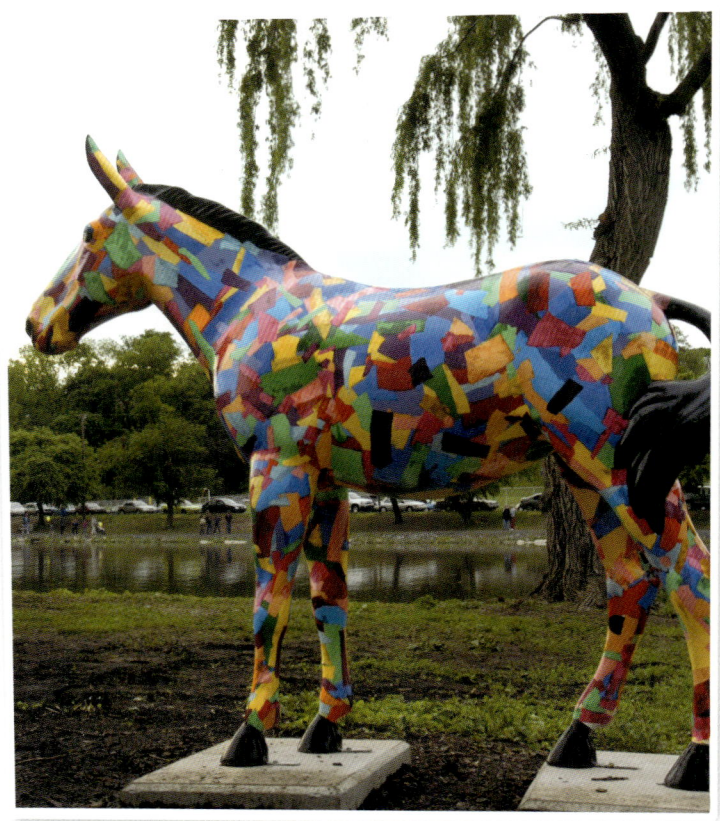

20 MULE TEAM PROUD! YIPPIE YI YAY-BRAY!

BETHLEHEM, PA

Several views of the West are showcased in full color. This mule was influenced by the artist's life in Tucson, Ariz., where the animals were also important to the region's history.

CARNIMULE

BETHLEHEM, PA

A colorful collage of paper captures the fun and festivities of a carnival.

Artist: Lehigh Valley Plastics Design Team
Sponsor: Lehigh Valley Plastics, Wachovia & Quadrant EPP

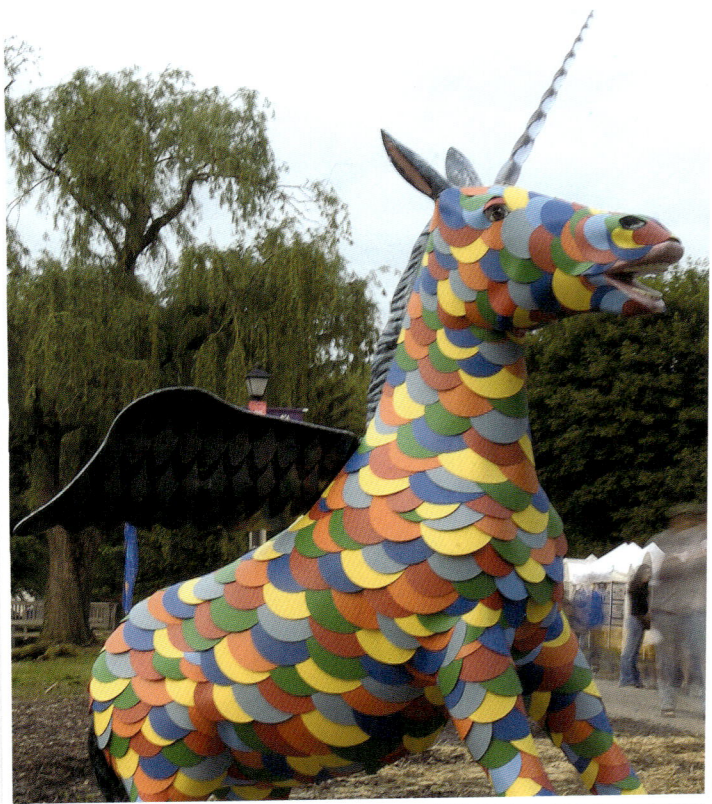

Artist: Rebekah Simonds and Rosemary Geseck
Sponsor: Lehigh Carbon Community College

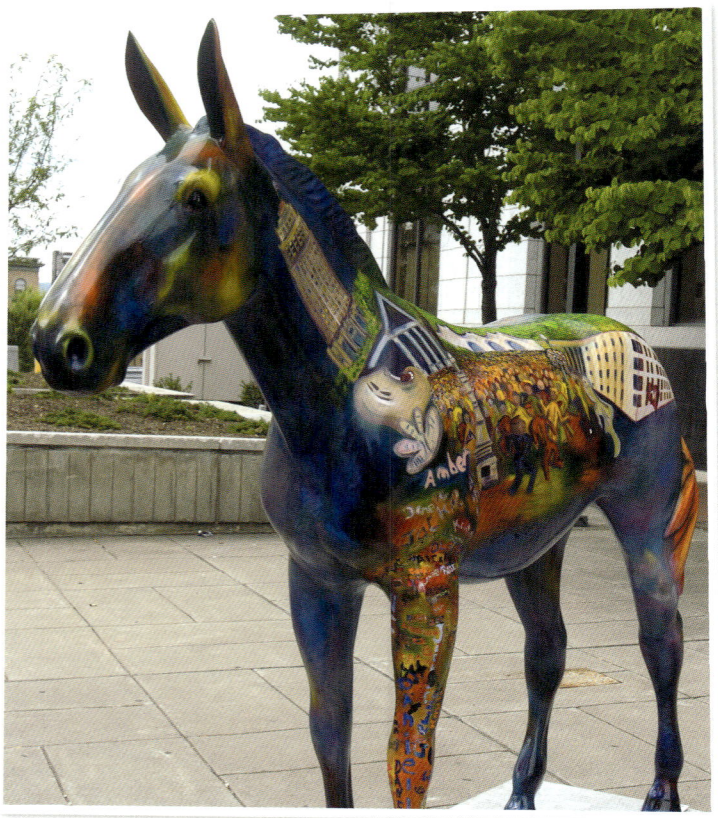

FLY "MULE" to the MOON

ALLENTOWN, PA

Completely decorated in Lehigh Valley Plastics' products. Multicolored plastic scallops cover the body while beautiful wings and a whimsical horn add to its unique features.

IMAGES OF ALLENTOWN

ALLENTOWN, PA

Several cityscapes of Allentown are depicted, including vibrantly painted visions of pedestrians interacting in the streets of this county seat.

Artist: Rosemary Geseck's Baum School of Art Students
Sponsor: The Baum School of Art

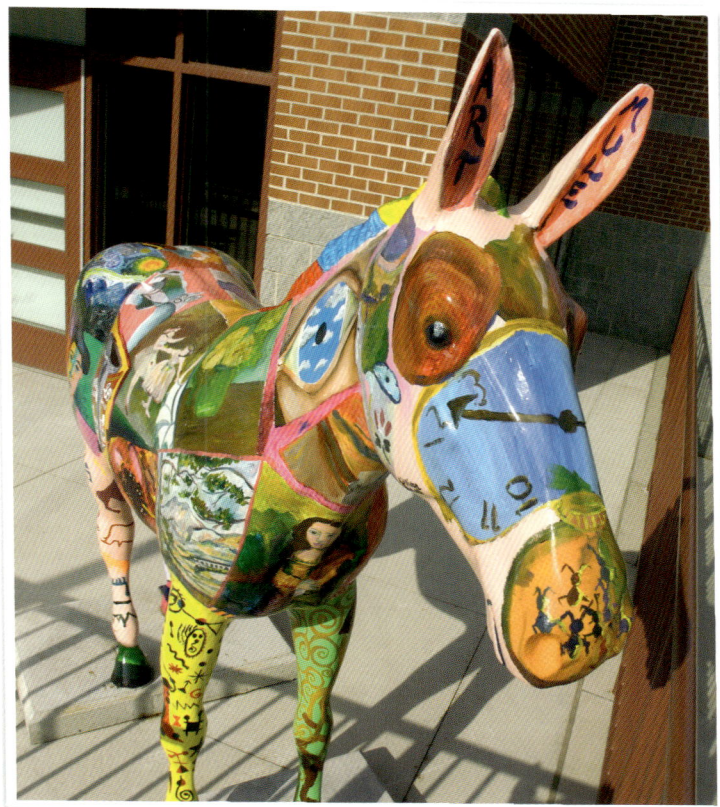

Artist: Haifa Bint-Kadi
Sponsor: Allentown Manor

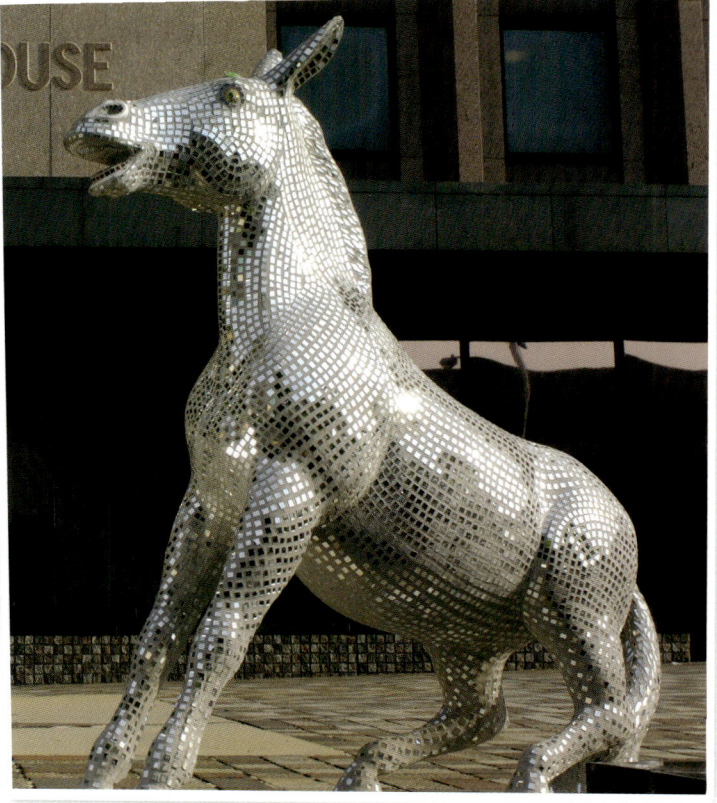

MULE OF MASTERS

ALLENTOWN, PA

Students studied the different painting styles of the Masters, including Monet, Degas, Picasso, da Vinci and van Gogh, and created a collage of miniature paintings depicting them.

MULE-TIDE REFLECTIONS

ALLENTOWN, PA

Enveloped in small mirror tiles, this mule is an exquisite, interactive piece allowing those who view it to see themselves in a multitude of reflections.

Artist: Bill Harris
Sponsor: Linny Fowler

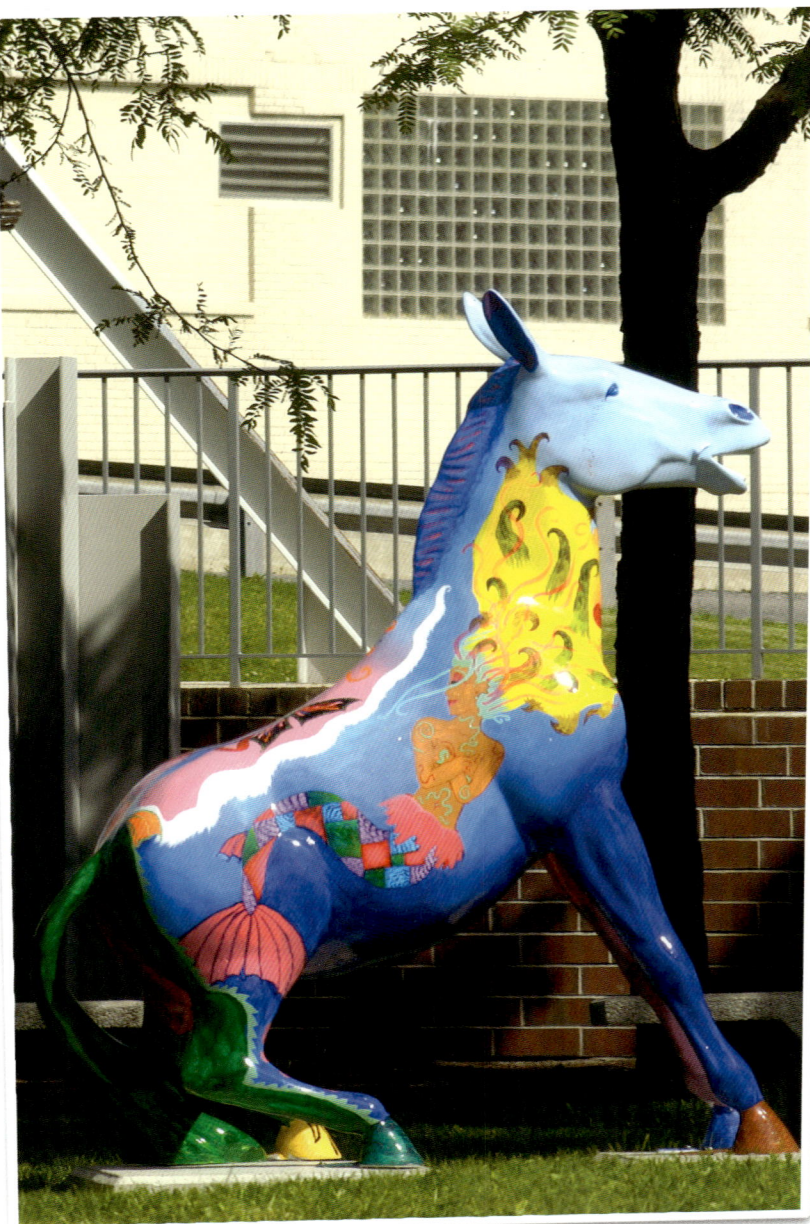

MYTHICAL MULE

BETHLEHEM, PA

Whenever there's a cause or an organization in need of a helping hand – especially if it involves young people and the arts – Marlene Fowler of Bethlehem is there. Her financial support has given many area children access to a positive creative outlet, allowing them to learn, grow and explore.

Fowler, simply known as "Linny" by those who know and love her, was one of the first sponsors to jump on board with the **Miles of Mules** public art project. Through her generosity, some amazingly talented young artists, some only 6 or 7 years old, were able to create and implement designs of which their communities can be extremely proud.

Fountain Hill Elementary School students crafted *Mule T. Cultural*, a vehicle to support cultural unity and expression; aspiring 18-year-old artist Bill Harris of Bethlehem designed the magical *Mythical Mule;* Broughal Middle School students created *The Broughal Middle School Mule;* and students from Donegan Elementary School crafted *Mona Mule.* In addition, Lehigh Valley Child Care staff created the *"Hands On"* mule, which features tracings of children's hands.

By being such an integral part of the **Miles of Mules** project, Linny has given young people an opportunity – to dream, to hope, to have fun, to create. There's little doubt this generous lady has made a positive impact on these young lives that will last well after the mules have been retired to the corral.

"...to dream, to hope, to have fun, to create."

Artist: Patricia Sonne
Sponsor: Lehigh Cement Company

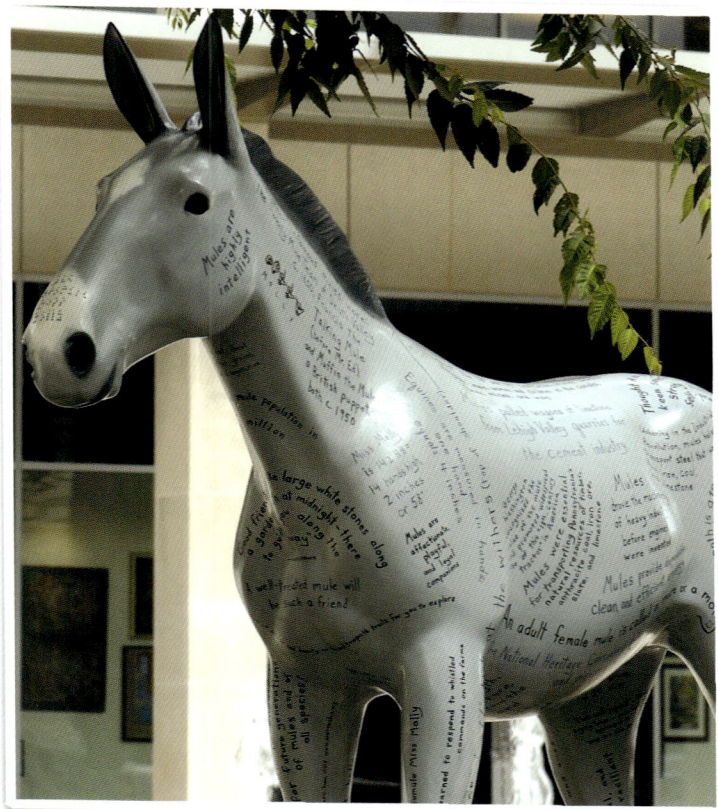

Artist: Sheckler Elementary School Students and Teacher Bill Nothstein
Sponsor: Catasauqua Home & School Association

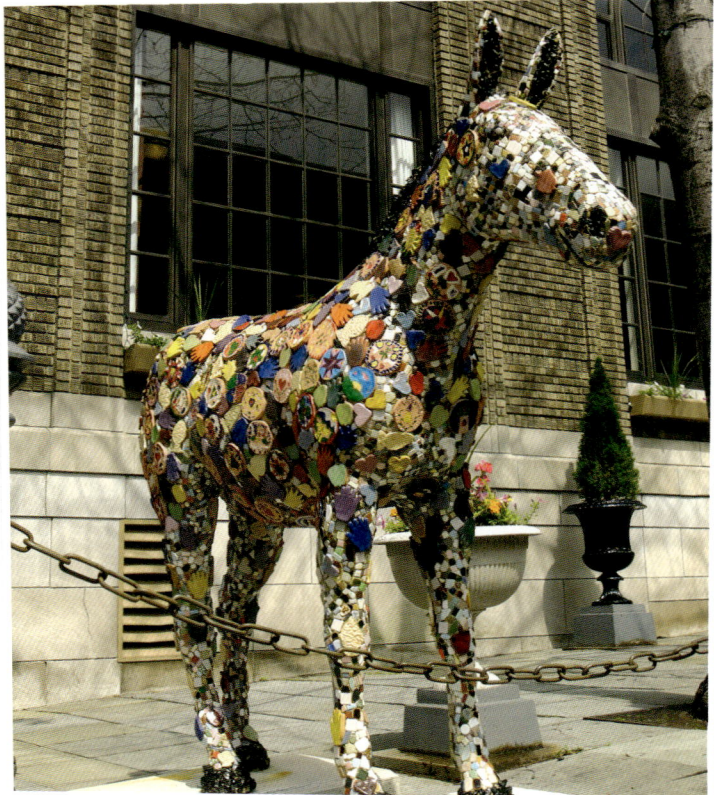

THE INFOMULE MISS MOLLY

ALLENTOWN, PA

Its wealth of historical and scientific data educates the public about mules, the region's dependence upon the canals and the canal corridor.

CATASAUQUA, "OUR RICH HISTORY"

BETHLEHEM, PA

More than 500 Sheckler Elementary students in kindergarten through fourth grade each created an individual clay tile of a specified theme. Each tile was glazed, fired and then affixed to the mule.

Artist: Moravian College Art Club
Sponsor: Payne Gallery of Moravian College

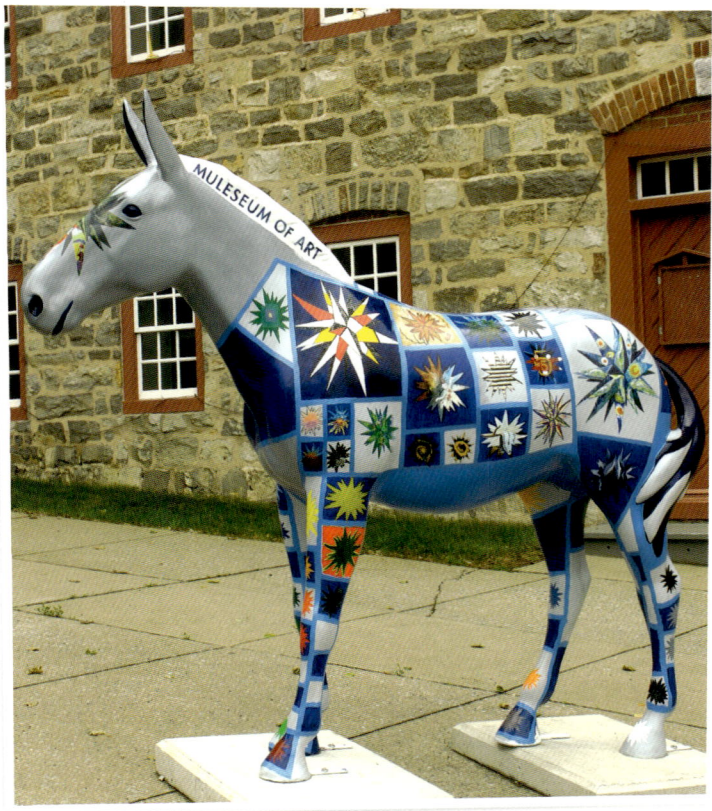

Artist: Tara Czujak
Sponsor: Wegmans Food Markets, Inc.

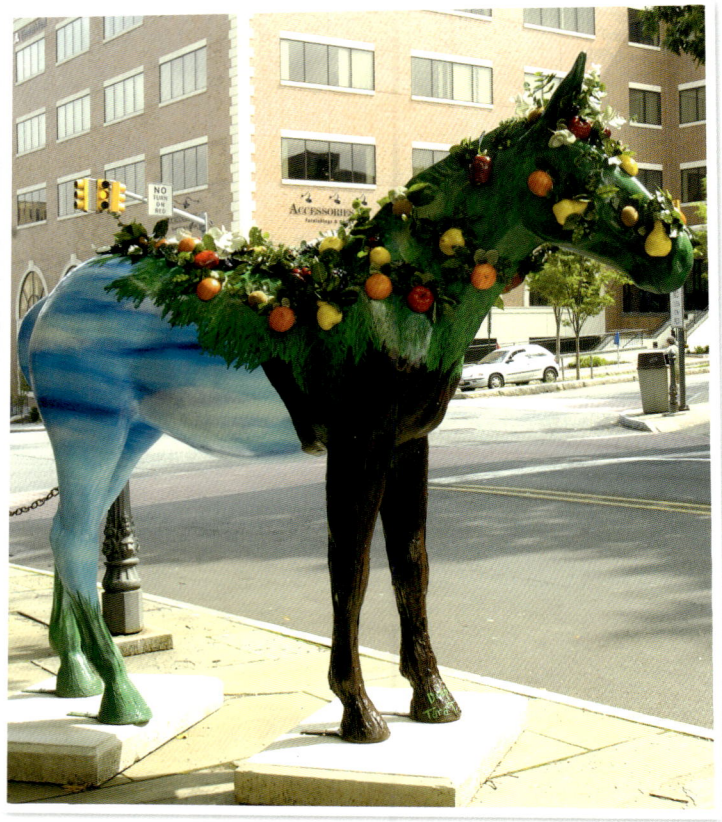

MORAVIAN COLLEGE MULESEUM OF ART

BETHLEHEM, PA

Students in the art club each created a Moravian Star in the style of a famous artist. The techniques emulated include those of Keith Haring, Monet and Degas.

DEEP ROOTED

BETHLEHEM, PA

A bountiful three-dimensional fruit-bearing tree and blue sky embody *Deep Rooted*. Wegmans Food Markets, which has three stores in the Lehigh Valley, chose this design to reflect its business philosophy and mission.

Artist: Jenny Leggett & Students of Lehigh Valley Academy Regional Charter School
Sponsor: Lehigh Valley Academy Regional Charter School

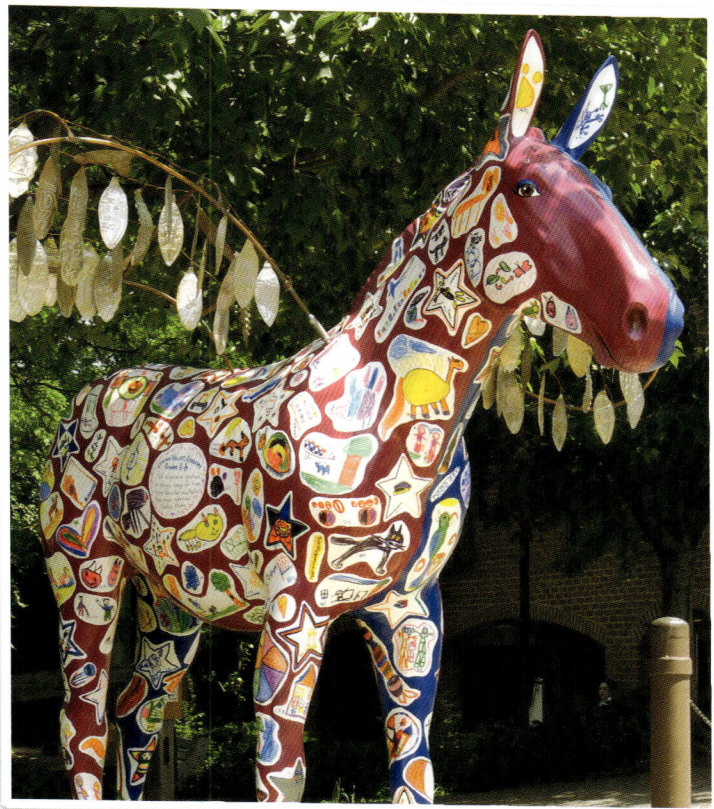

GREETINGS

BETHLEHEM, PA

With *Greetings,* "Hello" and "Goodbye" are stated in many languages, expressing the global emphasis of this new charter school. Wings represent the change and freedom the institution ignites in its students.

Artist: Salma Arastu
Sponsor: Indian Families of Lehigh Valley

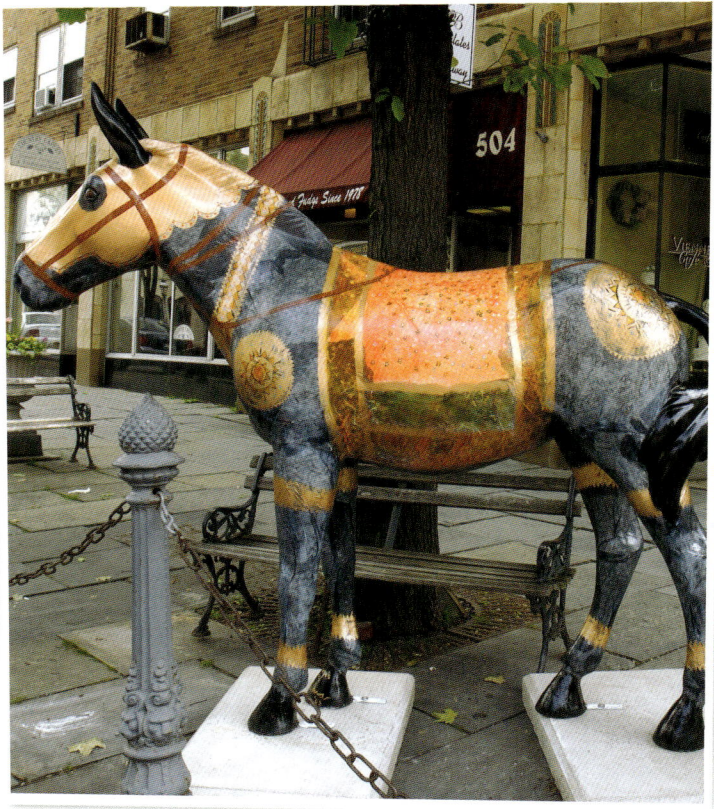

MAHARAJA'S MULE

BETHLEHEM, PA

The thought of mules evoked the artist's memories of Indian Kings and their horses adorned with special occasion velvet and jewels.

Artist: The Early Childhood Education Association, Parents, Students & Children
Sponsor: Northampton Community College

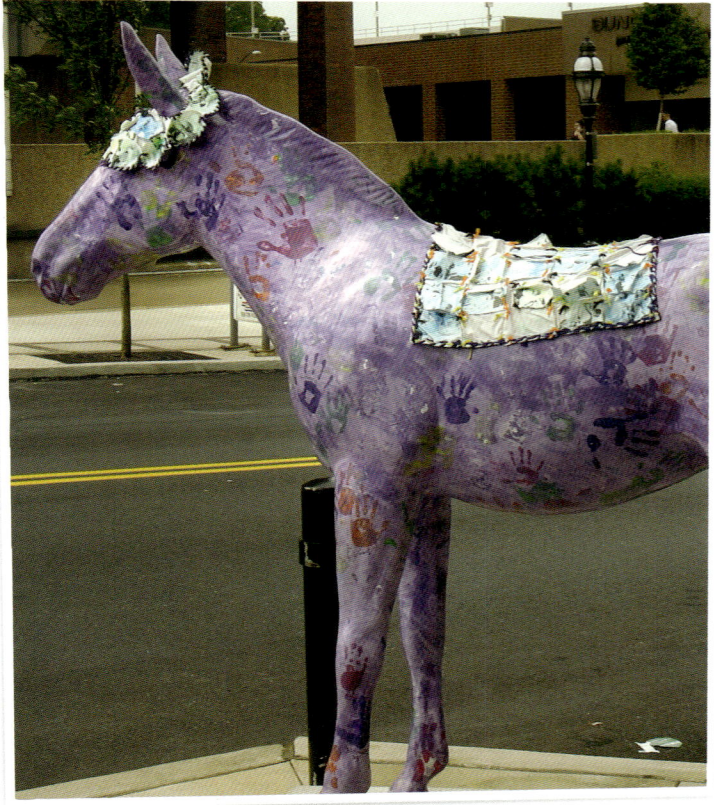

MULLAGE

BETHLEHEM, PA

Created at the community college's annual Springfest, children and adults pressed paint-covered hands in a collage pattern onto the mule. Photographs of the event fashioned its quilt-like hat and blanket.

Artist: Holy Infancy School Students
Sponsor: Holy Infancy School, thanks to Jack and Barbara Yaissle

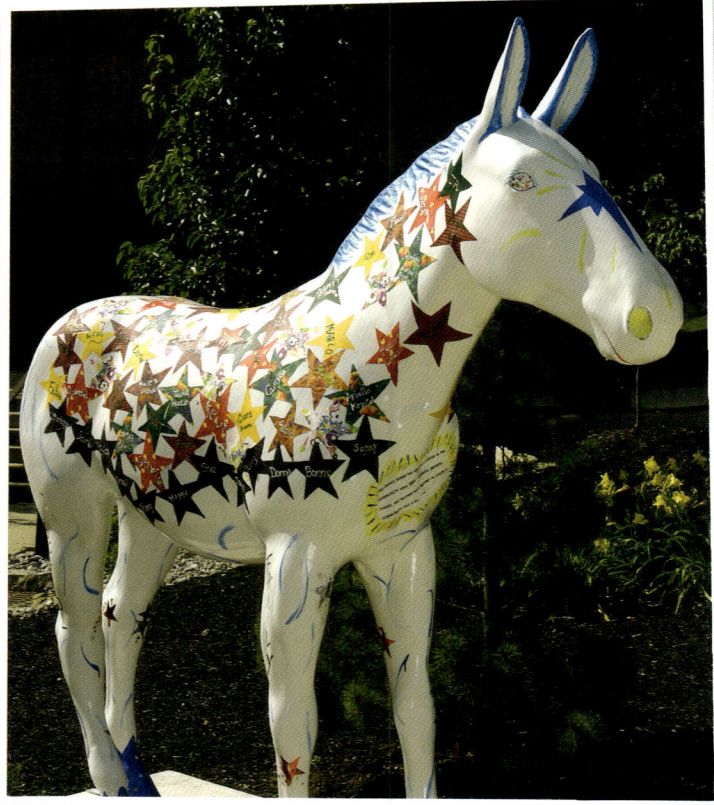

COM"MULE"ITY

BETHLEHEM, PA

Church, Family, School and Work – the four legs of the mule – support the children's efforts to become good citizens. Multicolored fabric stars represent their families and school staff.

Artist: Mr. Imagination
Sponsor: Lehigh University

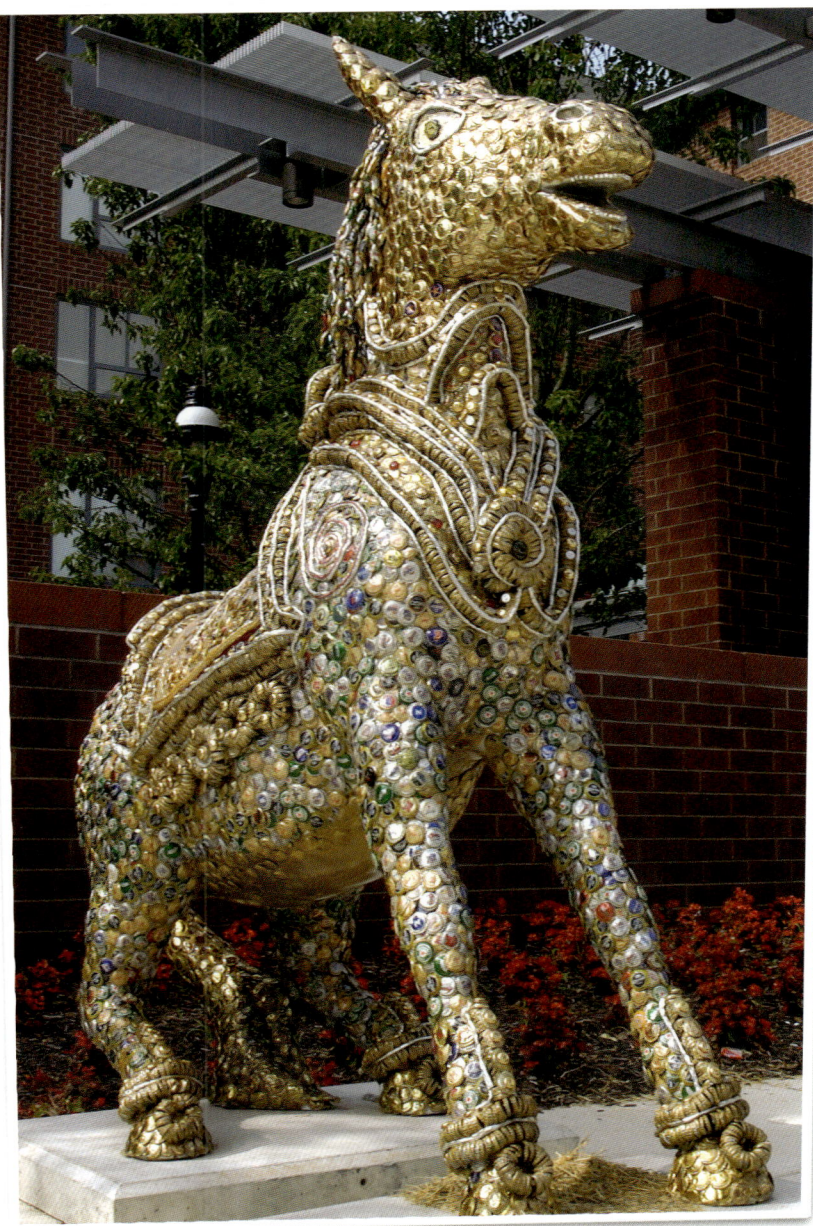

ALFRED THE MOUNTAIN MULE
BETHLEHEM, PA

Gregory Warmack, Mr. Imagination, is a renowned self-taught visionary artist who hails from Chicago, Ill. Famed as the world's greatest living bottle cap artist, Mr. Imagination is a master at creating art from recycled materials.

He has made concrete sculptures embedded with resurrected junk, sandstone carvings from industrial by-products and figural "memory" sculptures from found wood, plaster and castoff materials.

He also created an award-winning bottle cap cow sculpture for the famed **Cows on Parade** public art project in Chicago. So it is especially appropriate that Warmack, now a resident of Bethlehem, produced two bottle cap mules for the **Miles of Mules** public art project.

A standing mule, *Capshaw,* was created for the Banana Factory and a stubborn sitting mule named *Alfred* was commissioned by Lehigh University.

Each mule engages the imaginative curiosity of people who encounter it on the sidewalks of south Bethlehem. One needs only to observe the wide-eyed wonder of those who happen upon these works for the first time – an amazement that naturally leads to exploratory touch, spontaneous laughter and joyful questions.

"…Mr. Imagination is a master at creating art from recycled materials."

Artist: Fountain Hill Elementary School Students and Teacher Sue Berkenstock
Sponsor: Fountain Hill Elementary School, thanks to Linny Fowler

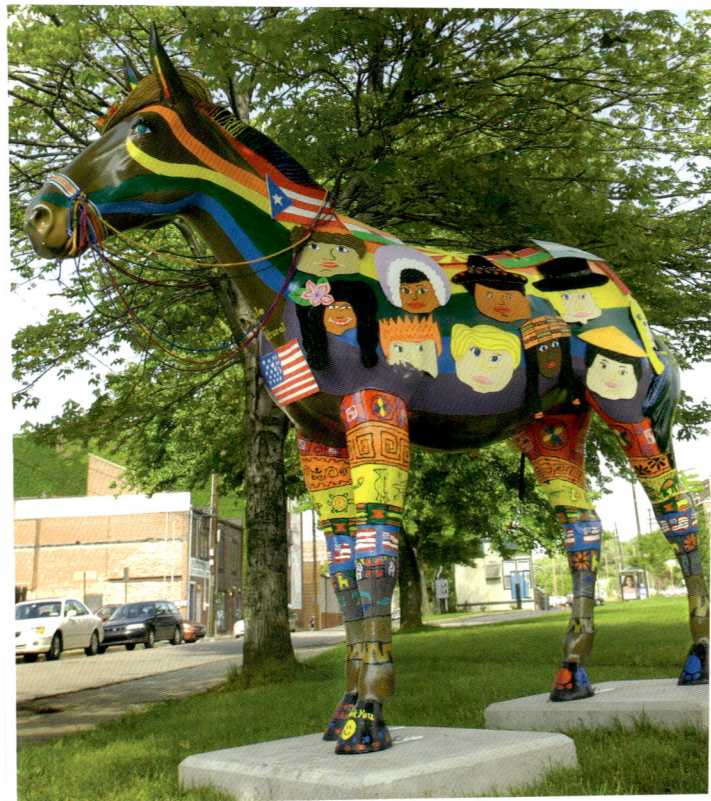

MULE t. CULTURAL

BETHLEHEM, PA

In honor of the world's children, Fountain Hill Elementary School students created smiling faces and flags in bright colors representative of a variety of countries.

Artist: Donegan Elementary School Students and Teacher Bob Schantz
Sponsor: Donegan Elementary School, thanks to Linny Fowler

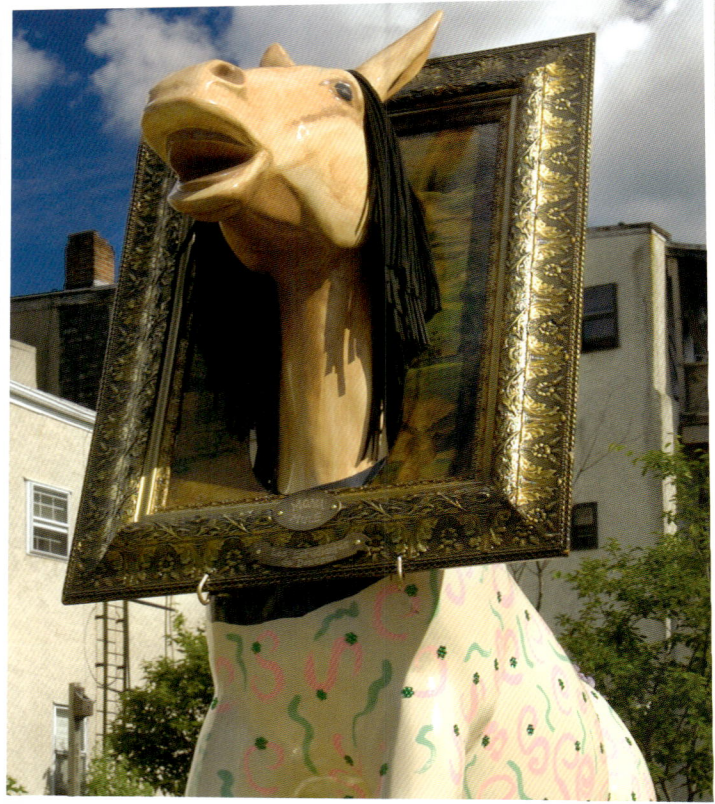

MONA MULE

BETHLEHEM, PA

This mule resembles the famous "Mona Lisa" painting by da Vinci. With an elegant frame, flowers and ribbons, this version of the masterpiece is just as striking!

*Artist: Southern Lehigh High School Art Students
and Teacher Anne Sikorski-Schneider*
Sponsor: Just Born, Inc.

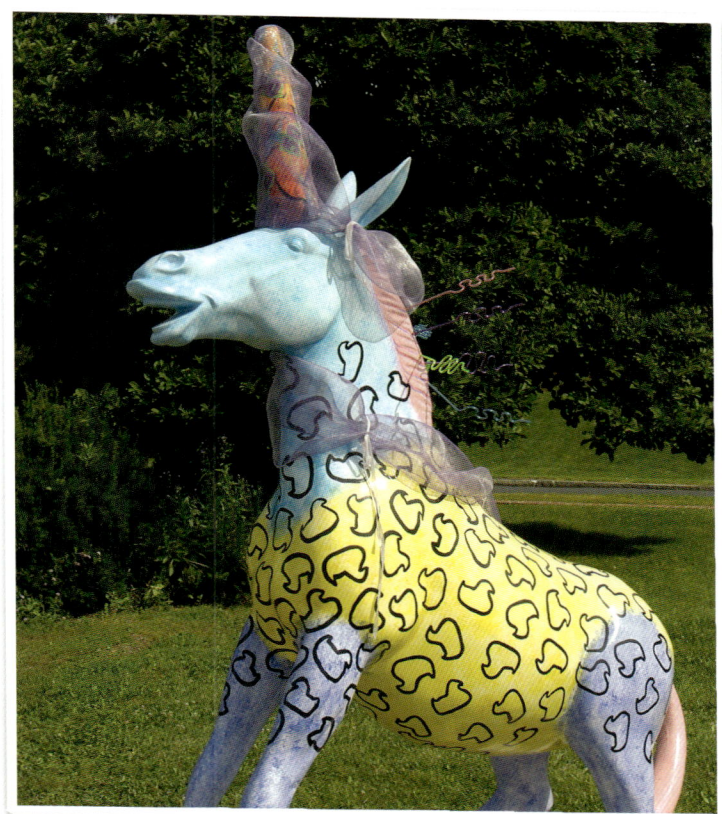

Artist: Katie Behler
Sponsor: A. Donald & Mary G. Behler

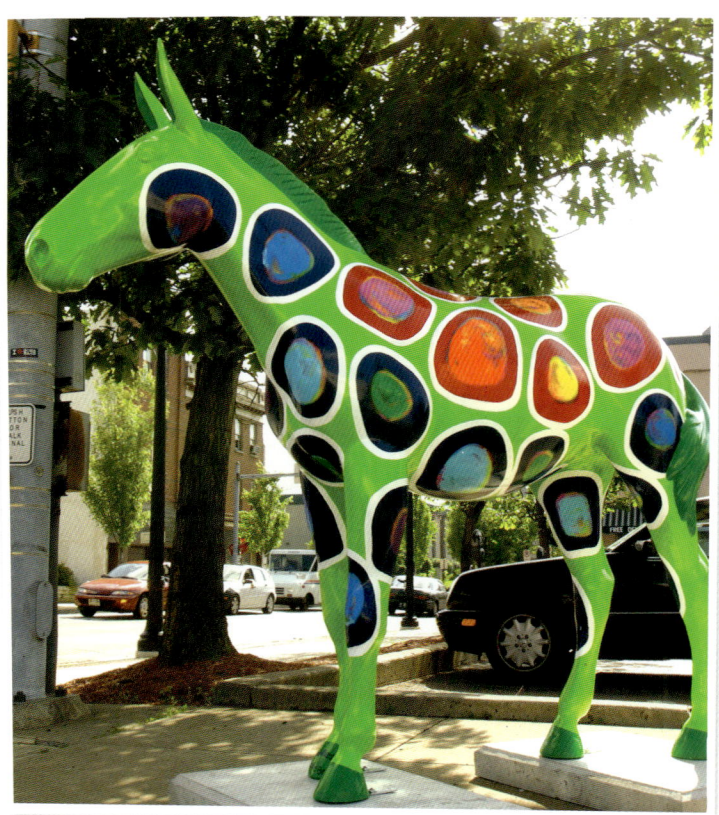

PEEPS OF MANY COLORS

BETHLEHEM, PA

This creation was designed to celebrate the 50th Anniversary of Just Born's Marshmallow Peep. It's painted in pastel colors, covered in a stylish peep pattern and dons a party hat.

PUDDLES

BETHLEHEM, PA

With bright, colorful puddle shapes, artist Katie Behler transferred her abstract style of painting to this vibrant creature.

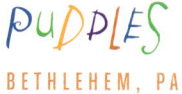

Artist: Children of the Lehigh Valley and Julie Benjamin
Sponsor: Lehigh Valley PBS/WLVT

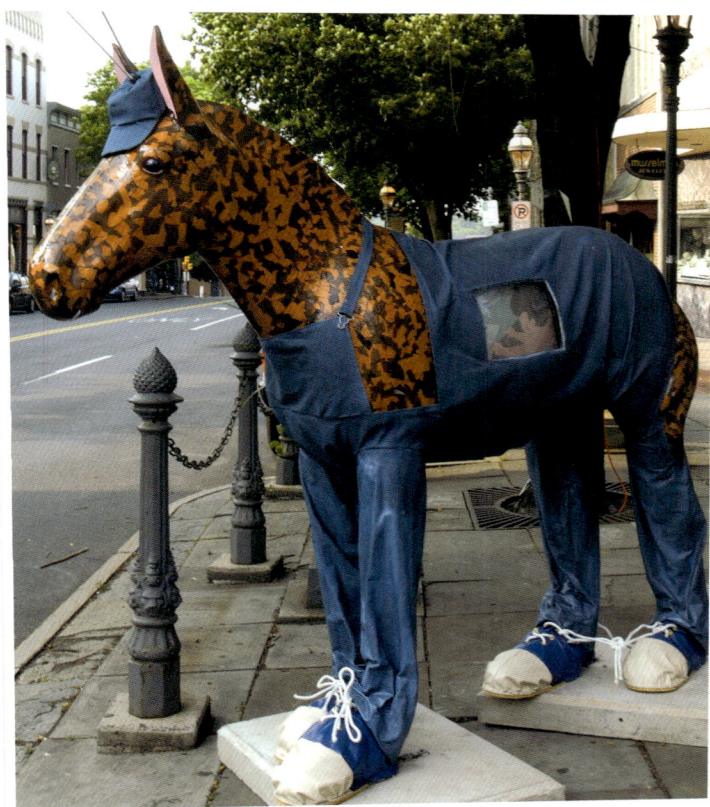

Artist: Broughal Middle School Students
and Teachers Ave Cassell Barr and Stacy DiSipio
Sponsor: Broughal Middle School, thanks to Linny Fowler

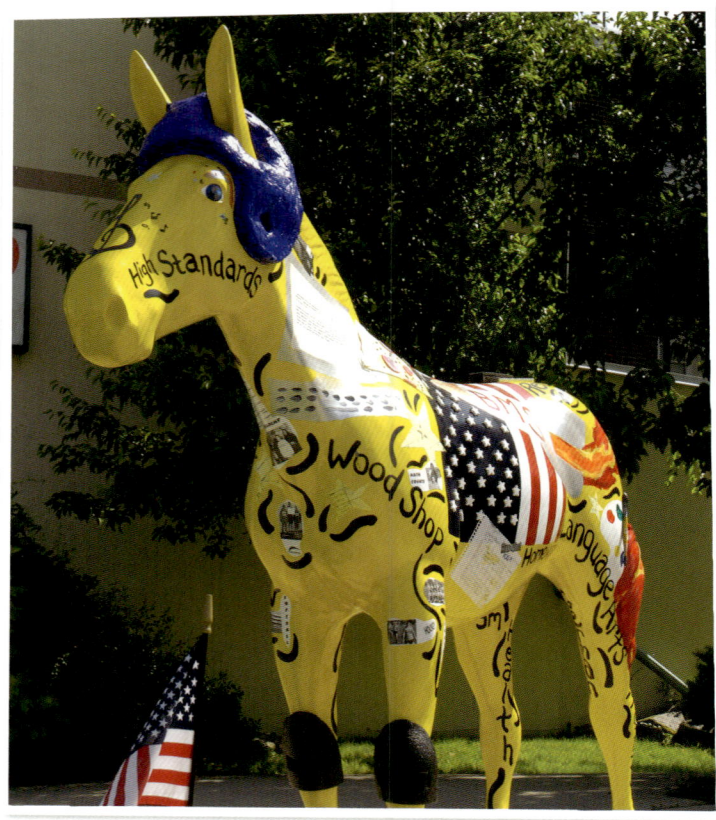

TELEBELLY

BETHLEHEM, PA

This mule was inspired by PBS's mascot TeleBear, a friend to all the youngsters in the Lehigh Valley. Eighteen area children helped decorate this mule, which contains a television in its belly.

THE BROUGHAL MIDDLE SCHOOL MULE

BETHLEHEM, PA

With its gold and blue school colors and rocket mascot, this mule represents the students, activities, classes, faculty and staff of Broughal Middle School.

Artist: Northampton Community College Art Students and Teacher Virginia Abbott
Sponsor: Northampton Community College

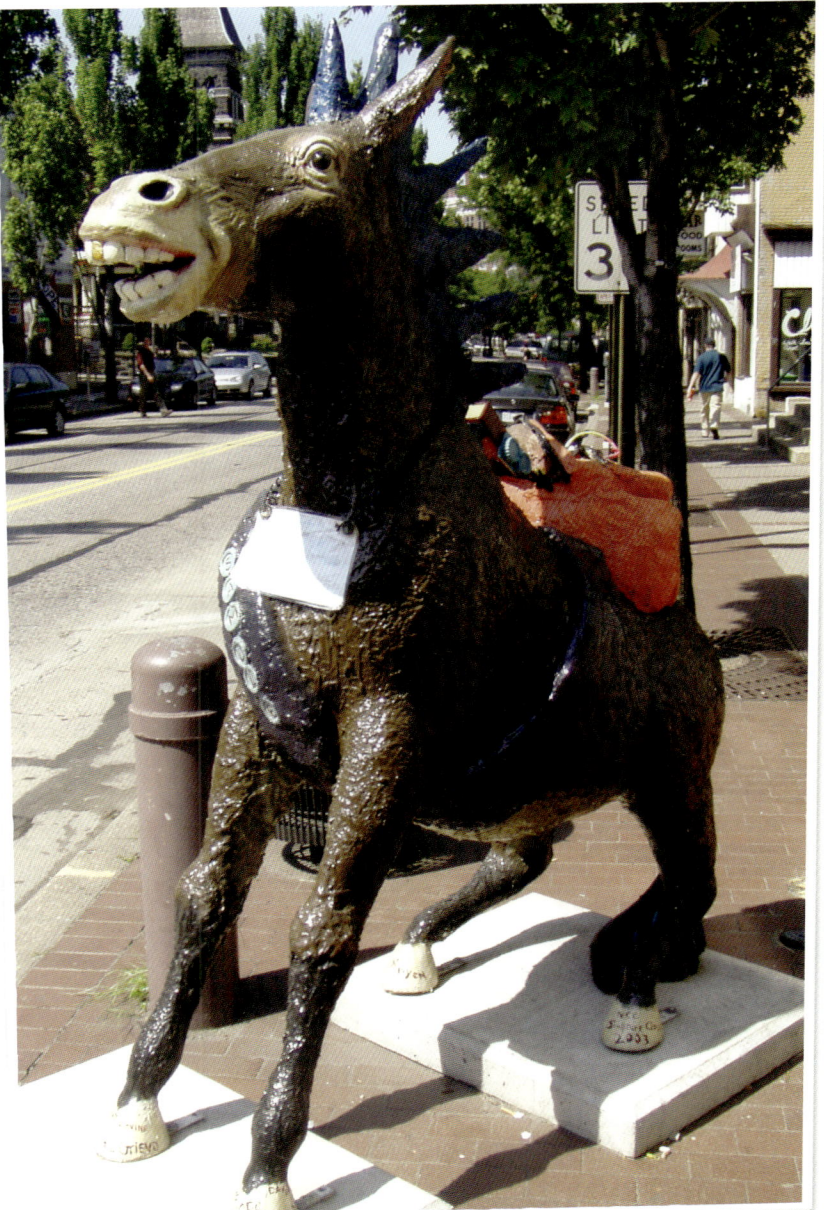

Photo by Mark Demko

SAM-MULE THE PACK MULE

BETHLEHEM, PA

Virginia Abbott and her student artists were eager to participate in the **Miles of Mules** public art project. Little did they know that their mule creation was destined to become an icon for community spirit on the SouthSide of Bethlehem. *Sam-mule the Pack Mule* – sporting a blue Mohawk, an earring and a backpack – sparked interest about the area's heritage among the college students. His presence evoked discussion on the history and importance of these animals to the canal in the Lehigh Valley.

After the mule creation was completed, they excitedly awaited his debut in south Bethlehem. However, exhilaration soon turned to sadness. Within two days of being in the community *Sam-mule* lay broken in pieces on the sidewalk. Dynamite had been placed in his mouth and ignited, causing what many believed to be irreparable damage. A town that had embraced these artful mules stood in dismay at this senseless vandalism. The residents mourned and the newspapers and television stations captured the sorrowful cleanup where *Sam-mule* once stood.

Everyone thought the mule was gone forever – everyone, except for two people. Mr. Imagination, or in this case Dr. Imagination, wielded his brand of artistic healing power and liquid nails as sutures to put *Sam-mule* back together again. Then Virginia Abbott worked her medicinal magic and made the mule look as good as new. Within two weeks, the once damaged creature returned to the streets of Bethlehem to become a symbol of hope for the saddened community.

"…an icon for community spirit on the SouthSide of Bethlehem."

Artist: Paula & Kevin Zelienka
Sponsor: Palmerton Area Chamber of Commerce

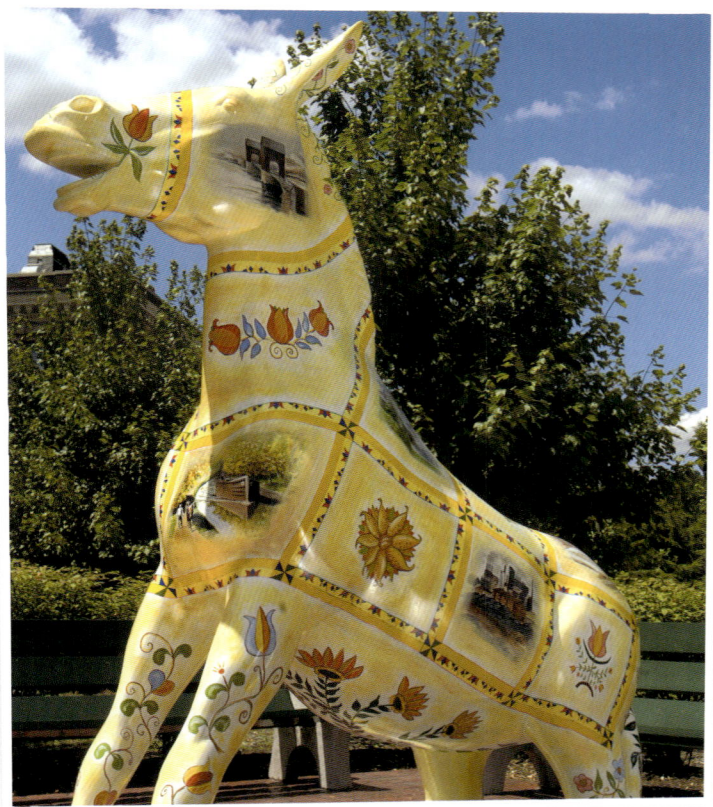

Artist: Lehigh Valley Child Care Staff
Sponsor: Lehigh Valley Child Care, Inc., thanks to Linny Fowler

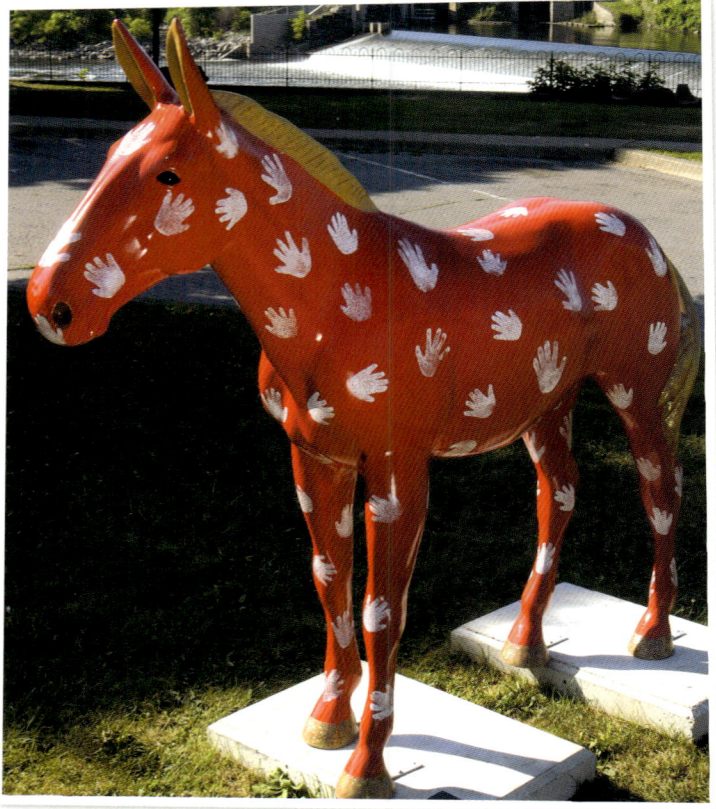

PALMERTON "PATCHES"

PALMERTON, PA

A Pennsylvania Dutch design serves as an outline for this quilt-like mule, with the interior of the squares containing painted images of beautifully rendered Palmerton landmarks.

"HANDS ON"

EASTON, PA

Designed to reflect the child care facility's "Hands On" approach, this mule is painted red, one of the daycare's colors, and includes handprints of adults and children.

Artist: Kathy Bruce
Sponsor: Binney & Smith, Inc.

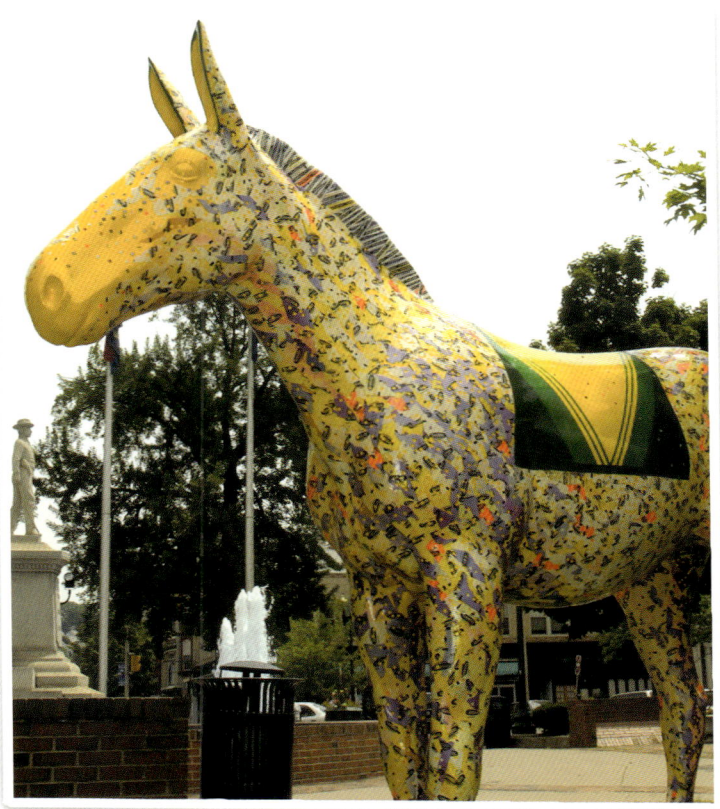

CRAIE-OLA

EASTON, PA

Covered with a base coat of Binney & Smith yellow, a confetti collage of Crayola Crayon wrappers and a green saddle, this mule embodies color and creativity.

Artist: Janice M. Truszkowski & Marisa Damiano
Sponsor: Hugh Moore Historical Park & Museums

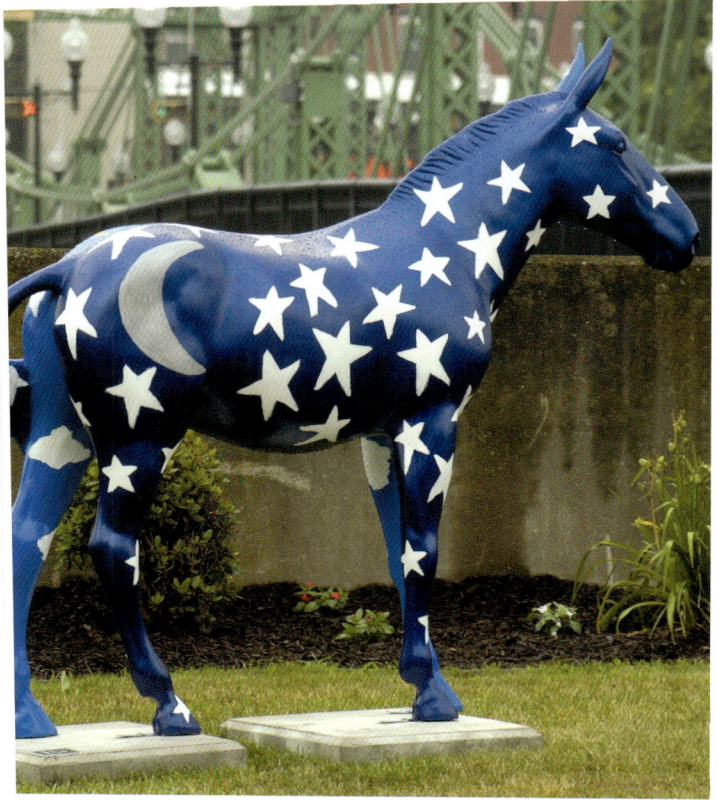

EQUINOX

EASTON, PA

This creation depicts the time of year when there is an equal amount of daylight and darkness. It's painted with stars on one side and a bright, sunny sky on the other.

Artist: Alison Scudder
Sponsor: Lafayette College

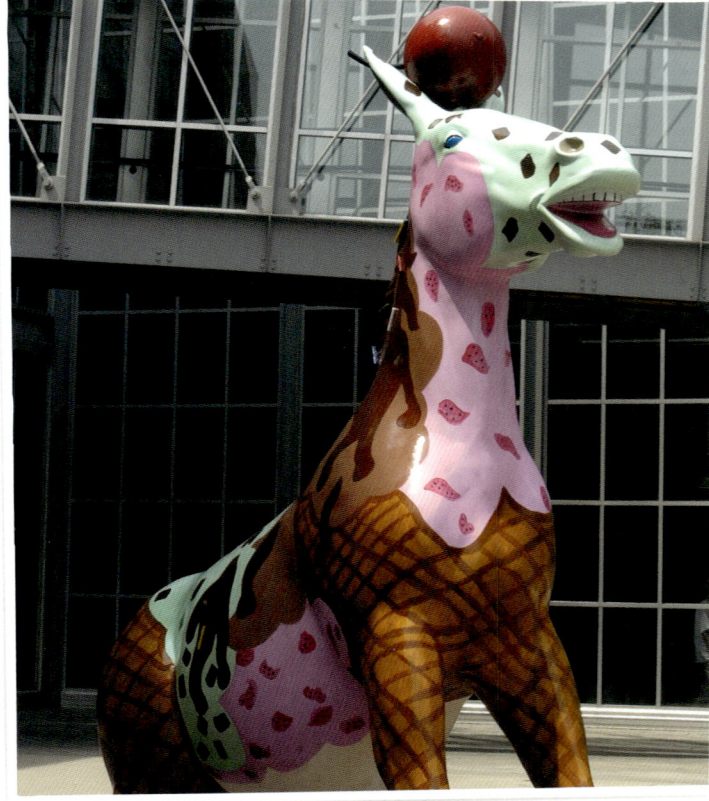

MULE A LA MODE

EASTON, PA

This cheerful, fun mule is painted as a giant ice cream sundae. "Ice cream sundaes make everyone happy. Why not apply this idea to a mule?" thought the artist.

Artist: Bruce J. Ward
Sponsor: County of Northampton

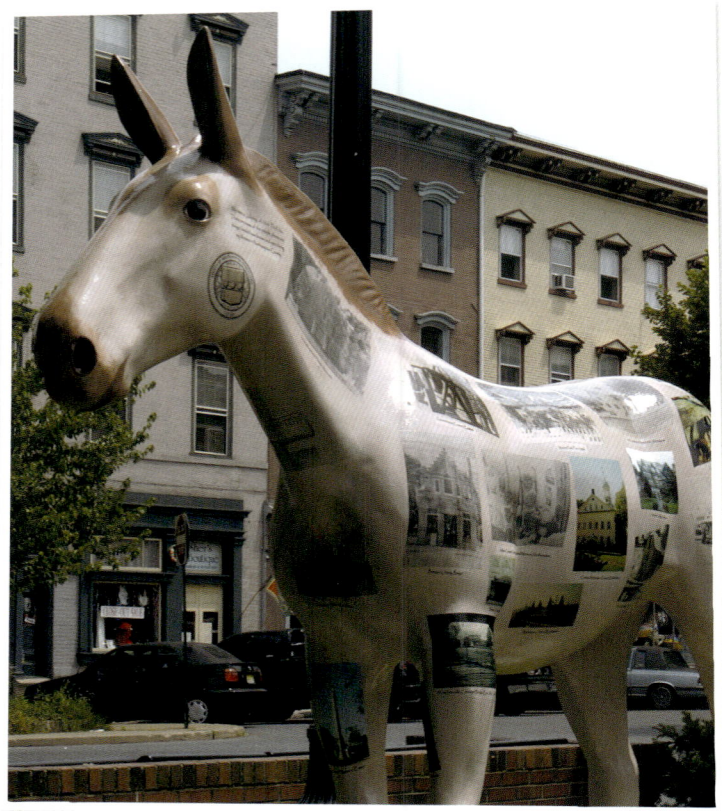

A MULE TO A VIEW

EASTON, PA

This mule is decorated with many images of Northampton County landmarks. Different photographic techniques were used to create this visually interesting and informative mule.

Artist: Second Chance Academy School Students and Teacher Tim Glick
Sponsor: PenTeleData

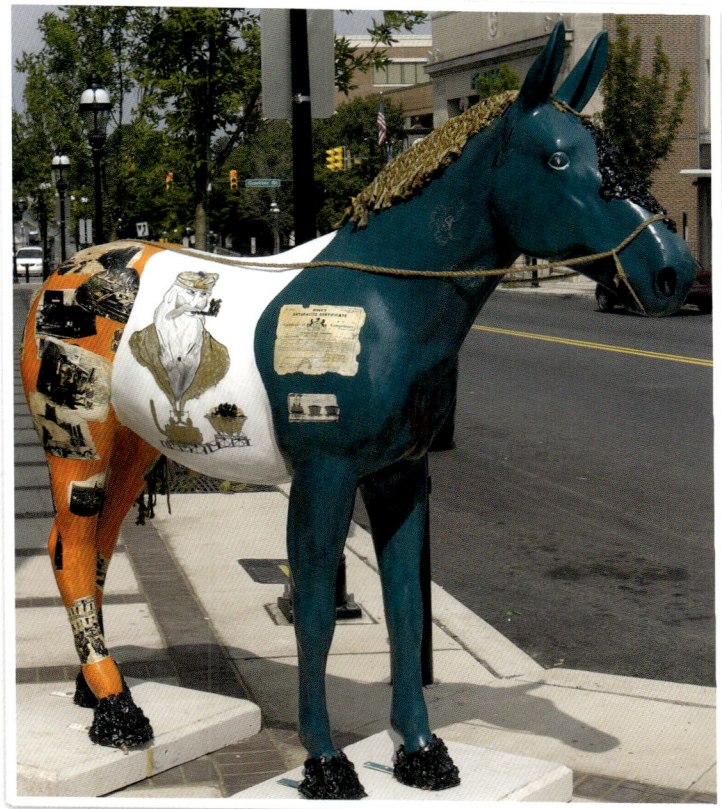

Artist: Ann Elizabeth Schlegel
Sponsor: Adams Outdoor Advertising of the Lehigh Valley

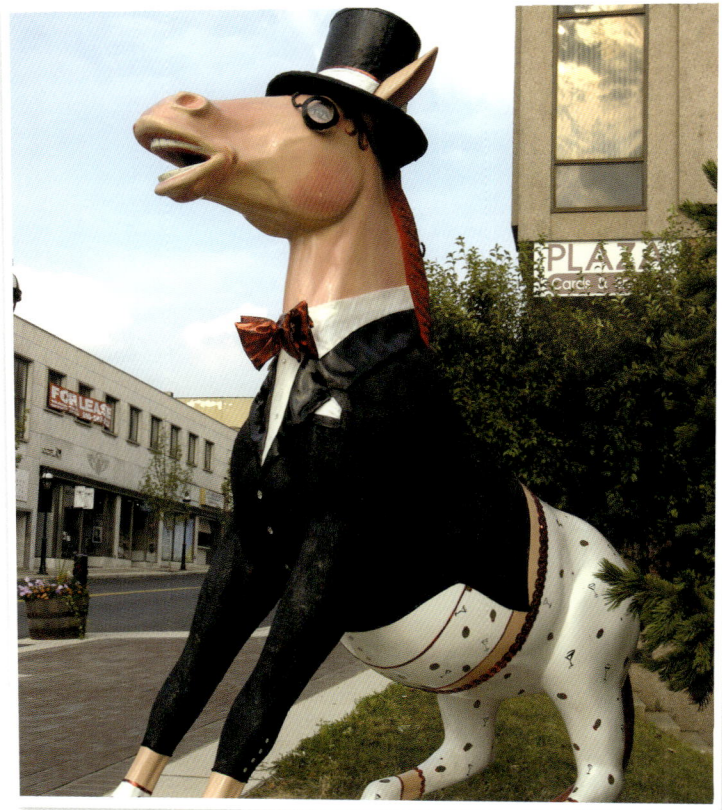

MULEY MAGUIRE – "COAL IS POWER"

BETHLEHEM/PALMERTON, PA

This mule depicts the history of coal mining in the regions surrounding the Lehigh Valley. A painted portrait, landscape and a collage of old photographs invite viewers to learn about coal mining.

MR. MULETINI

BETHLEHEM, PA

The mule about town looks dapper decked in top hat, coattails and a signature monocle. This is one mule that's definitely ready to be the life of the party.

Artist: Tracy Elementary School Students and Teacher Cindy Sames
Sponsor: Tracy Elementary PTA

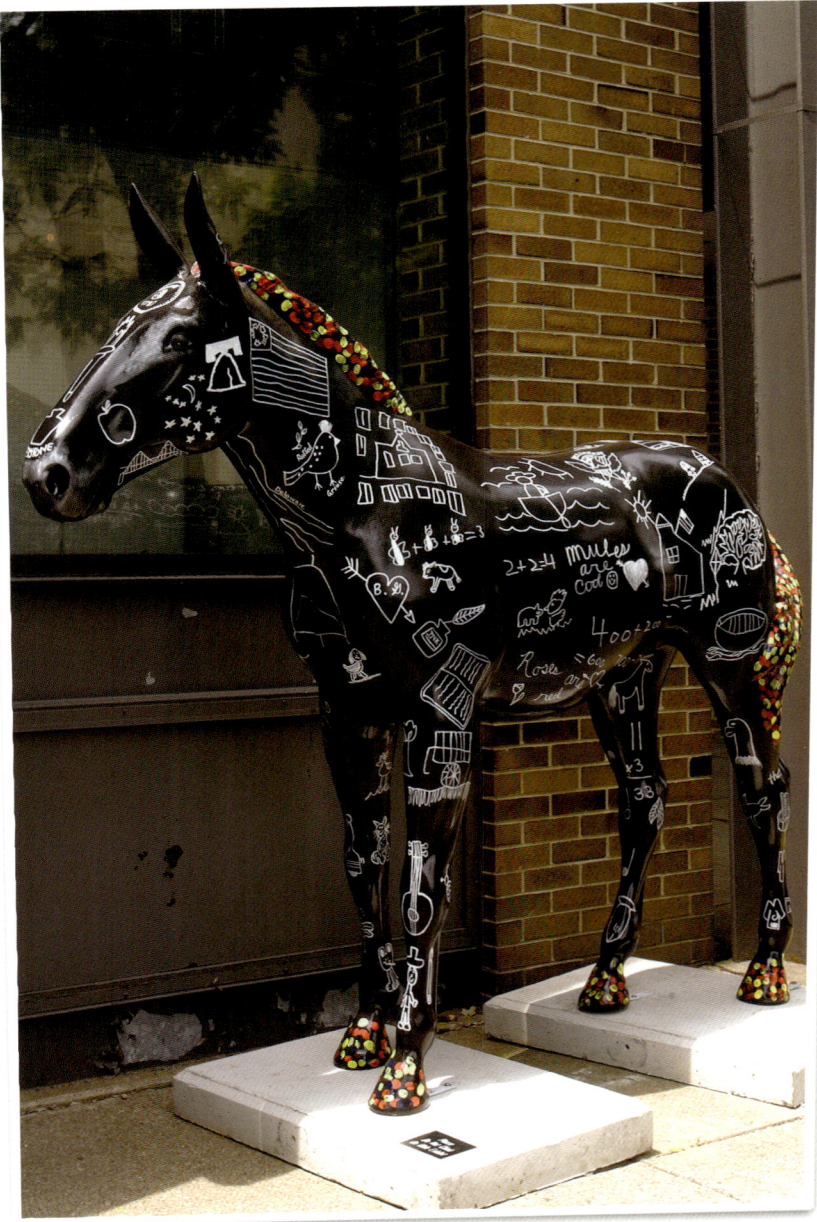

SKETCH

EASTON, PA

With its dull, black finish, *Sketch* resembles a chalkboard and symbolizes student involvement and the value of learning. Utilized during the school year as a teaching tool in art and social studies classes, the mule helped students at Tracy Elementary School in Easton learn about the history of the canals.

It also educated them about the Delaware and Lehigh Canals as a method of transportation and what schools were like during that time period. The mule's design, chosen from two through a student vote, incorporates this new-found knowledge.

Drawing on black paper with wet chalk, students created various sketches of what life was like during the canal era. They included math problems, an old-fashioned school and canal boats. The winning sketches, also voted on by the students, were then drawn directly on the mule with chalk. As each design was completed, it was covered with a paint pen to keep the chalk from smearing.

Everyone at the school became involved. Painted thumb-prints were added. The kindergarten students covered the hooves, the staff marked the mane and all the students and teachers decorated the tail!

"...a teaching tool in art and social studies classes..."

Artist: Catherine Fackenthal a.k.a. Anita Vacation
Sponsor: Online Computer Library Center (OCLC) Preservation Service Center

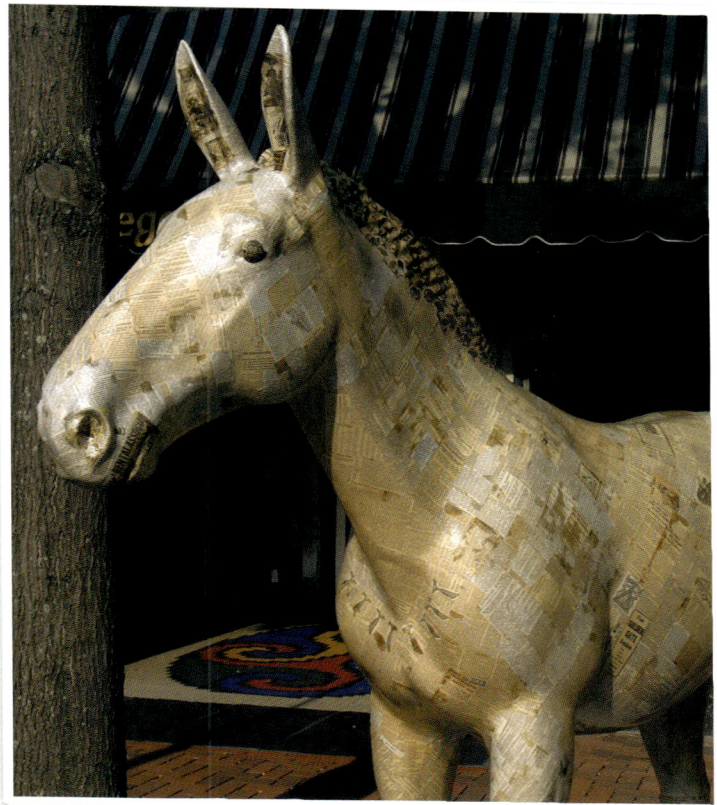

Artist: Randi Pavlick and Inger Olsen
Sponsor: The Downtown Bethlehem Association – SouthSide

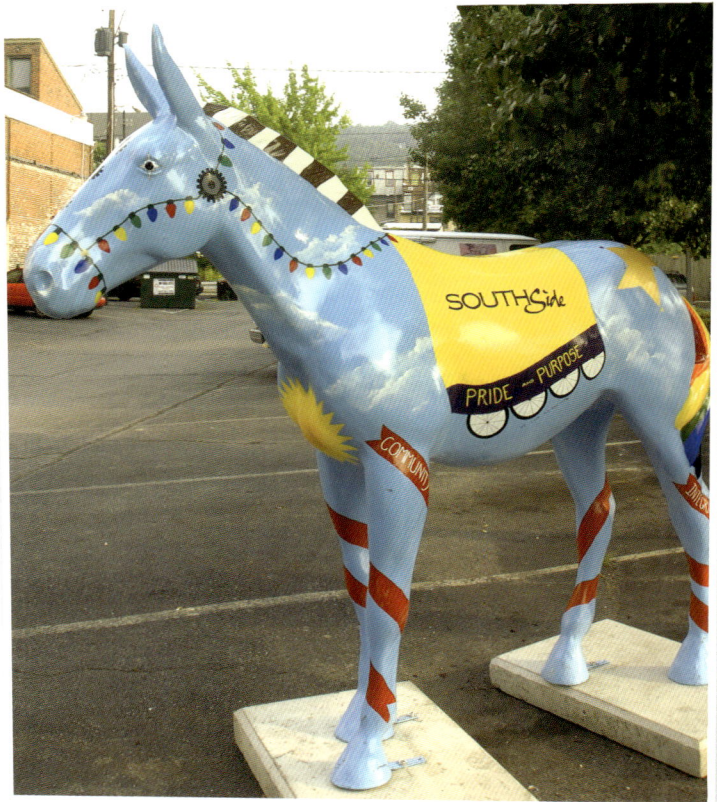

EMULATING THE PAST (EMMY)

BETHLEHEM, PA

Hundreds of articles and advertisements from the early 1900s are cleverly collaged to represent the business of OCLC and creatively indicate the mule's anatomy.

SOUTHSIDE PRIDE

BETHLEHEM, PA

Colorful symbolism imbues this mule with the vibrant spirit found on Bethlehem's SouthSide. It's designed to represent the partnership between commerce and community.

Artist: Michael Sayre
Sponsor: The Downtown Bethlehem Association – Historical District

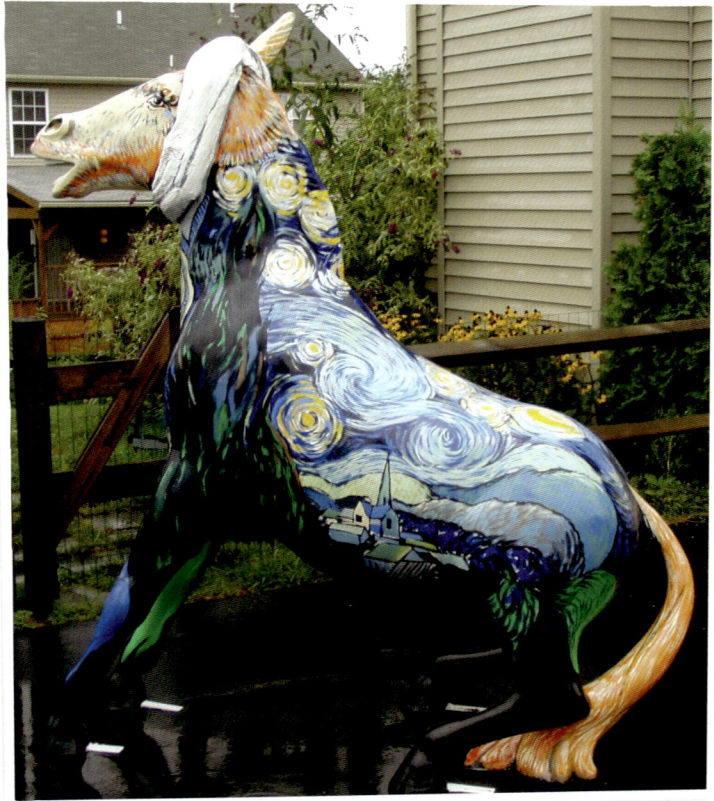

Photo by Steve Truscott

STARRY, STARRY NIGHT
BETHLEHEM, PA

A humorous homage to van Gogh based on two of his most familiar works, "Starry Night" and "Self Portrait."

Artist: Donna Alrich
Sponsor: Hospital Service Association of Northeastern Pennsylvania

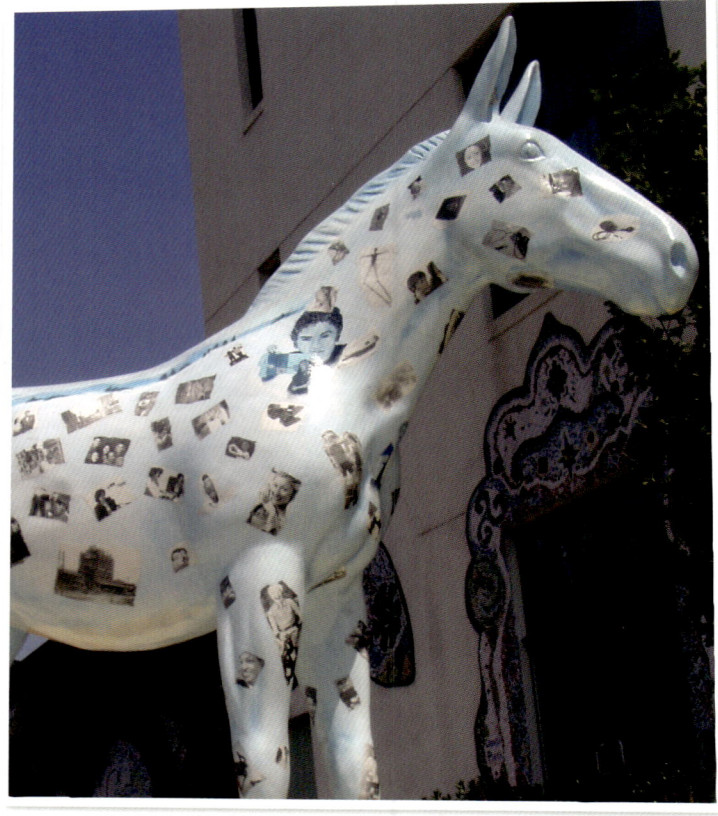

Photo by Mark Demko

MULE WITH A MISSION
BETHLEHEM, PA

Mule with a Mission depicts the history of our area and Blue Cross, while charting a steady path to better health for our community.

Artist: The Citizens of Emmaus
Sponsor: Emmaus Main Street Program

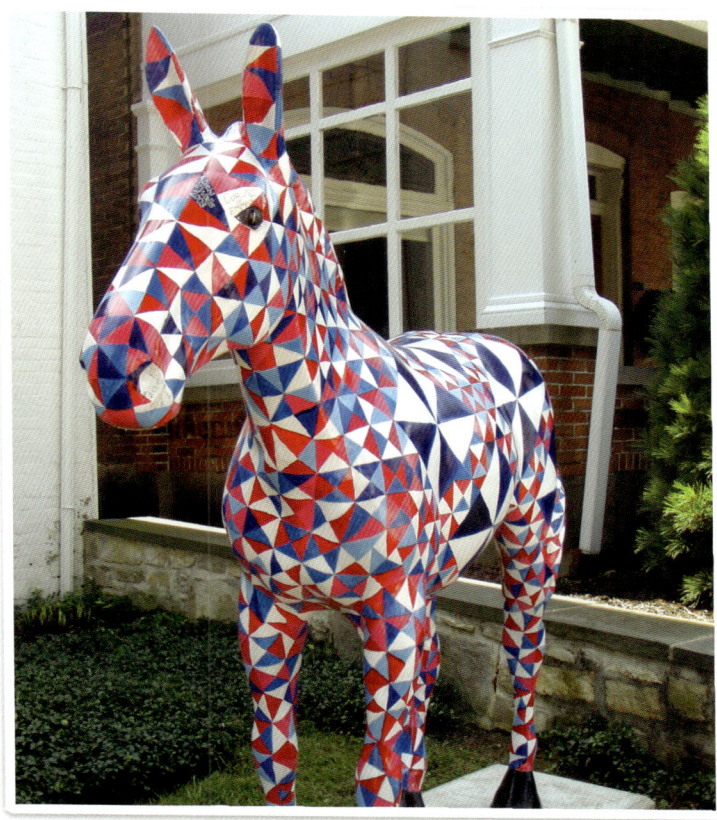

Photo by Mark Demko

EMMA, tHE EMMAUS tRiANGLE COMMUNiTY QUiLt

EMMAUS, PA

Covered by a community quilt with a patriotic design of red, white and blue triangles, *Emma* provides a focal point for Emmaus' downtown revitalization and heritage celebrations.

S ☆ UTHERN CORRAL

Housed on the site of the former Bucks County Prison, the James A. Michener Art Museum in Doylestown opened in 1988 and has since served as an independent, non-profit cultural institution dedicated to preserving, interpreting and exhibiting the art and cultural heritage of the Bucks County region. The museum is named for Doylestown's most famous son, a Pulitzer Prize-winning author and avid supporter of the arts.

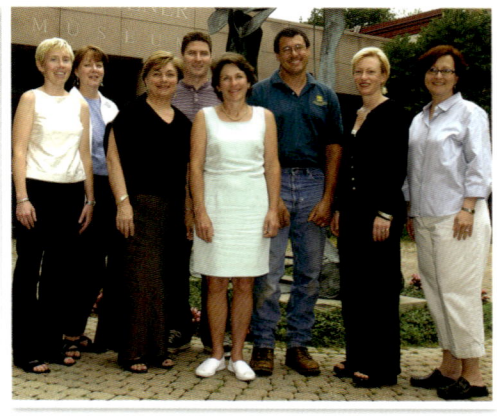

From left to right:
Elisabeth Flynn,
Joan Welcker,
Carole Hurst,
Bryan Brems,
Benita Ryan,
Hugh Marshall,
Amy Lent,
Chris Hacker
Not shown:
Laura Biersmith,
Gilbert Winner

At the heart of the Museum's permanent collection are some of the finest Pennsylvania Impressionist paintings, including works by Edward Redfield, Daniel Garber, and Fern Coppedge. The Museum also hosts nationally touring exhibitions and showcases regional artists.

A satellite facility at Union Square in New Hope features the multi-media interactive exhibition *Creative Bucks County: A Celebration of Art and Artists.* This exhibit brings to life the work of many visual artists, authors, playwrights, lyricists and composers who lived and worked in Bucks County.

When seeking an artist to design their prototype mule, the Museum approached acclaimed Newtown artist Robert Dodge, who has worked on re-creating and redefining the chair through paintings, drawings and sculptures.

Dodge's ongoing exploration of this everyday object shaped his mule design as well. Hundreds of tiny chairs were hand painted onto a black background to create an overall texture similar to galaxies in a night sky.

The mule's name, *Chairman of the Barge,* was decided through a contest in the local newspaper, *The Intelligencer.*

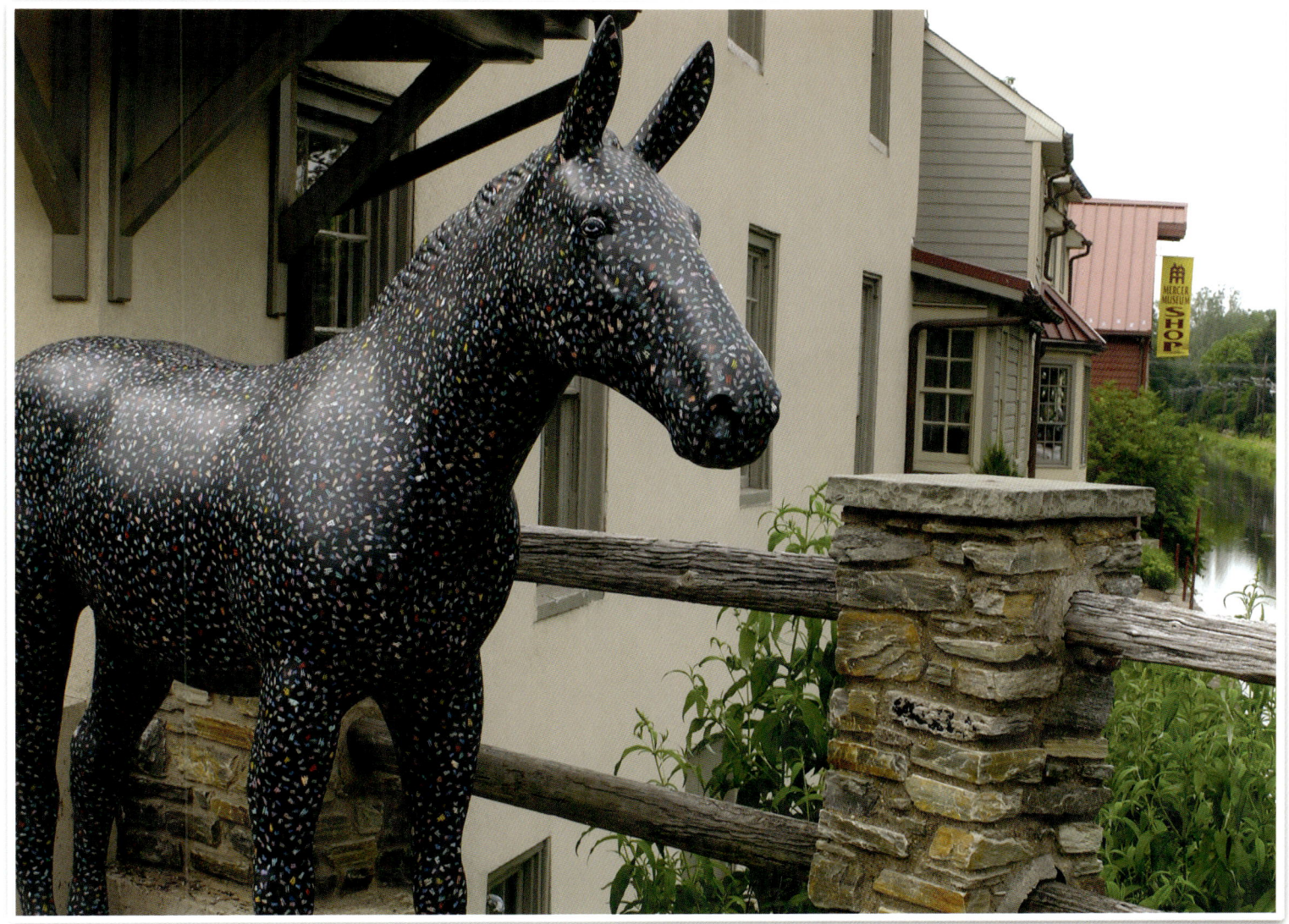

CHAIRMAN OF THE BARGE
NEW HOPE, PA

Artist: Robert Dodge
Sponsor: James A. Michener Art Museum, The D&L National Heritage Corridor, DCNR

"Hundreds of tiny chairs…create an overall texture similar to galaxies in a night sky."

Artist: Linda Williams
Sponsor: Christine and Dan Taylor of Taylor Made Carpets & Flooring

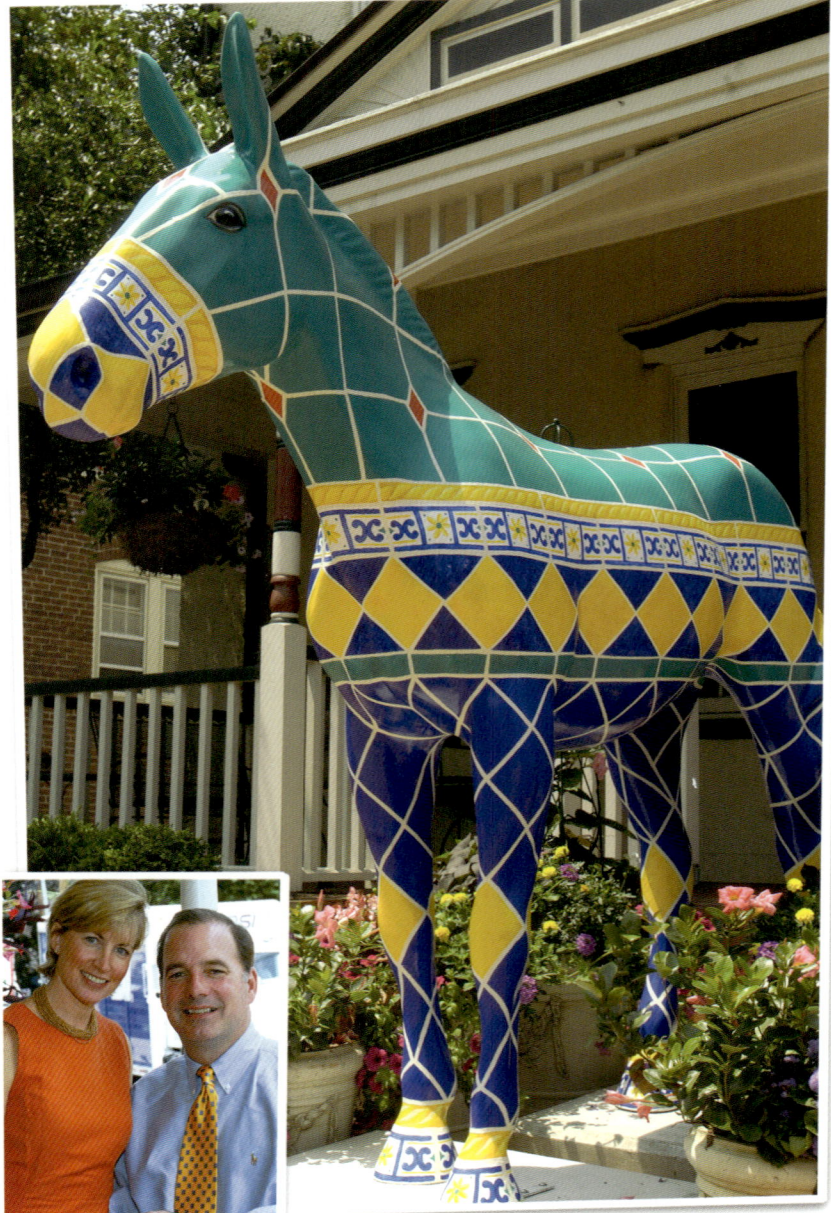

Christine and Dan Taylor
Photo by Jared Polin

BURRO OF DOYLESTOWN

DOYLESTOWN, PA

Bucks County artist Linda Williams worked closely with sponsors Christine and Dan Taylor to create a design that would effectively reflect their Doylestown business, a custom flooring company. The Taylors supplied the artist with actual tile and floor samples in a variety of colors.

Williams chose the brightest, most colorful tiles and developed six different sketches before settling on the final design. She painted mainly with acrylics to create the ceramic tile effect, but also used sand paint to simulate the grout.

Williams has created several large murals, but this mule is the biggest three-dimensional item she's ever painted. She said it was a bit tricky matching up the tile design around the animal's underside and legs.

Called *Burro of Doylestown*, the mule's name is a play on words for Taylor Made Carpets & Flooring's location in the Borough of Doylestown.

The Taylors have been Business Partner members of the James A. Michener Art Museum since its inception. They were among the first to become sponsors of the **Miles of Mules** public art project.

"…the biggest three-dimensional item she's ever painted."

Artist: Katy Powell
Sponsor: Friends of the Artist

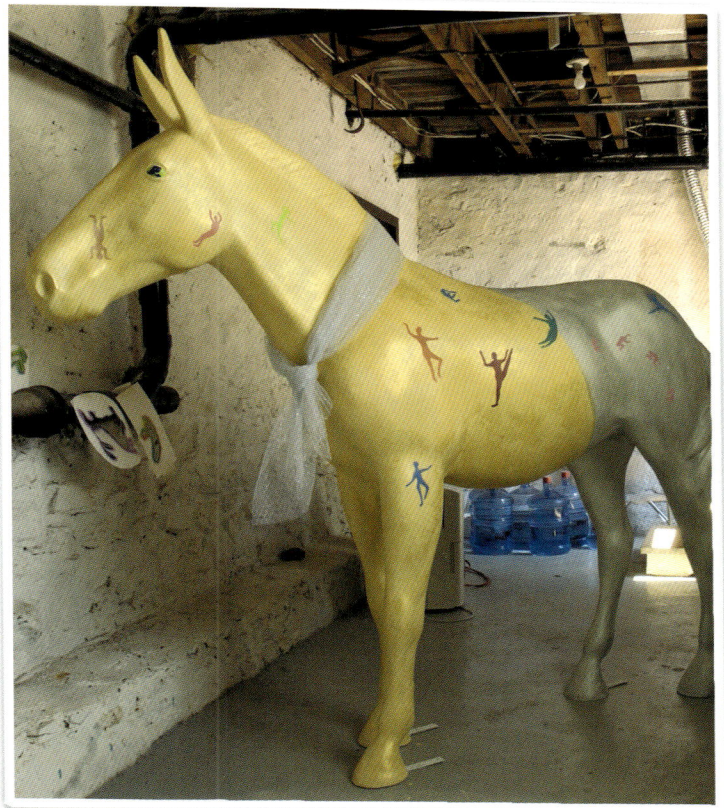

WHAt i CAN'T SAY iN WORDS
DEBUT AT AUCTION

Eleven-year-old artist Katy Powell spent the summer on this unique project. She worked with a local school art teacher to express her artistic thoughts and feelings.

Artist: Walt Disney Elementary School Students
Sponsor: Walt Disney Elementary School, thanks to Tullytown Council and First Federal Savings of Bucks County

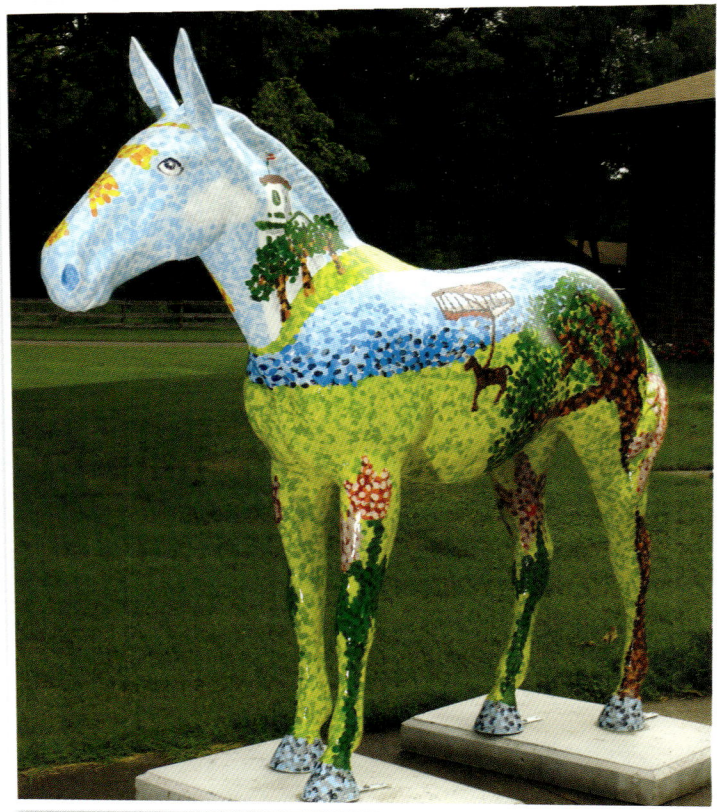

AN AFTERNOON ON tHE CANAL OF LA GRANDE MULE-AtTE
MORRISVILLE, PA

Thumbs ups! School art teacher Danyelle Lala had her students emulate the technique of French Impressionist painter Georges Seurat, with each one contributing a thumbprint in various colors.

Artist: Gale S. Scotch
Sponsor: Bristol Cultural & Historical Foundation

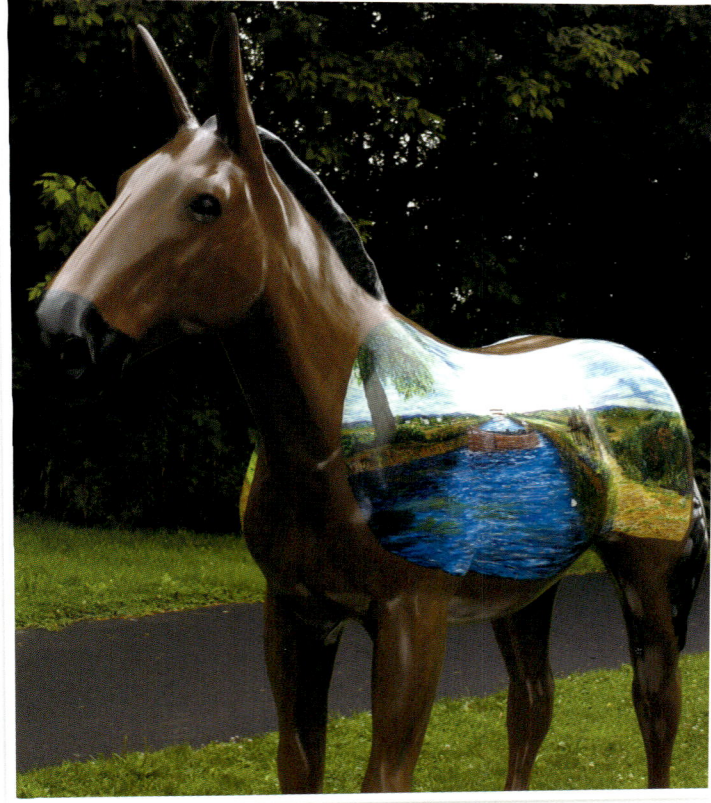

Artist: Kutz Elementary School Students
Sponsor: Township of Doylestown

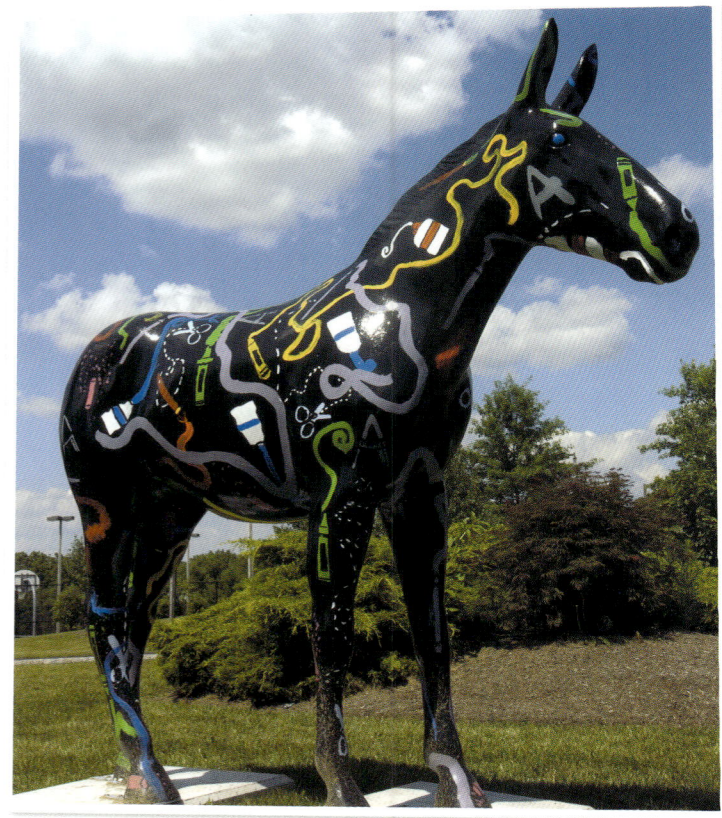

REFLECTIVE MULE

BRISTOL, PA

Inspiration for this peaceful scene was found as the artist floated down the Delaware Canal on an authentic mule-drawn barge, now used by tourists to travel the waterway.

A MASTERPIECE OF A MULE

DOYLESTOWN, PA

"Arty," as the student artists fondly dubbed him, is decorated with splashes of color and art tools to resemble a masterpiece in progress.

Artist: Angela Mikula
Sponsor: Doylestown Business and Community Alliance, thanks to Heritage Towers, Whitney Photography and Community Conservatory of Music

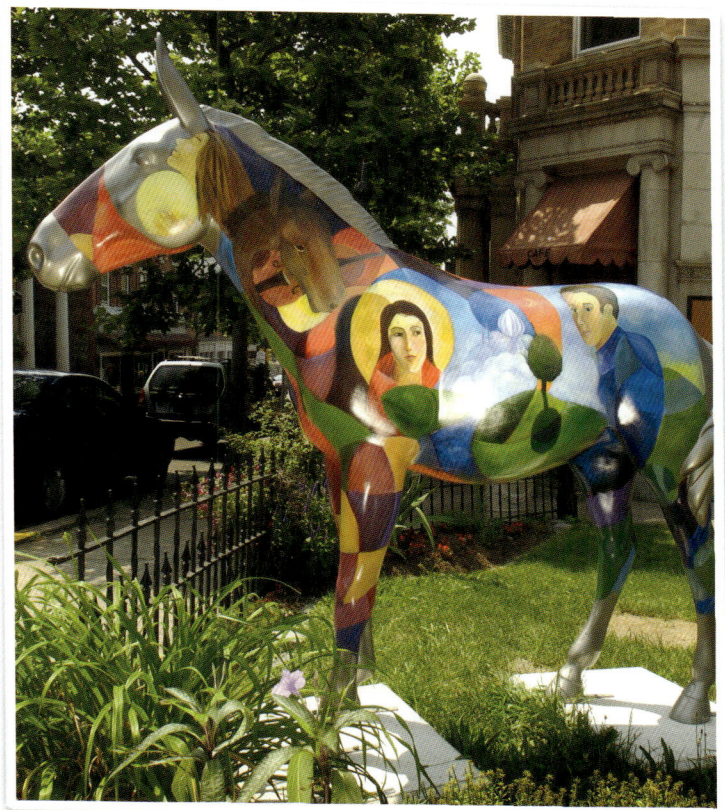

Artist: William Sloan
Sponsor: Habitat for Humanity, thanks to Fox Rothschild, LLP

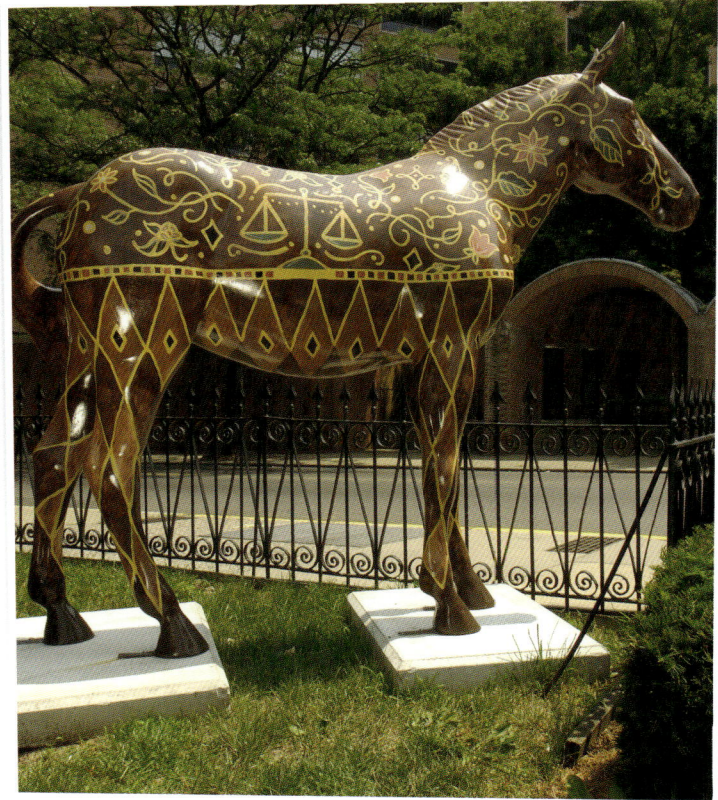

BY THE LIGHT OF THE SILVERY MULE
DOYLESTOWN, PA

A young girl whispers her wish for a land of castles into the mule's ear. On its other side her wish is granted, and the streets of her hometown are transformed.

CHESTER
DOYLESTOWN, PA

The simple, utilitarian and beloved mule stands for loyalty, hard work and dignity. *Chester* is decorated in the style of traditional Pennsylvania furniture that displays some of these same qualities.

Artist: Kathy Moniot
Sponsor: Big Brothers Big Sisters of Bucks County, thanks to Square One and Fred and Shary Koenig

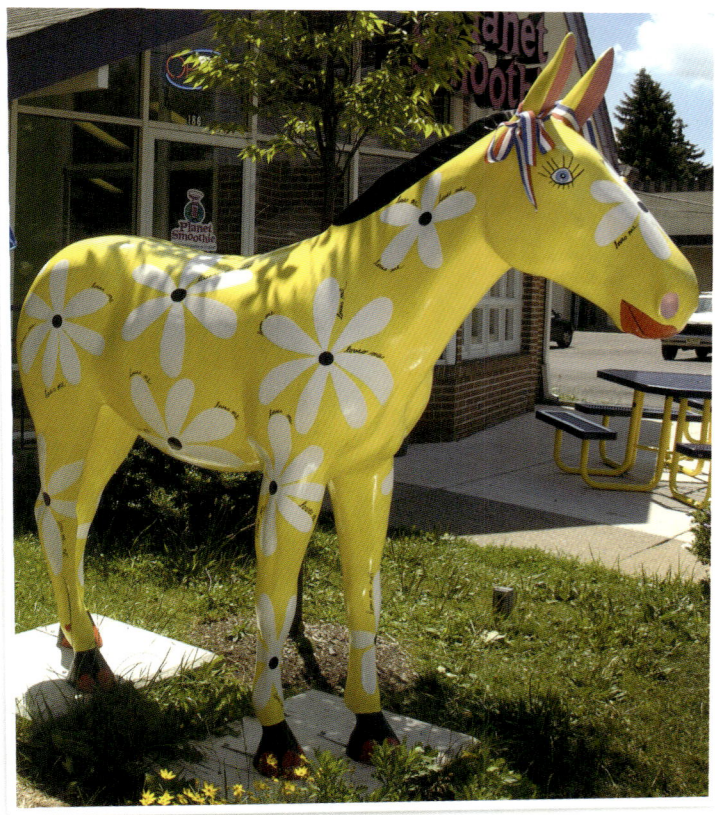

Artist: Beverly Meredith Garnett
Sponsor: Kurfiss Real Estate, Inc.

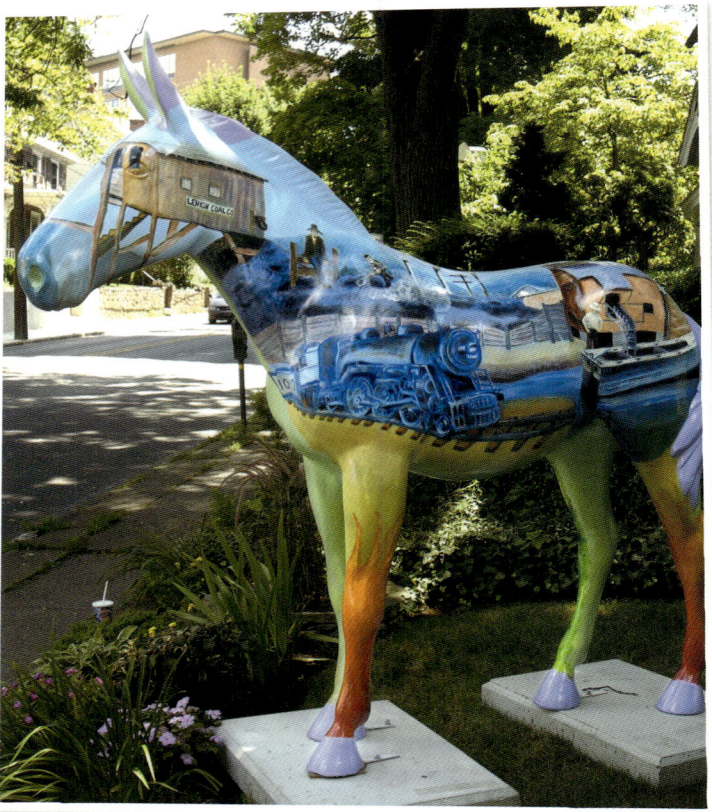

DAISY IN LOVE

DOYLESTOWN, PA

With its red lips, daisies and sunny background, this is a tribute to romantic summer love. The artist gained inspiration from a mule on her grandparents' farm.

FROM THE COAL YARD to THE CANAL

DOYLESTOWN, PA

A history lesson on four legs! This design illustrates how mules were utilized along the canals to transport coal. One side represents the Delaware Canal, the other the Lehigh.

Artist: Susan Roseman
Sponsor: County of Bucks, Office of the Commissioners

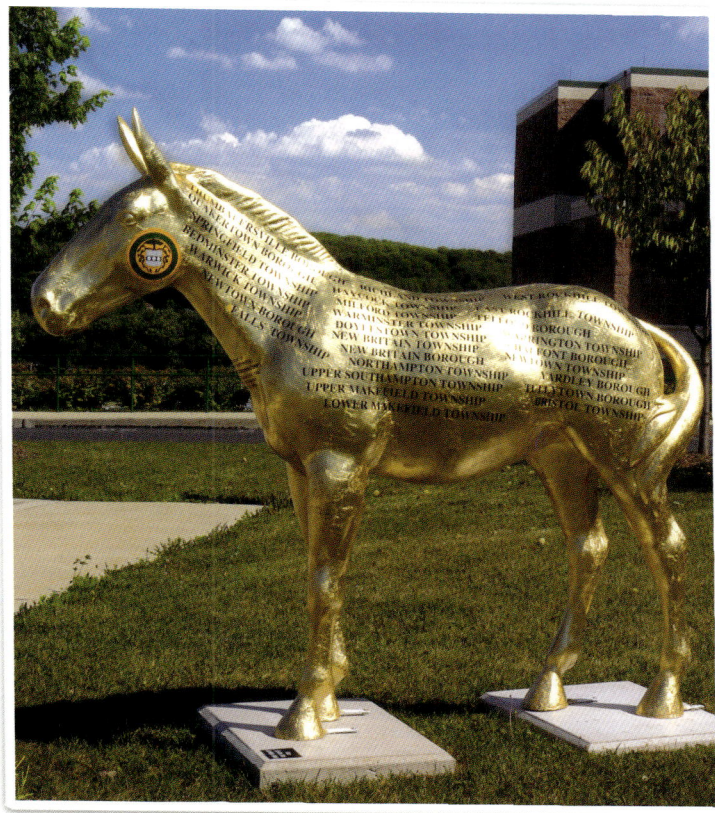

Artist: Jean D. Johnson Lang
Sponsor: F. Lang Family

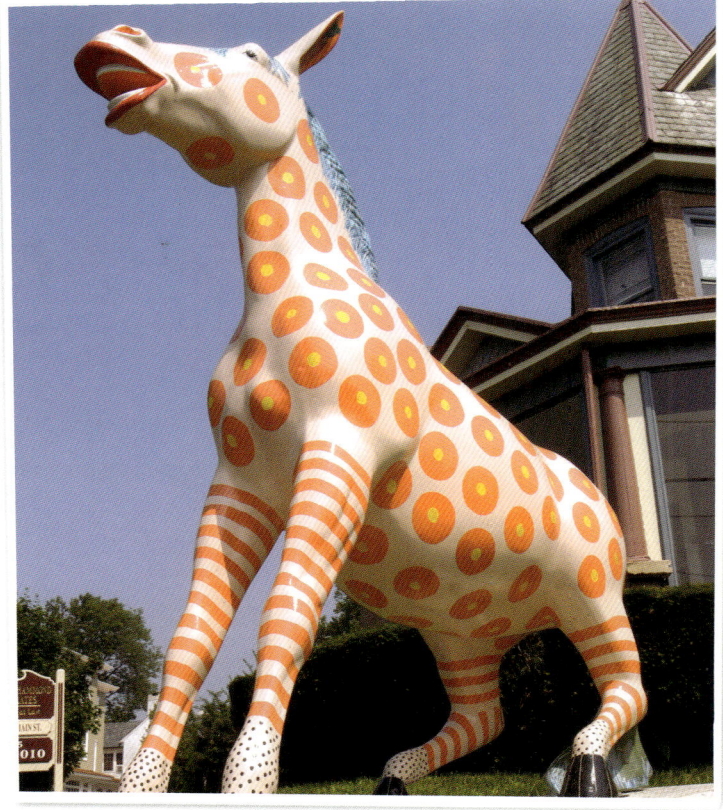

DESTINATIONS

DOYLESTOWN, PA

The artist, also a sign painter, applied her craft to the mule, which lists all of the original towns in Bucks County, at one time called Buckinghamshire.

DAUCUS CAROTA

DOYLESTOWN, PA

Completely covered in carrots, including its 24k gold leaf tooth, the concept was inspired by the artist's grandchildren laughing at the notion of tempting a stubborn mule with carrots.

Artist: Dora Siemel
Sponsor: WOLF

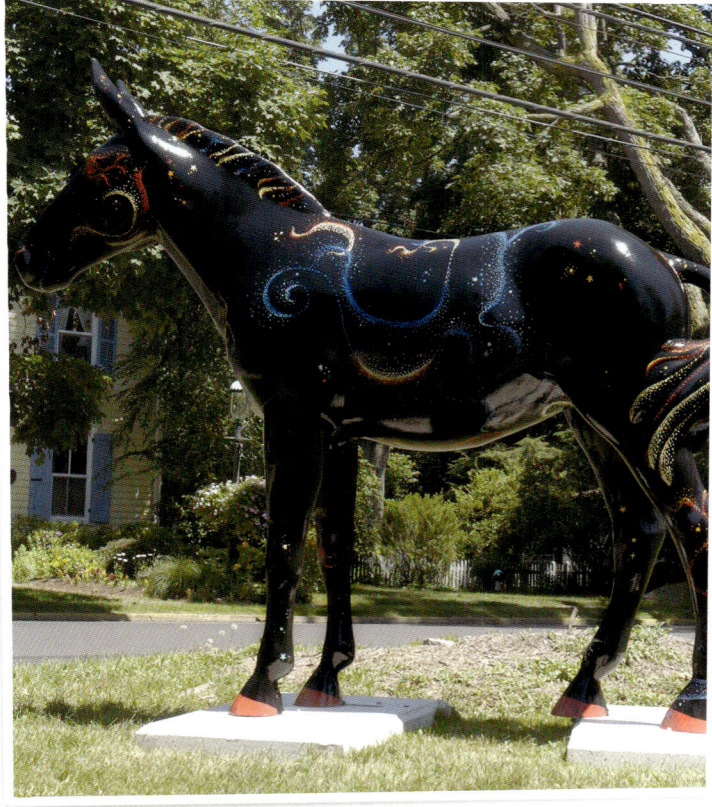

Artist: Joseph Dougherty
Sponsor: Gale Nurseries, Inc.

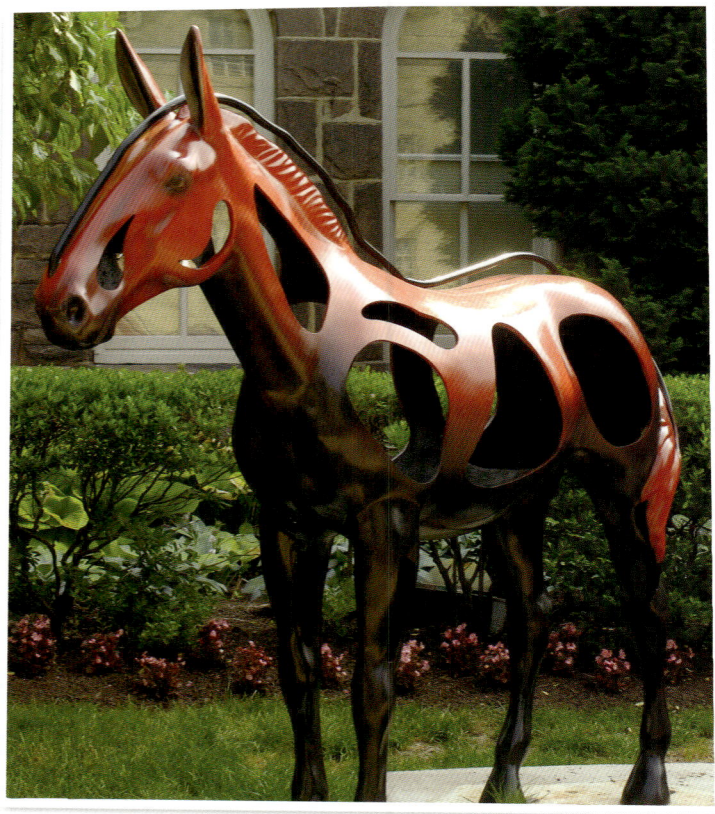

GALACTIC MULE

DOYLESTOWN, PA

An "out of this world" surprise birthday gift from her husband, artist Dora Siemel's mule reflects the grandeur of the cosmos in brilliant color.

INSIDE OUT MULE

DOYLESTOWN, PA

A mule was a major departure for figurative sculptor Joseph Dougherty, whose previous work includes a monument to Thomas Paine. His eye-catching, contemporary design explores the mystery of negative spaces.

Artist: Diana Vincent
Sponsor: Breast Cancer Awareness in Memory of Judy Schwartz, thanks to Helene and Mark Hankin and Libby and Marvin Schwartz

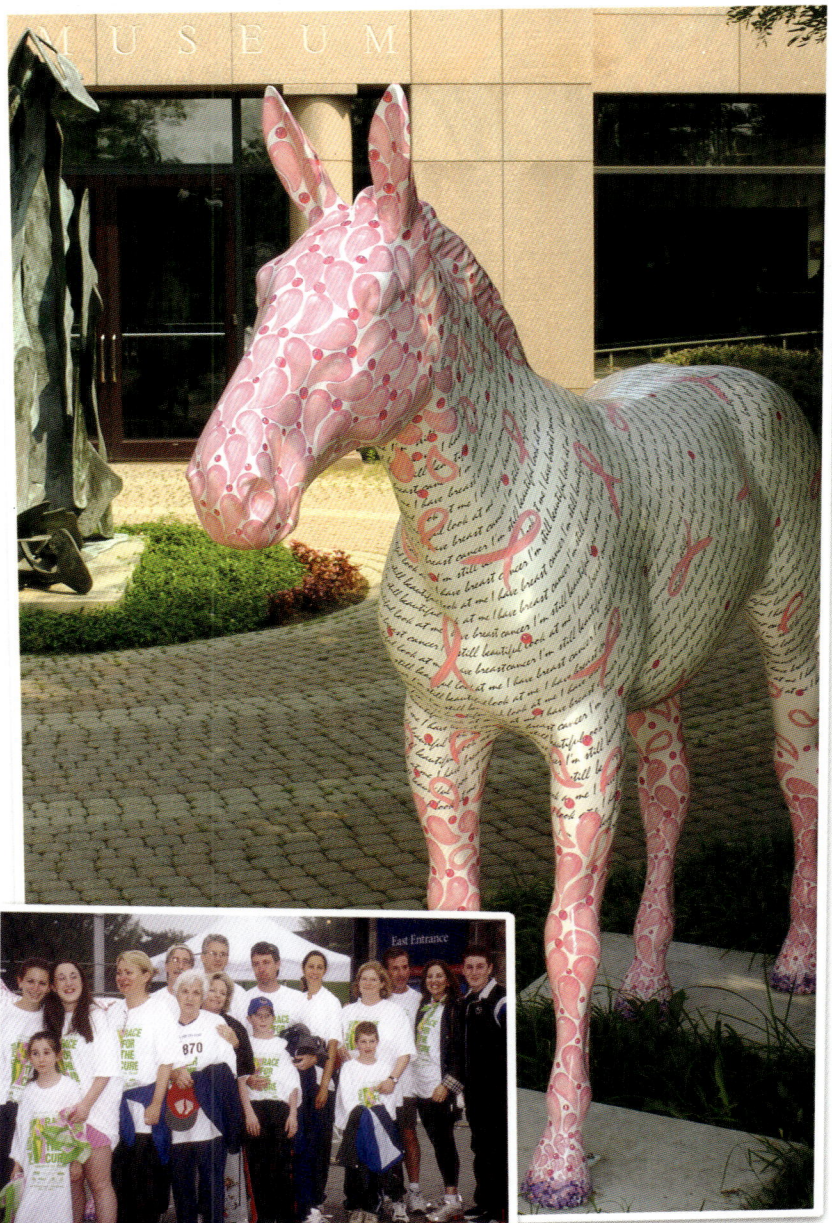

Friends and Family of Judy Schwartz at Race for the Cure
Photo by Carole Hurst

JUDY'S JEWEL
DOYLESTOWN, PA

Judy's Jewel serves as a wake-up call for women and those who love them. It was created in memory of Judy Schwartz, who lost her six-year battle with breast cancer in 2002. Sponsors Helene Hankin and Libby Schwartz say the **Miles of Mules** project was an opportunity to raise awareness of the disease in a unique and creative fashion.

Award-winning jewelry artist Diana Vincent adapted an original design she submitted, working with both Judy's cousin, Hankin, and her stepmother, Schwartz, to create a fitting tribute. Vincent decorated the mule in a teardrop pattern with pink ribbons, cabochon cut jewels and faceted crystals to represent the spirit of every woman, precious to someone, who has suffered from the disease. The mule carries the repeated inscription: "I have breast cancer, I'm still beautiful, look at me." On its hooves are pretty purple violets adapted from a pair of Judy's favorite shoes.

This spring, *Judy's Jewel* made an appearance in Philadelphia at the annual Race for the Cure. As breast cancer survivors walked down the art museum steps to the theme from "Rocky" they passed by the mule. Hundreds of race participants, including Judy's friends and family (who have participated in the race every year in honor of Judy), stopped to touch, hug and admire this beautiful symbol of strength.

"I have breast cancer, I'm still beautiful, look at me."

Artist: Annelies van Dommelen
Sponsor: Habitat for Humanity, thanks to Prudential Fox and Roach Realtors,
Bucks County Offices: Doylestown, New Hope, Newtown, Southampton and Yardley

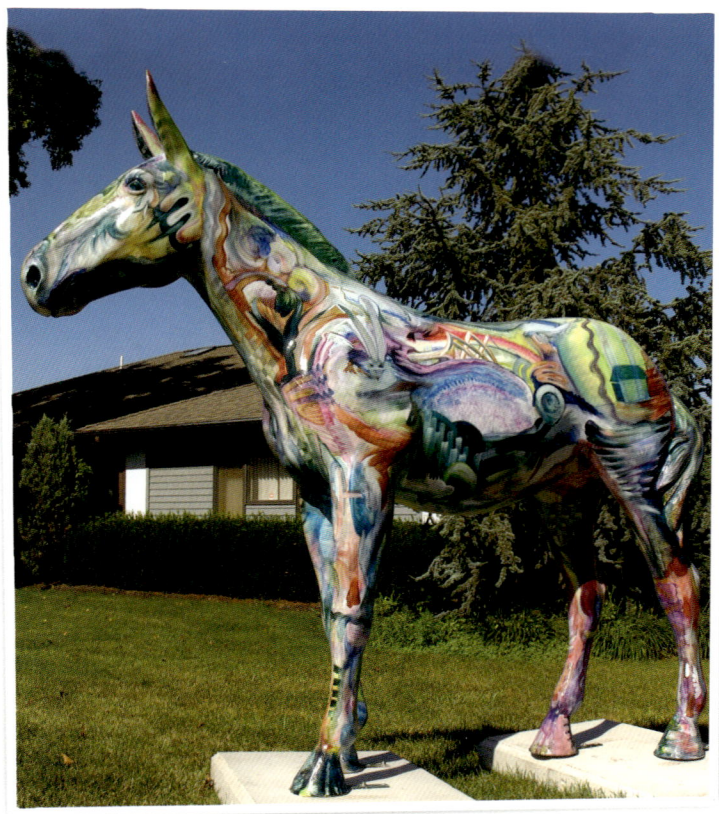

Artist: Jo Thompson Mercer
Sponsor: Premier Bank

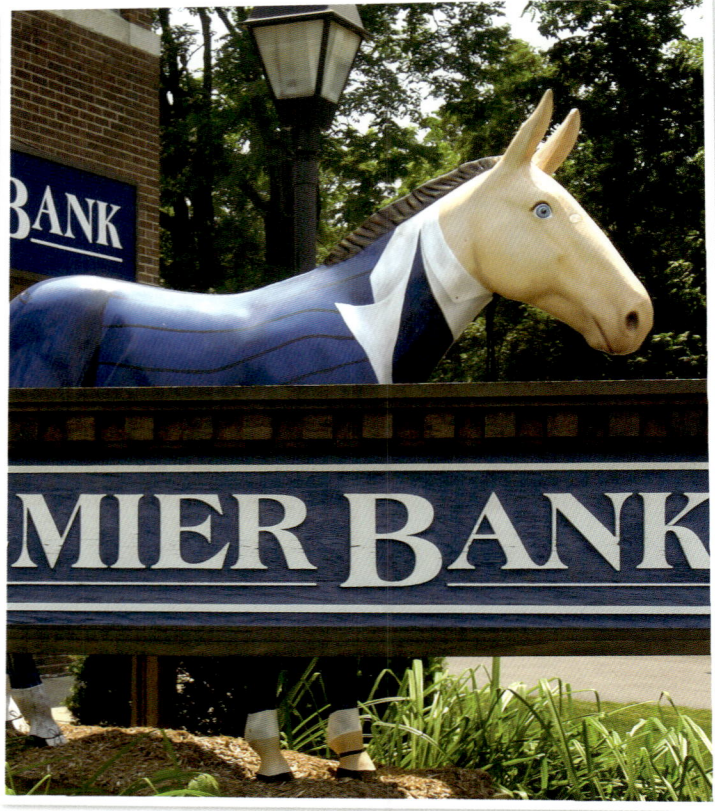

KANDINSKY'S LAST RIDE HOME

DOYLESTOWN, PA

Dedicated to the discovery of non-objective painting and true to Kandinsky's spirit of freedom, this design was executed with "the liberation of spirit and paint."

NORBUCK THE BANKER MULE

DOYLESTOWN, PA

Dapper in a pinstripe suit, wristwatch, pince-nez eyewear and an actual necktie, this mule transacts his way through history withdrawing miles of smiles from his clientele.

Artist: Karen Hartman
Sponsor: Delaware Valley College

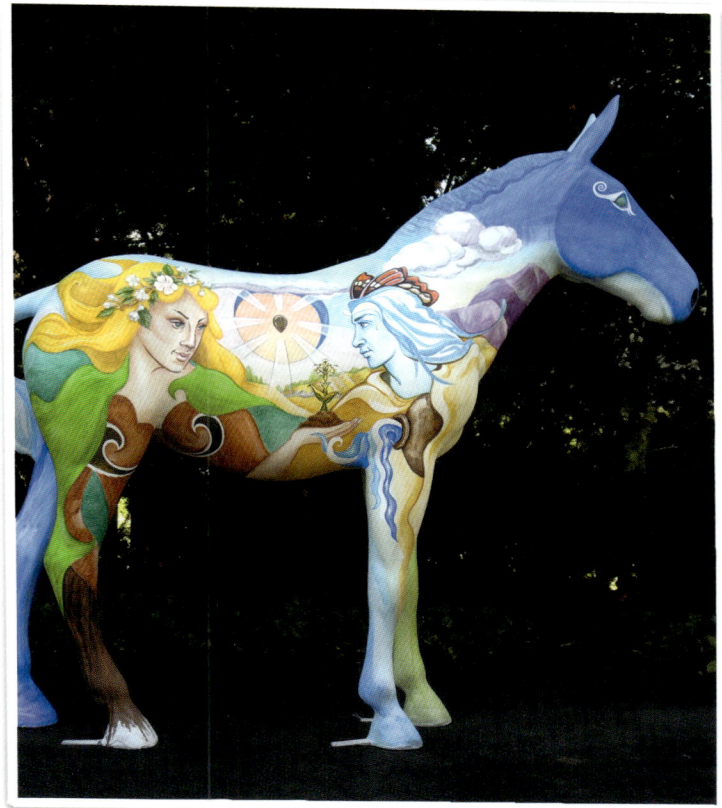

Artist: Marion Needham Krupp
Sponsor: Fox Chase Cancer Center, Bucks County Chapter, thanks to Jane and Bryce Sanders, William Berry and Kay Lopata Fine Arts

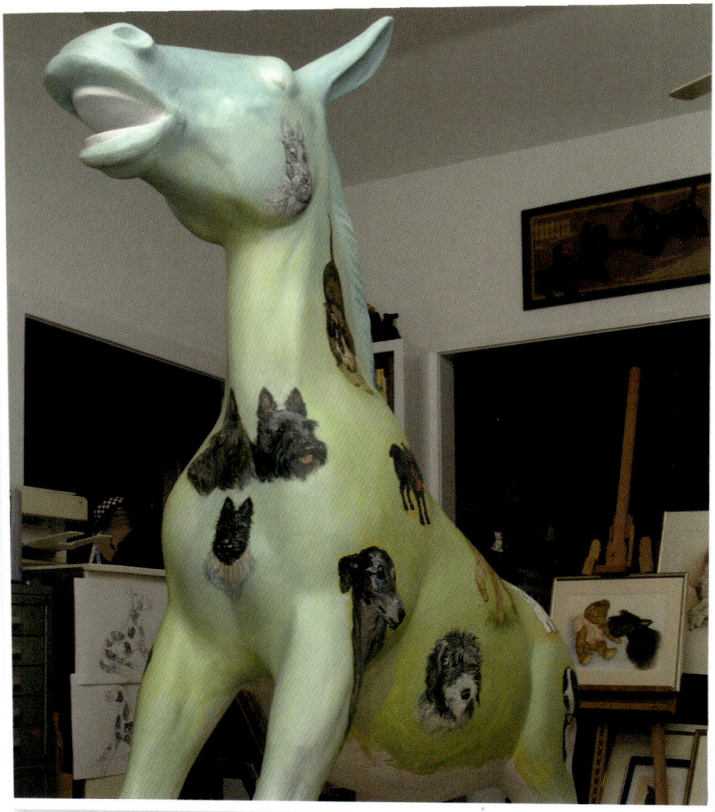

NOBLE WALKER

DOYLESTOWN, PA

Symbolism conveys the power of potential. Just as earth, air, sun and water help seeds to grow, Delaware Valley College seeks to cultivate and nurture innovative thinking.

MULE DOGGIE

DOYLESTOWN, PA

It's a Dog's Life! This design pays tribute to the many dogs that this nationally recognized artist has known and walked with along the Delaware Canal.

Artist: Rosemary Tottoroto
Sponsor: Robert G. Loughery

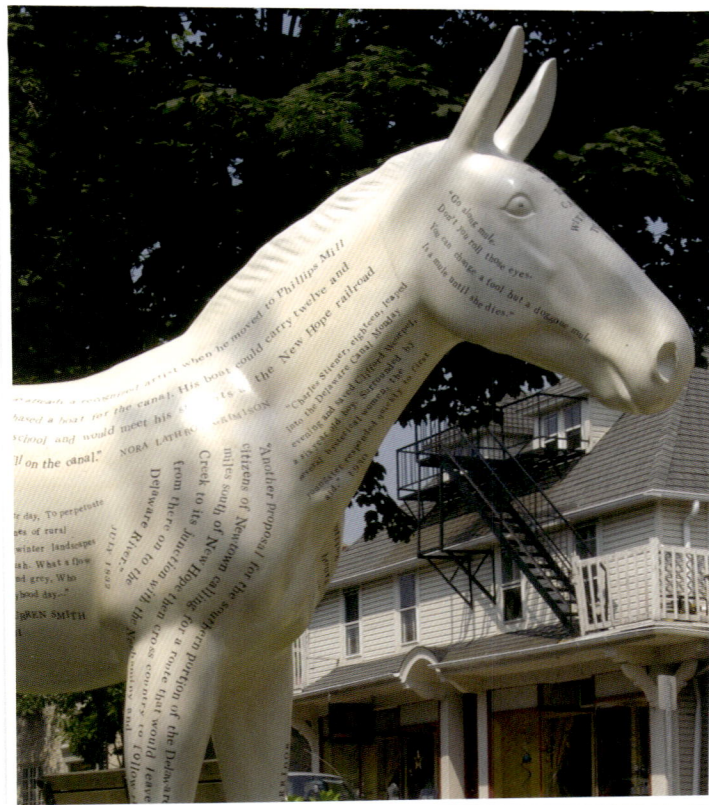

MULE tALES
DOYLESTOWN, PA

Graphic designer Tottoroto was inspired by the captivating stories of life on the canal that she discovered during extensive research at the Delaware & Lehigh archives in Easton.

Artist: Renny Reynolds
Sponsor: The Thompson Organization

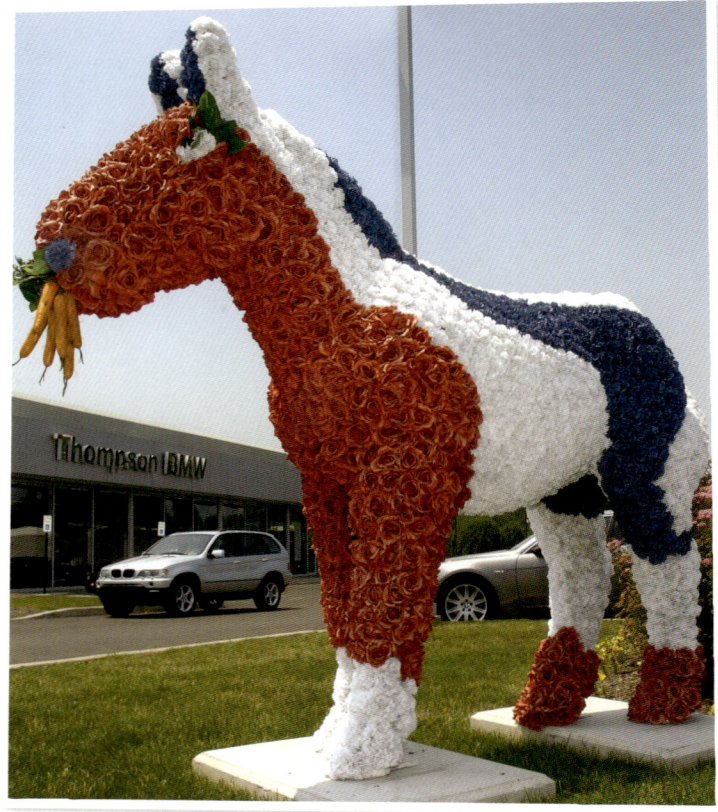

MiSS LiBERTiNE
DOYLESTOWN, PA

Renowned floral designer Renny Reynolds covered Miss Libertine in patriotic red, white and blue silk flowers; a reflection of his horticultural passions.

Artist: Jo Thompson Mercer
Sponsor: Keenan Motors

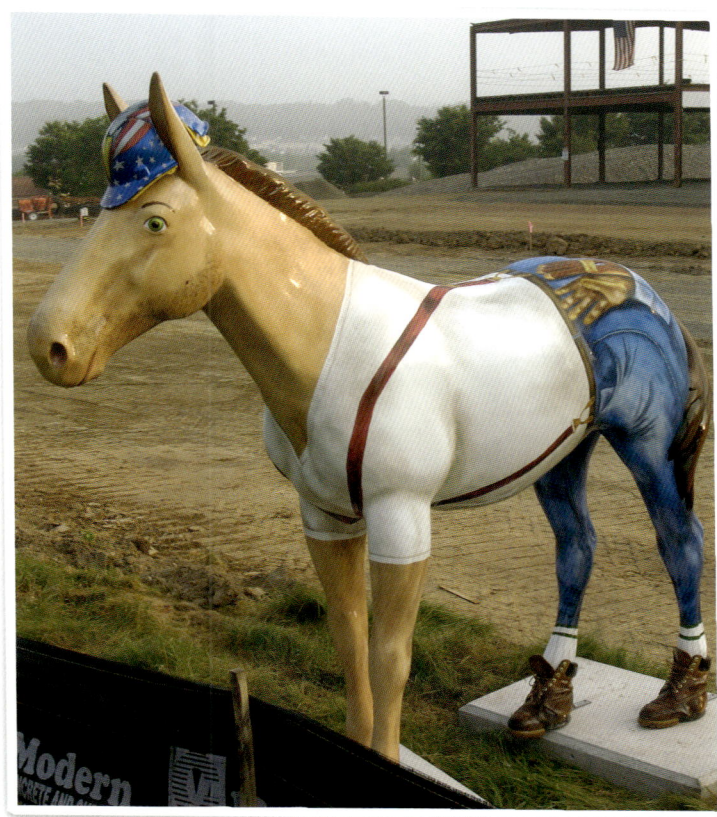

Artist: Mary V. Pearson
Sponsor: Penn Color

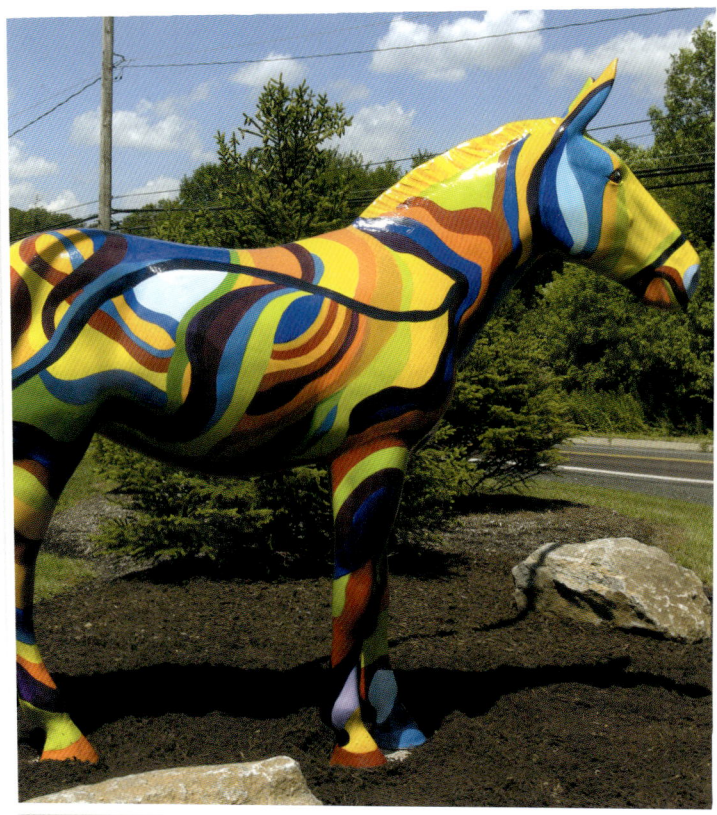

MERCEDES MULE

DOYLESTOWN, PA

The sponsor's concept of a construction worker mule was brought to life. Wearing a hardhat, dungarees and boots, it watches over the site of their future headquarters.

RAINBOW

DOYLESTOWN, PA

A reminder to look at the world around you with a fresh eye! Even as a young child the artist was inspired by combinations of colors and shapes in nature.

Artist: Jackie Simoné
Sponsor: The Intelligencer

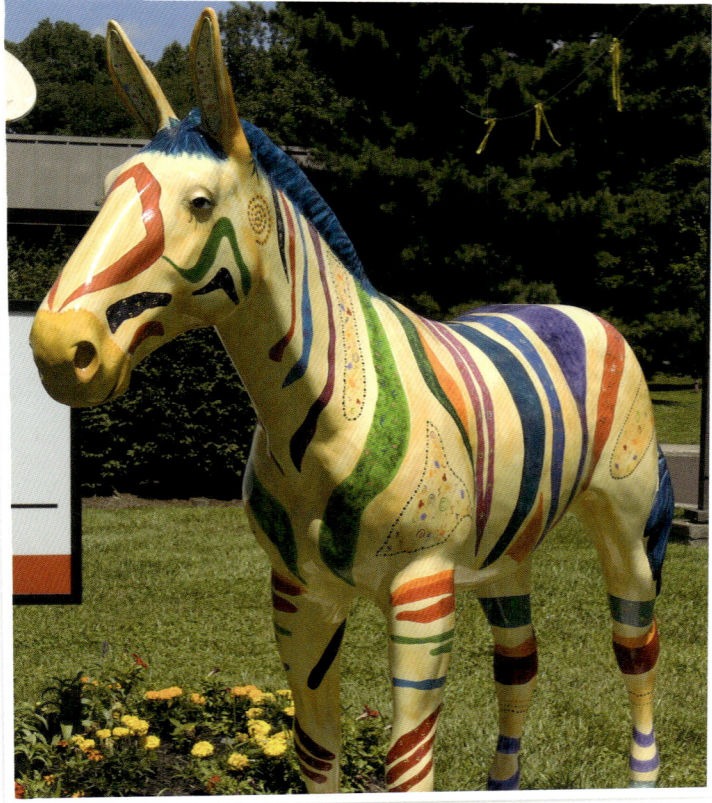

SPECIAL EDITION

DOYLESTOWN, PA

Just as color has transformed traditional newspapers, the artist used this zebra-striped mule to show the powerful impact of color.

Artist: Linden Elementary School Students
Sponsor: Doylestown Borough and Doylestown Revitalization Board

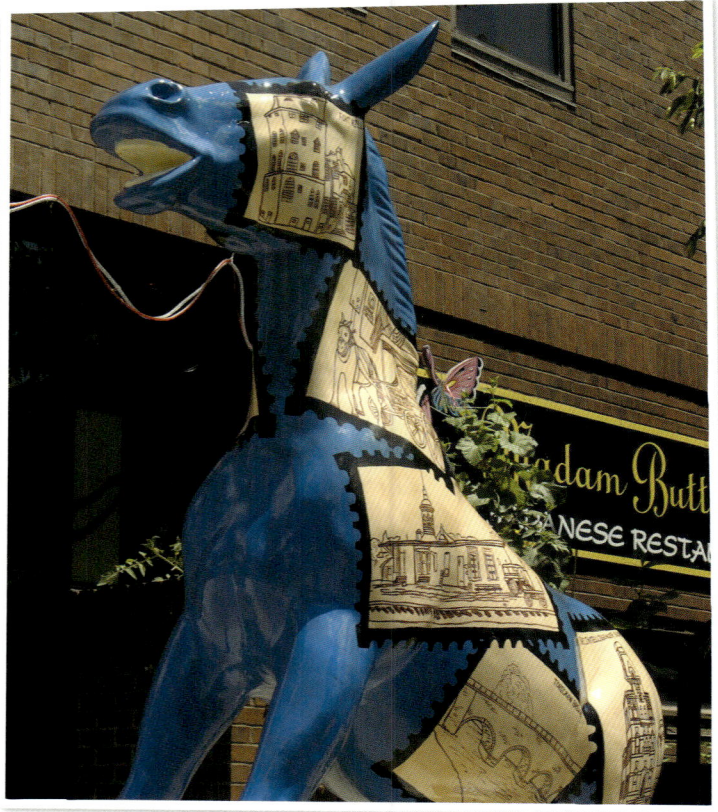

THE LINDEN COURIER

DOYLESTOWN, PA

Fifth and sixth grade art students created line drawings of local sites and painted them onto this mule's bright blue background to deliver a message about the history of Doylestown.

Artist: Jill P. Frazier
Sponsor: Doylestown Art League in memory of Anita Gronendahl, thanks to the Gronendahl Family

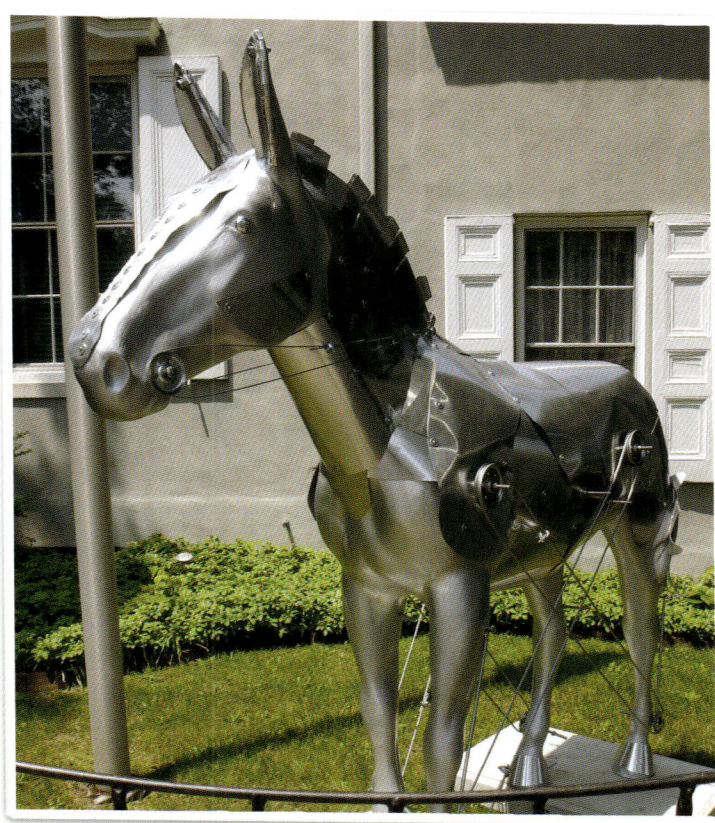

Artist: Geraldine Knock-Paul
Sponsor: Kelchner's Horseradish

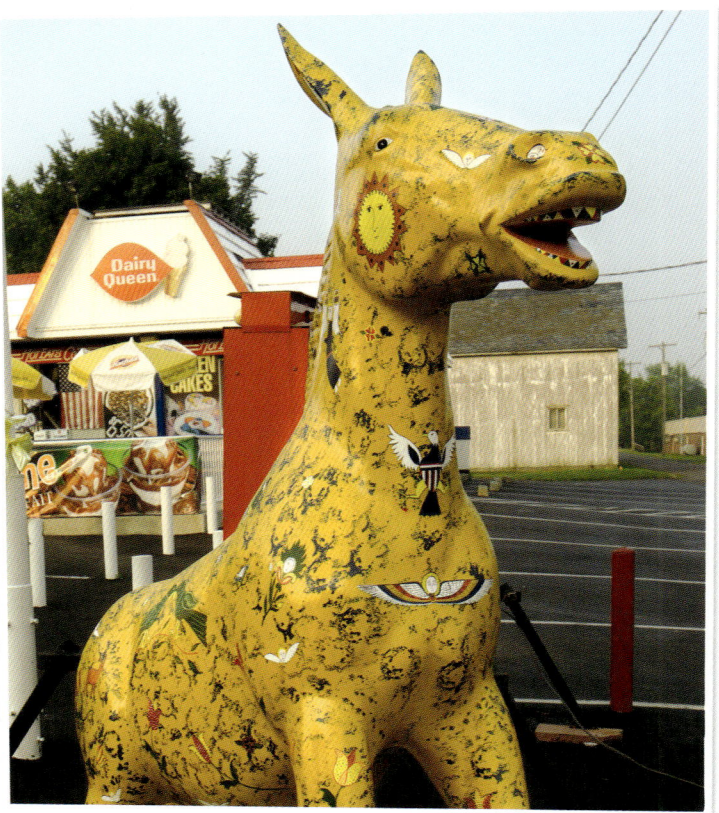

THE "CRANKY" MULE

DOYLESTOWN, PA

Cranky mules get the job done! In their heyday mules were the driving force behind the region's economy. This artist's design incorporates the idea of mules as machines.

EARL

DUBLIN, PA

Inspired by the Pennsylvania Dutch heritage of her grandfather Earl, the artist based her design on Pennsylvania German fraktur art and covered the mule with hearts, tulips and parrots.

Artist: Sally Getchel and Lynn Heath
Sponsor: The Faure Family

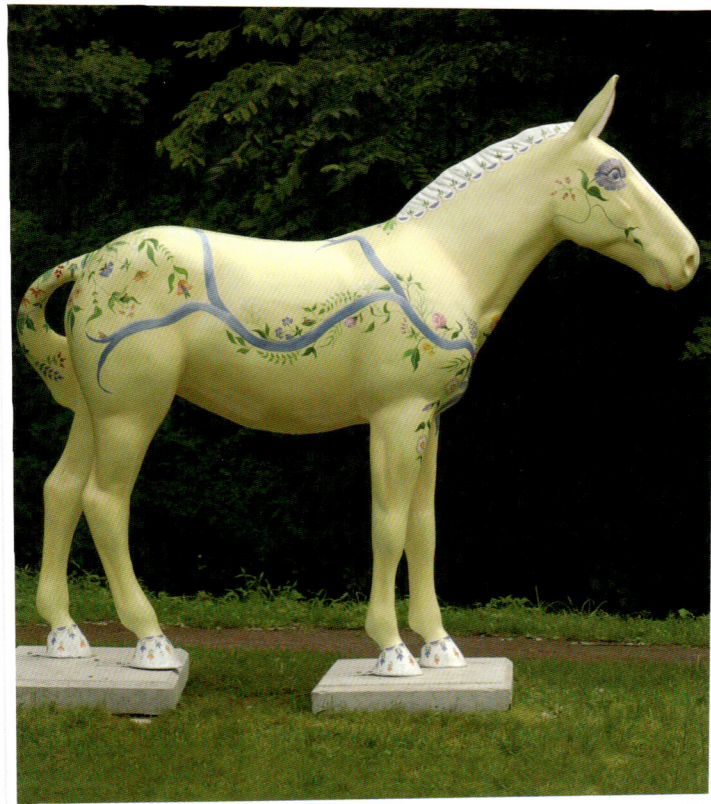

Artist: Kipp Sujet and Barry Sharplin
Sponsor: Kipp Sujet Memorial Scholarship Fund

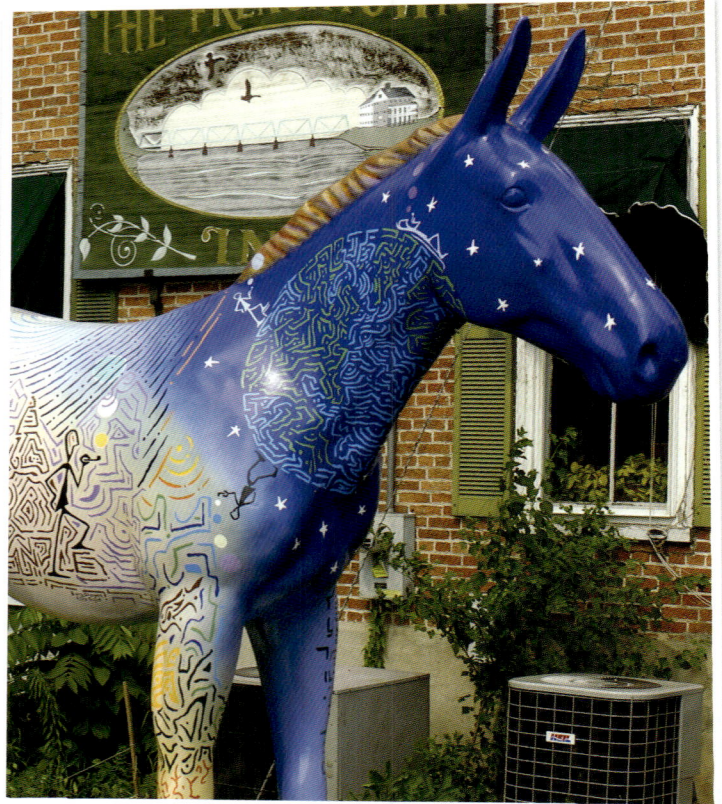

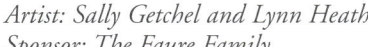

BÉBÉ

ERWINNA, PA

The Golden Pheasant Inn in Erwinna served as a mule barge stop during the Delaware Canal's commercial years. *BéBé* reflects the inn's colors, fabrics and French flair.

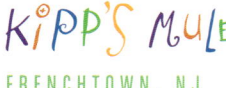

KIPP'S MULE

FRENCHTOWN, NJ

Kipp Sujet lived his 18 years in Hunterdon County and learned to bike along the canal towpath. Artist Sharplin interpreted artwork Sujet created when he was hospitalized for a bone marrow transplant.

Artist: Loraine Lovell Thompson
Sponsor: The Thompson Organization

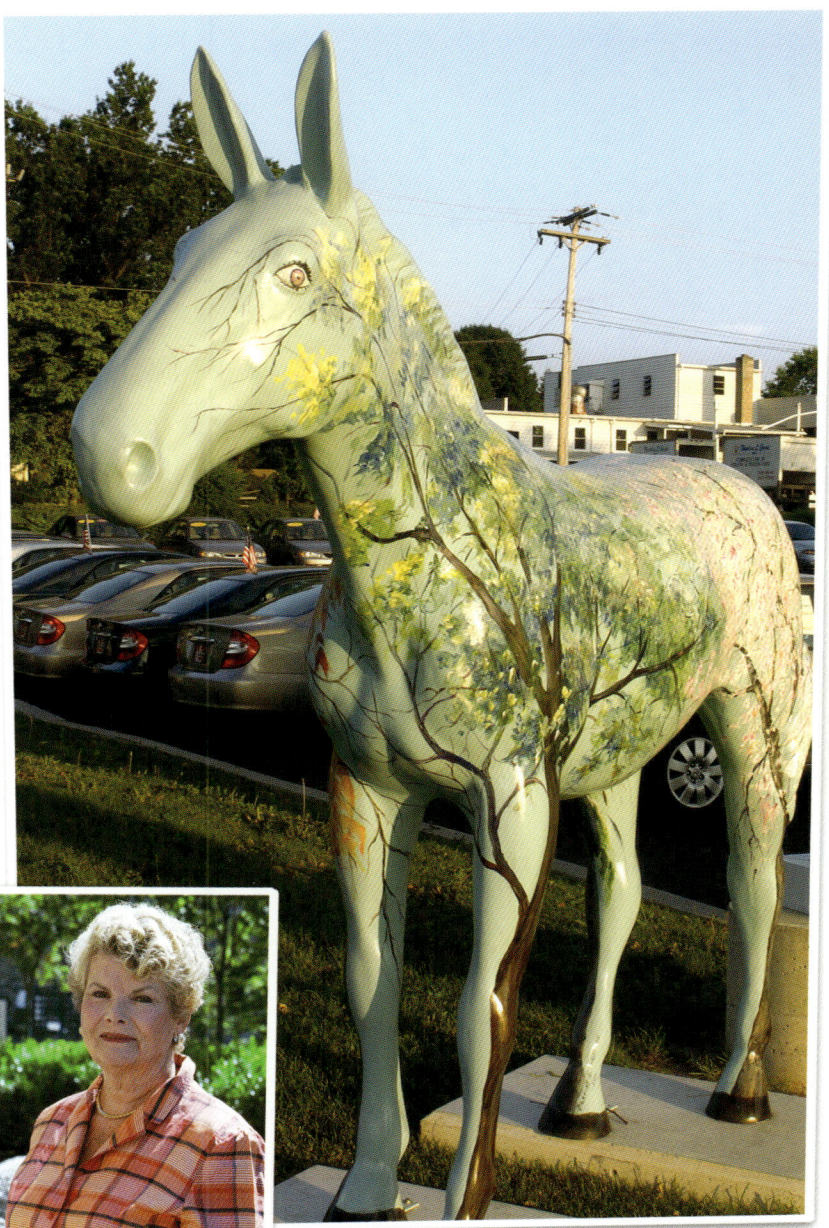

Loraine Lovell Thompson
Photo by Jared Polin

THE FOUR SEASONS

DOYLESTOWN, PA

The Thompson Organization in Doylestown was one of the first sponsors in Bucks County to recognize the importance and significance of the **Miles of Mules** project. Laura Barnes, a children's book author and vice president of marketing at the Thompson Organization, immediately recognized the impact the project would have.

Painting a life-sized, fiberglass mule would certainly have an impact on self-taught artist Loraine Lovell Thompson, Barnes' mother, who has worked in watercolors and oils for nearly 20 years. Having always concentrated on two-dimensional canvases, Thompson admitted the scale of this project was a bit daunting. Initially she housed the beast in her barn, until her husband Jack built a platform with wheels to help maneuver it.

Inspired by their bucolic Bucks County farm setting, the artist drew on childhood memories of the different trees along the Delaware Canal near her aunt's home in Morrisville. With a fondness for these perennial plants Thompson created her impressionist design, which depicts the changing beauty of the seasons.

A newcomer to working with acrylic paints, the artist received advice and guidance from a number of resources, including family and friends like painter Brad Redfield, great-grandson of well-known Pennsylvania Impressionist artist Edward Redfield.

"...memories of the different trees along the Delaware Canal."

95

Artist: Barry Sharplin
Sponsor: River Union Stage, thanks to Frenchtown Business Association

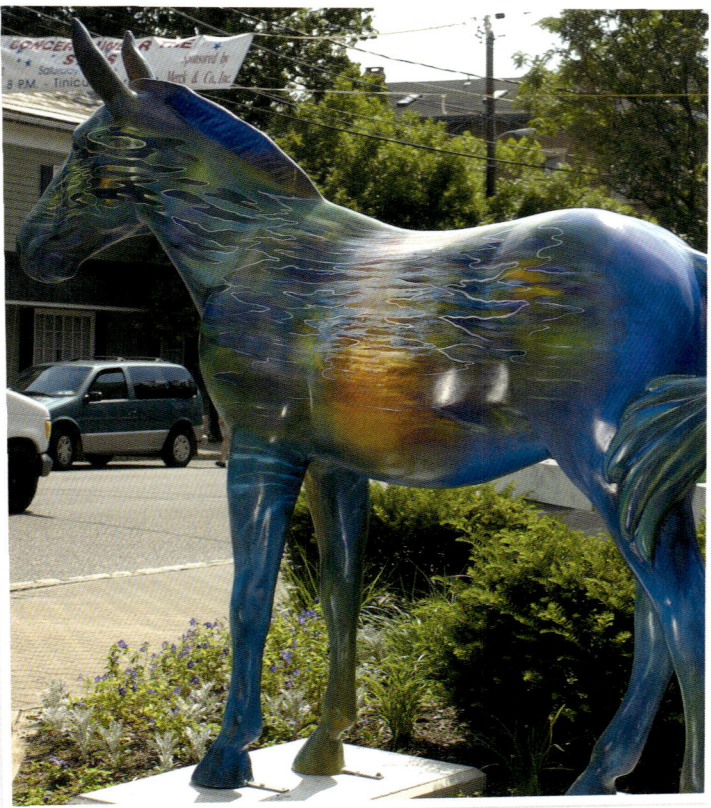

Artist: Selma Bortner
Sponsor: Peddler's Village

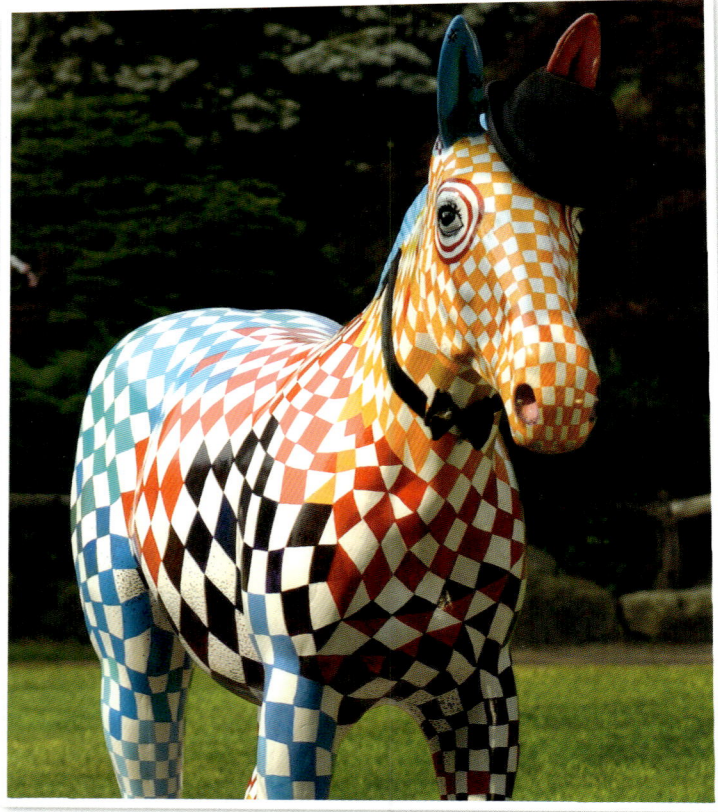

RIVER MULE

FRENCHTOWN, NJ

Originally from New Zealand, Sharplin is a multimedia artist and art teacher. His design depicts the swirls, eddies and graceful flow of the Delaware River, which served as his inspiration.

CITY SLICKER

LAHASKA, PA

A throwback to the days of the old-fashioned dandy, this mule sports a checkered coat, derby hat and a bow tie originally worn by the artist's husband to his high school prom.

Artist: Jo Thompson Mercer
Sponsor: Bucks County Herald

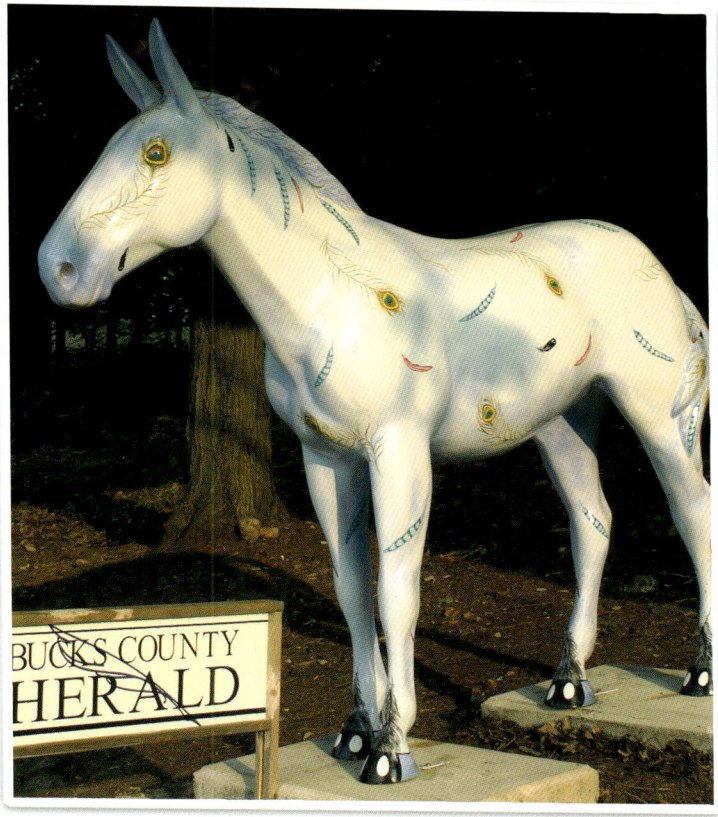

Artist: Susannah Hart Thomer
Sponsor: Knobs 'n Knockers

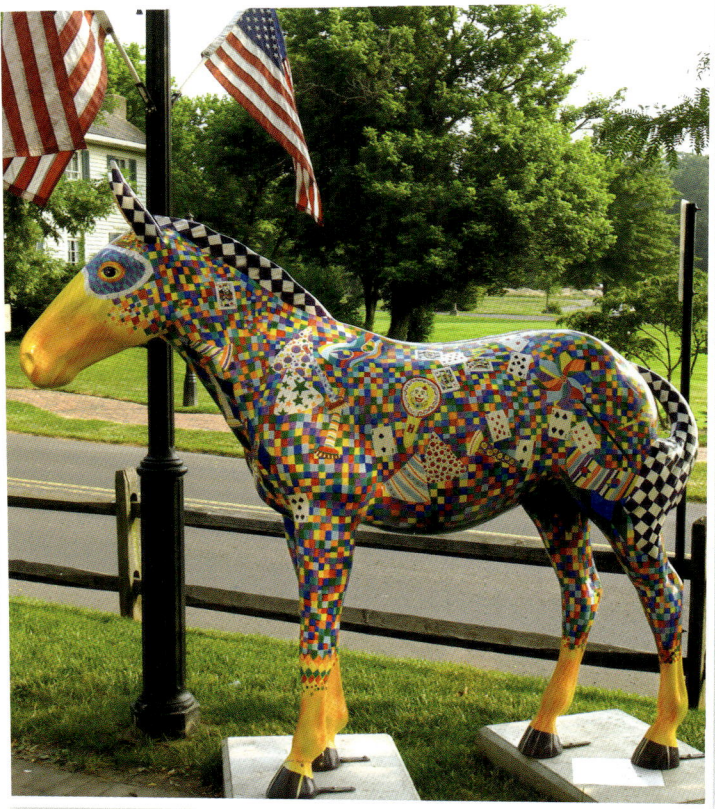

MULEFEATHERS

LAHASKA, PA

A single fallen blue jay feather inspired this creation. The mule features expressive peacock-feather eyes and a variety of hand-painted feathers that float lightly across a sky blue background.

PARTY ANIMULE

LAHASKA, PA

Created to elicit humor and pleasure with a hide-and-seek design that encourages viewers to find the disguised noisemakers, cards, party hats and other celebratory objects.

Artist: Groveland Elementary School Students
Sponsor: Groveland Elementary School friends and family

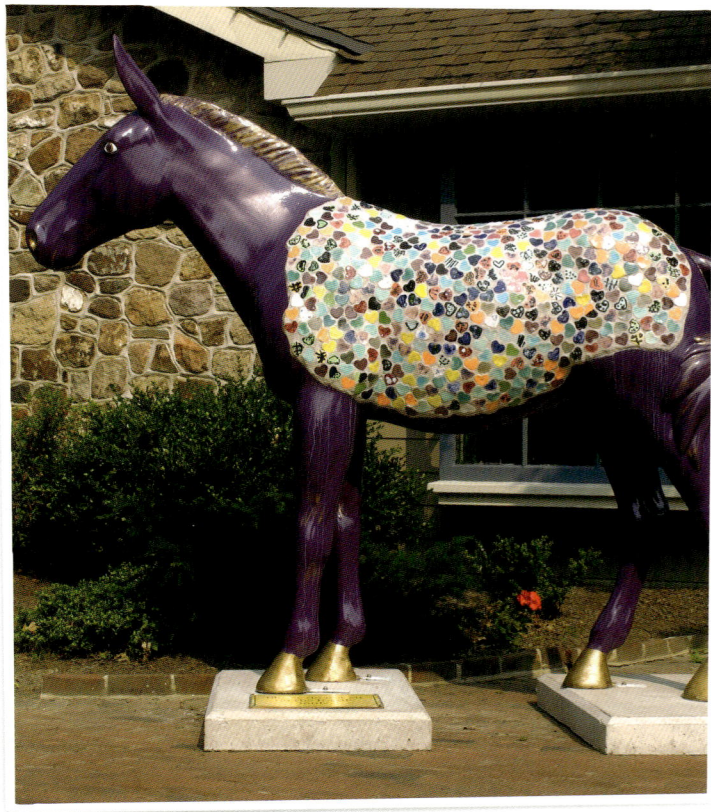

Artist: Unami Middle School Students
Sponsor: Unami Middle School

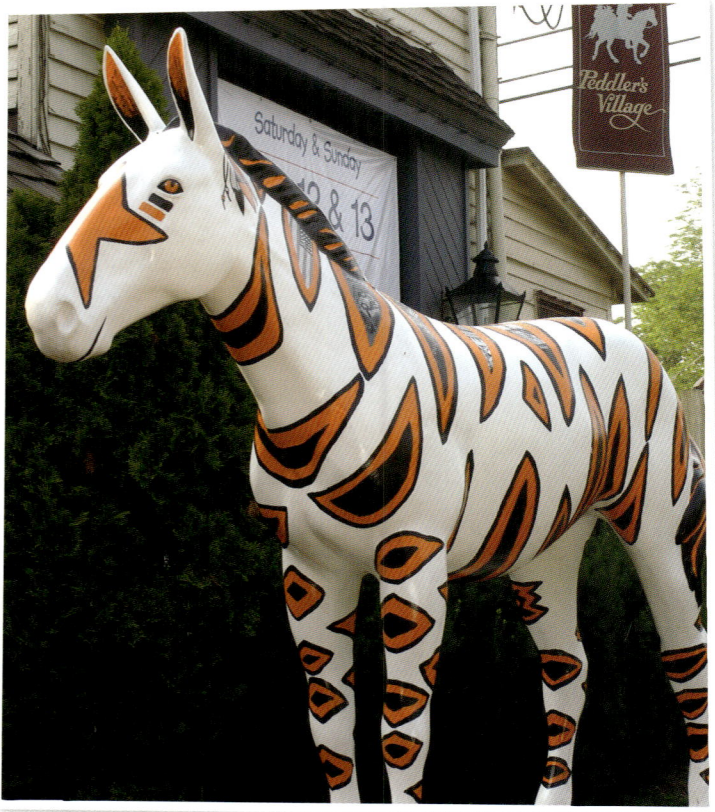

PURPLE HEART

LAHASKA, PA

Under art teacher Karen Houser's direction, each student created an individual clay tile heart affixed to the mule "honoring the heroes of yesterday, today and tomorrow."

UNAMI

LAHASKA, PA

Ninth-grader Amy Montella's design was chosen through a school-sponsored art contest. The area's Native American Unami tribe is the namesake for the school and this mule.

Artist: Butler Elementary School Students
Sponsor: Butler Elementary School Parent Teacher Organization

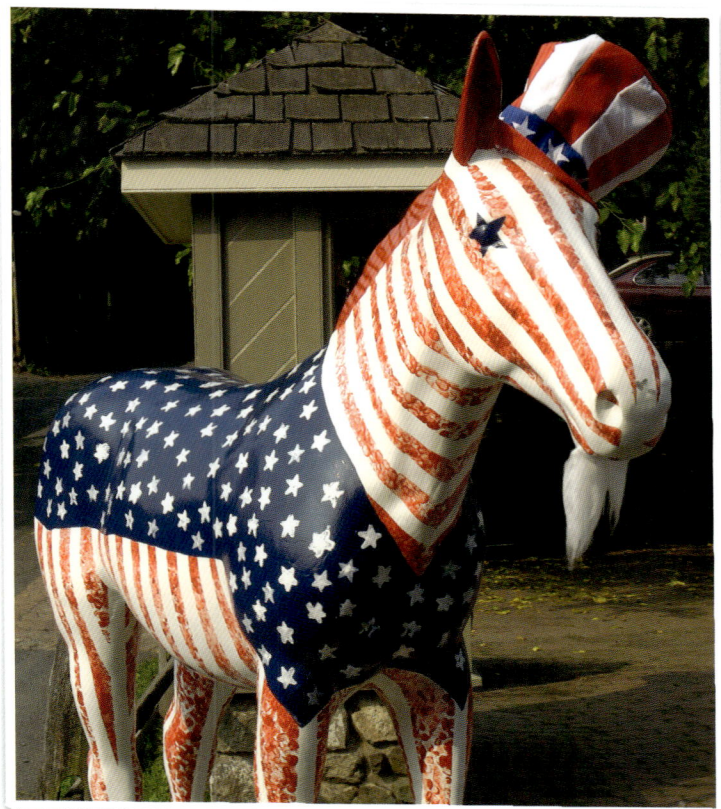

Uncle Samule
Lahaska, PA

Each Butler student contributed a red thumbprint to *Uncle Samule*. The upper classmen also stamped white stars on a field of blue to carry out this patriotic theme.

Artist: Dot Bunn
Sponsor: Crystal Springs Farm

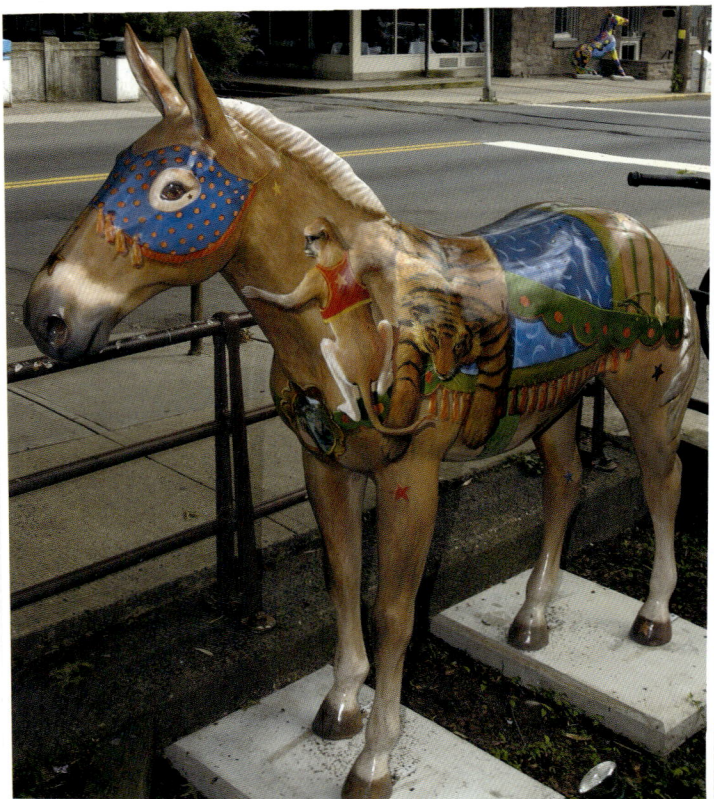

Circus Mule
Lambertville, NJ

Dot Bunn works in storybook illustration, custom artwork and murals. Here she has created a colorful three-dimensional look at the circus.

Artist: Patients at New Jersey's Ann Klein Forensic Center
Sponsor: AKFC Board of Trustees, and Art Therapists Susanne P. Davis and Carol Pletnick

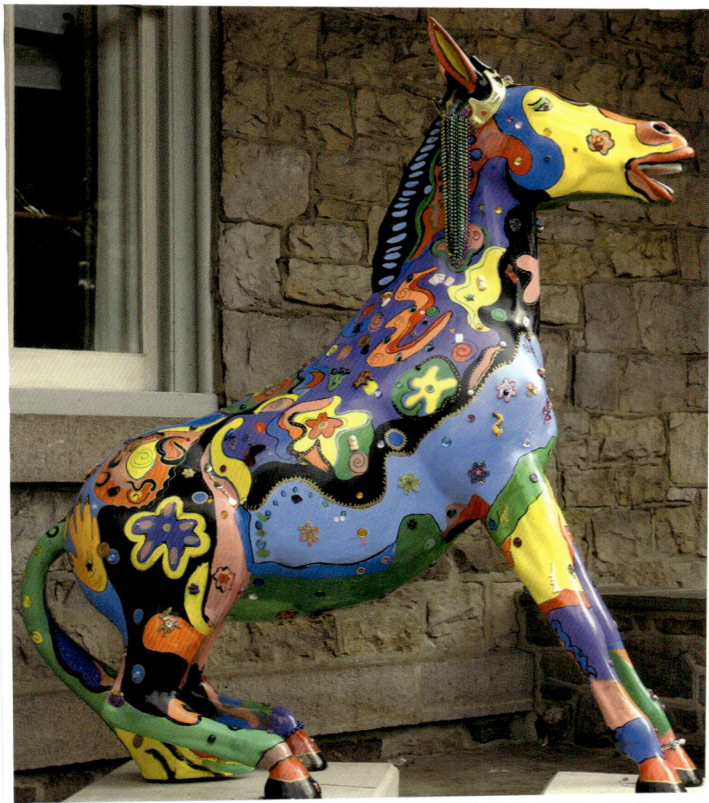

Artist: Yvonne Love
Sponsor: FACT and Artists in Residence, thanks to In Rare Form

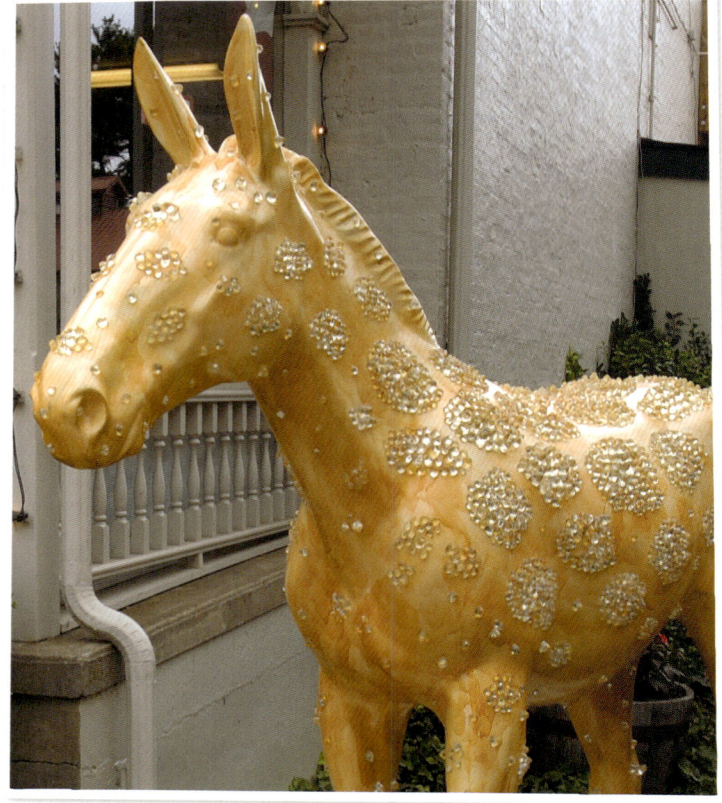

MARDI GRAS MULE

LAMBERTVILLE, NJ

"Don't worry! Be happy! Raise your voice with joyful singing all around you and you too shall be given shining beads and a golden crown to wear."

MEMORY MULE

LAMBERTVILLE, NJ

This abstract design draws on personal memories of the artist's sister who died from Leukemia at age 12. Clay cast clusters represent memory cells, aimed to provoke reflection.

*Artist: Kim Guenther, with a little help from
the Oxford Communications team
Sponsor: Oxford Communications*

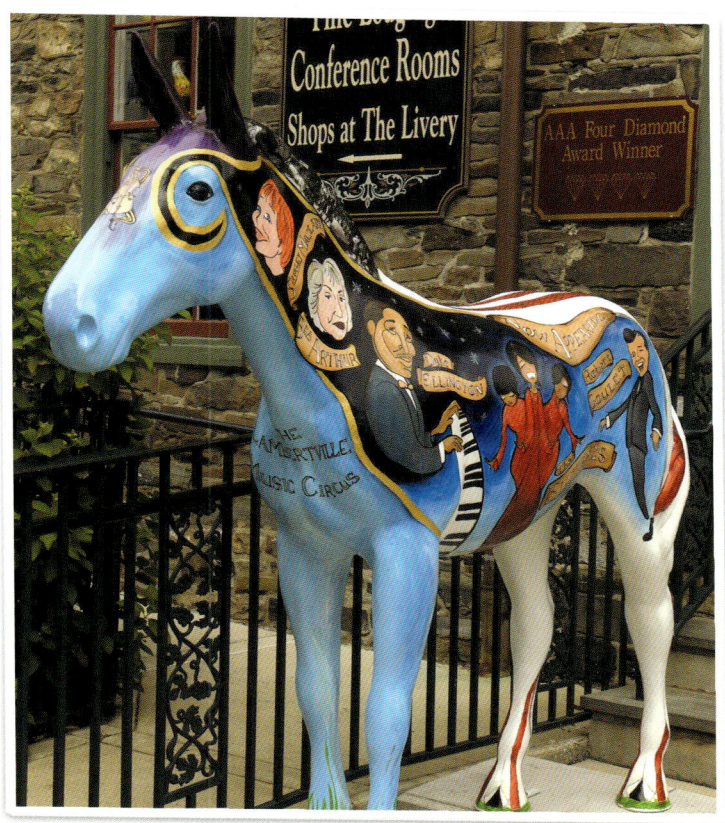

*Artist: Julie Marie Fischer
Sponsor: Bucks County Courier Times*

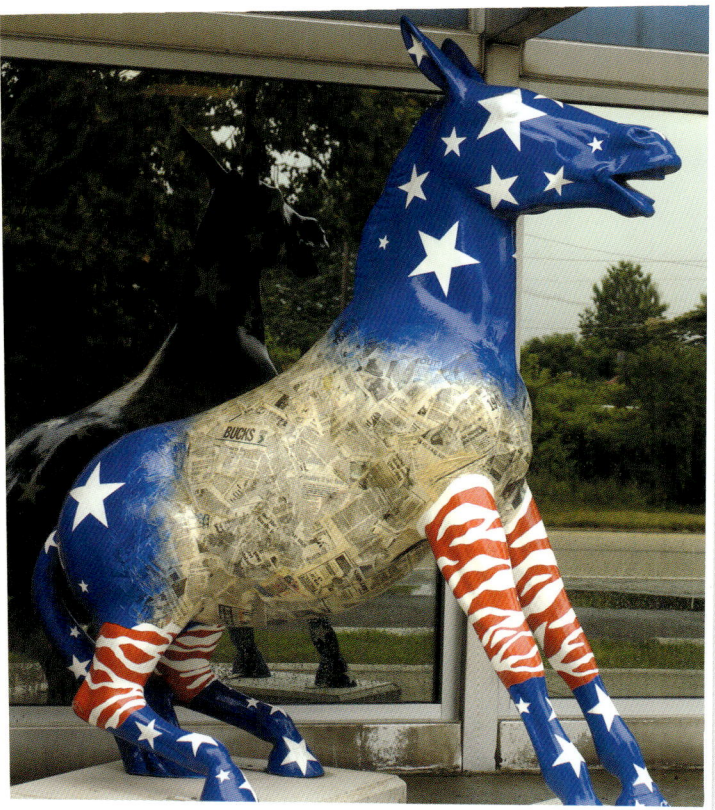

tHE SOUND OF MULE-SiC

LAMBERTVILLE, NJ

Inspired by their local roots and the location of their headquarters, the creative team at Oxford drew on the history of St. John Terrill and his famous Lambertville Music Circus.

FREEDOM OF tHE PRESS, FiRSt A"MULEMENt"

LEVITTOWN, PA

By overlaying elements of newspapers and the American flag, the artist created a tribute to the freedom of the written word.

Artist: The Michael Girls
Sponsor: The George Michael Family

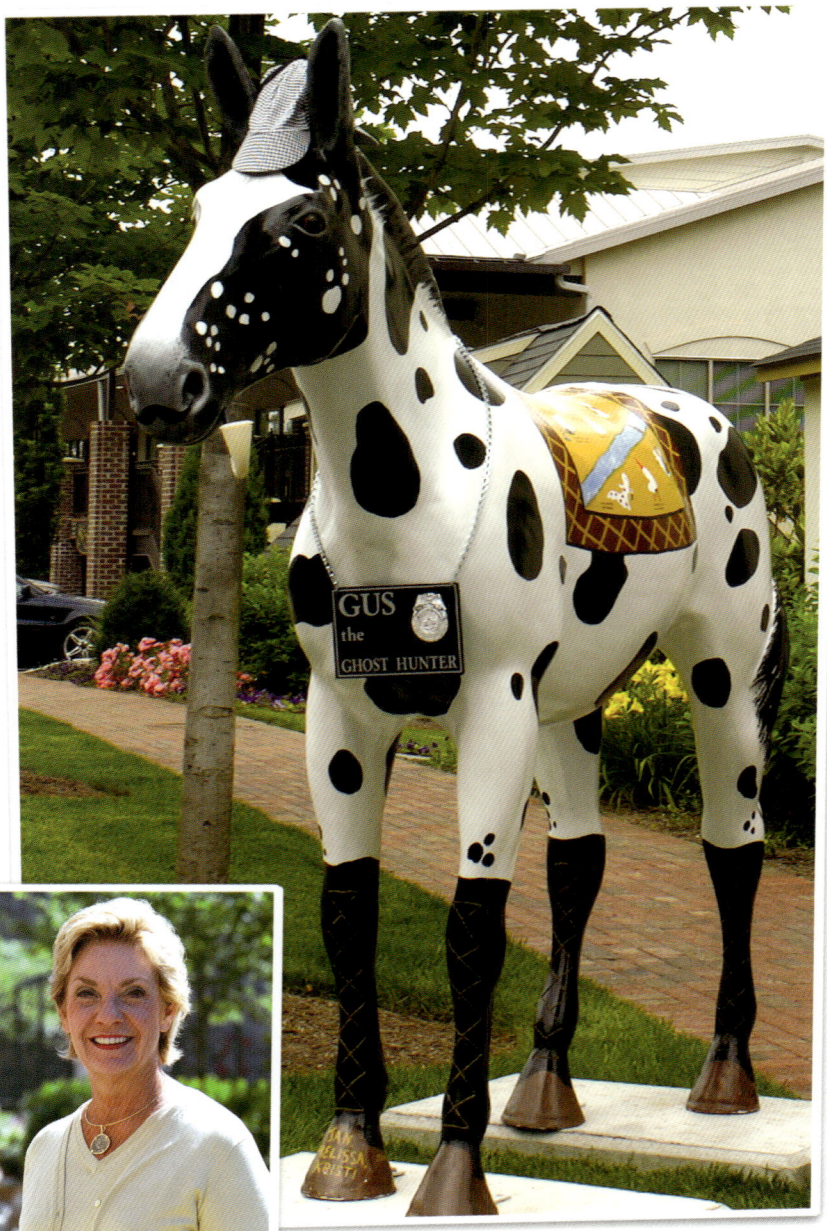

Jan Michael
Photo by Jared Polin

GUS THE GHOST HUNTER
NEW HOPE, PA

The New Hope area is known for many things: its rich heritage as an art colony, its scenic waterfront and its legends, including those about ghosts. These scary stories are only speculation, of course, but rumored hauntings of the town's historic properties have been commonplace for years.

Before designing *Gus,* Jan Michael and her daughters-in-law, Kristi Biello Michael and Melissa Michael, took a guided ghost tour of the area to learn more. The trio discovered specific ghosts who have been repeatedly seen. These include the famed hitchhiker who roams along Windy Bush Road and Route 202 and a little girl who lingers near the Wedgwood Inn.

Gus' garb, similar to the Scotland Yard variety worn by Sherlock Holmes, also features a dramatic black and white background pattern. On his blanket is an area map marked with rumored haunts including The Logan Inn and the Lambertville House.

Gus greets visitors to the Union Square complex, the home of the Michener Art Museum's satellite location. Not only was the George Michael family an early supporter of the **Miles of Mules** project, their generosity also made the Museum's New Hope satellite possible.

Despite the ghostly overtones, *Gus the Ghost Hunter* is one mule that never spooks!

"…Gus the Ghost Hunter is one mule that never spooks!"

Artist: Jeanne Elodie Matusky
Sponsor: Waste Management of Pennsylvania

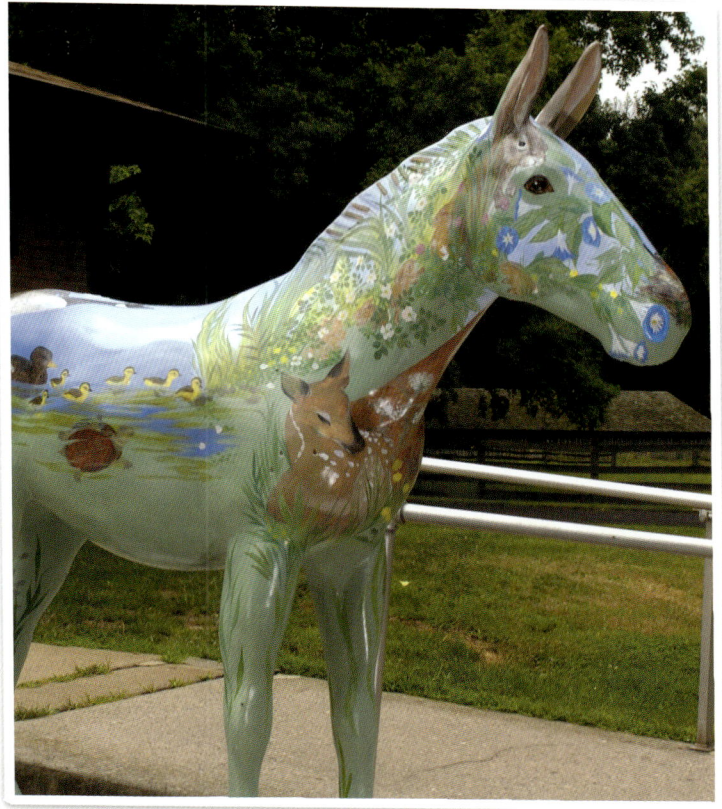

Artist: Edward Ward
Sponsor: Borough of New Hope, thanks to Scannapieco Development Corp.

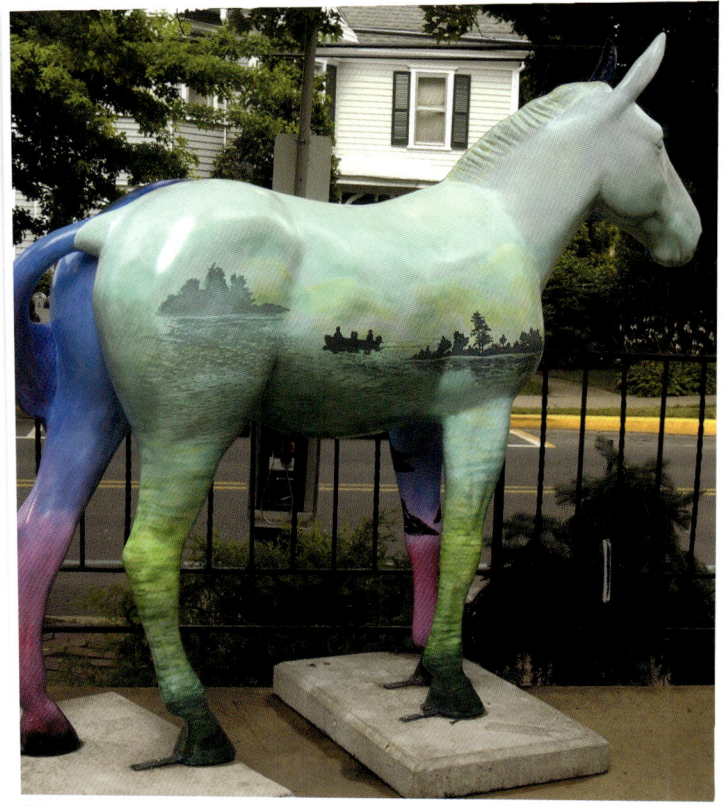

SANCTUARY

MORRISVILLE, PA

Sanctuary is a beautiful amalgam of land and water motifs that expresses the harmony of the natural world.

A DAY ALONG THE DELAWARE

NEW HOPE, PA

The Trenton artist based this concept on the many canoe trips taken by him and his family down the Delaware River near Scudders Falls.

Artist: Linda Guenste
Sponsor: Bill and Cathy Rieser

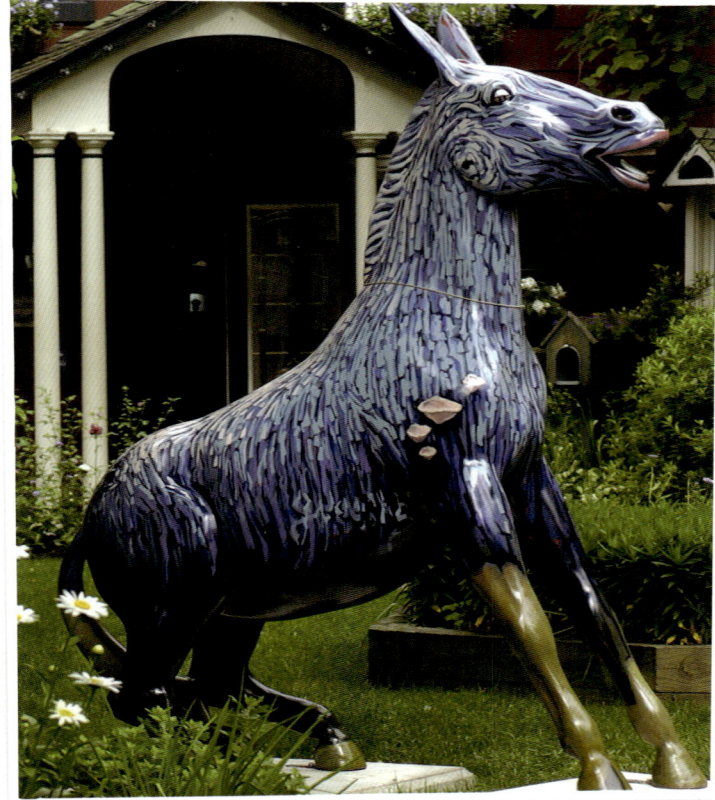

DELA-LE THE BARKING MULE

NEW HOPE, PA

Working in landscapes, artist Guenste developed an interest in the characteristics of trees. Here she includes colorful lichen, moss and bark to reflect an arboreal surface on the mule.

Artist: Brenda Lawson
Sponsor: Friends of the Artist

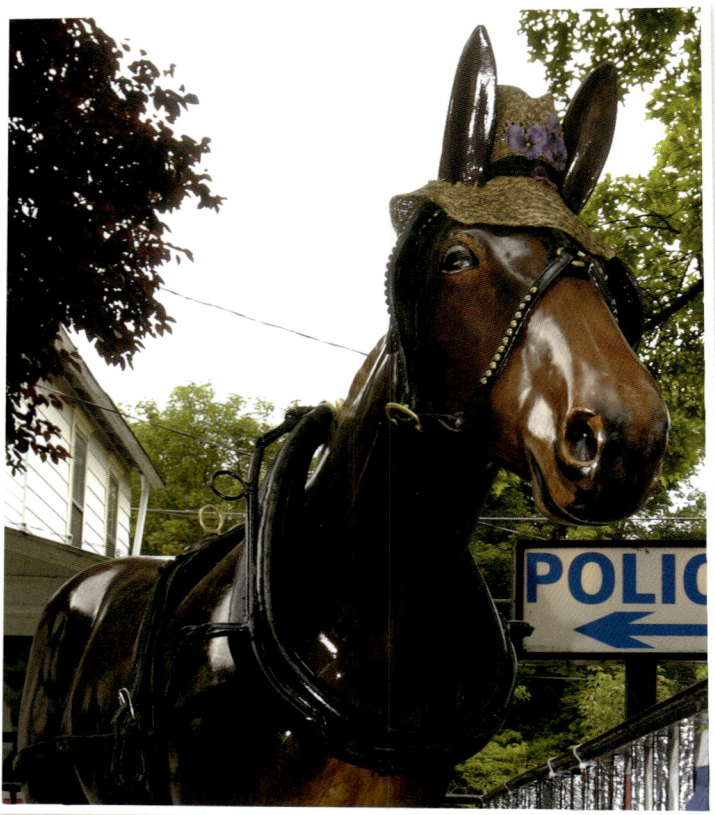

DELAWARE CANAL MULE

NEW HOPE, PA

Painted in realistic splendor, with a leather harness and straw hat, this mule looks real enough to pull a barge along the canal in New Hope.

Artist: Claudia Funke
Sponsor: Friends of the Artist

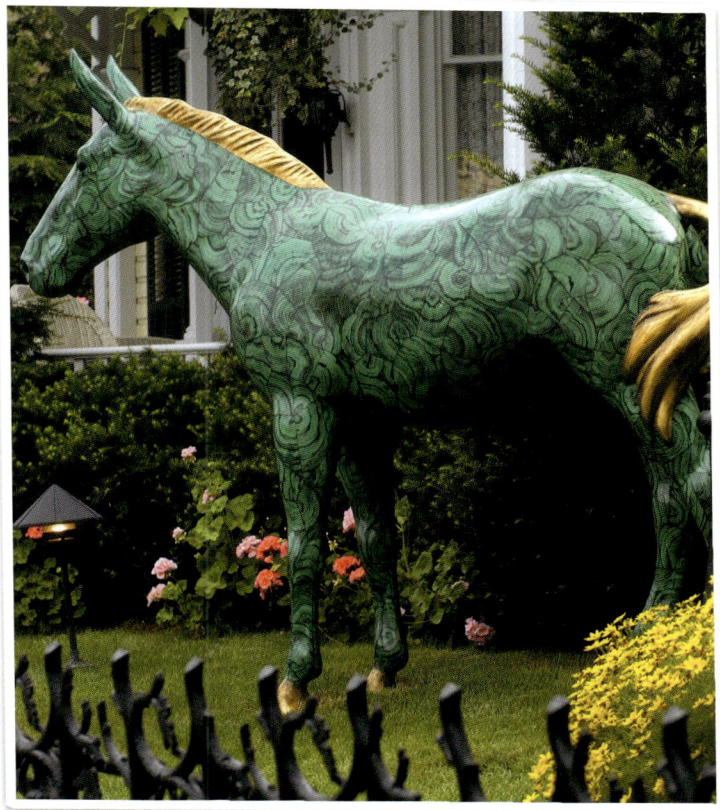

Artist: Barbara Surick
Sponsor: Pam and Carl Asplundh

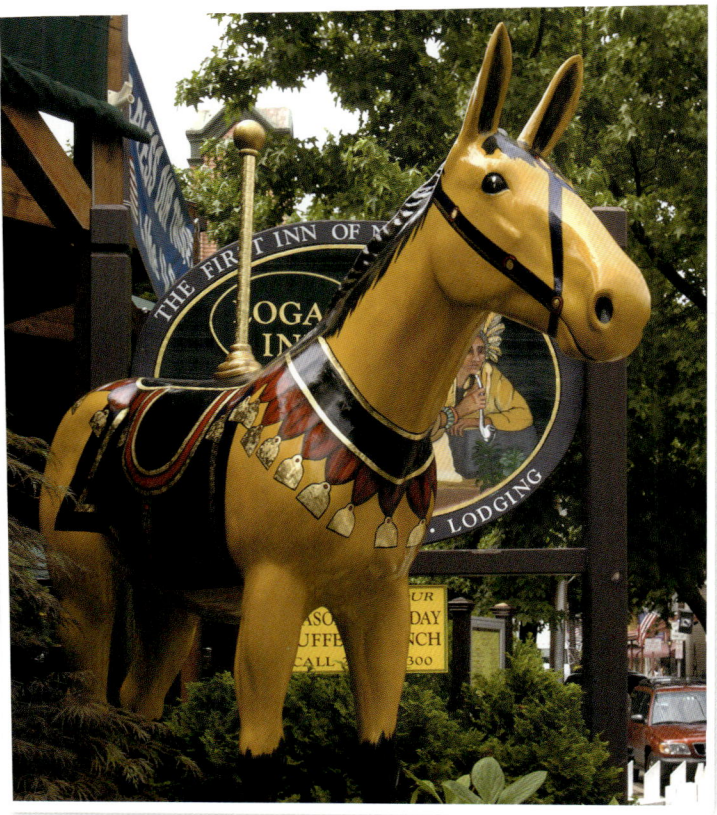

ORMA-LOU

NEW HOPE, PA

Decorative painting skills were brought to bear on this mule, which features a striking faux malachite finish and gold ormolu details.

MERRY GO MULE

NEW HOPE, PA

This mule is about pure joy, fun, memories, trips to fairs, vacations, starry nights, pretty lights, waving hands, small children, lovers, and grandparents…it's a heart thing, says the artist.

Artist: James Feehan
Sponsor: Friends of the Delaware Canal

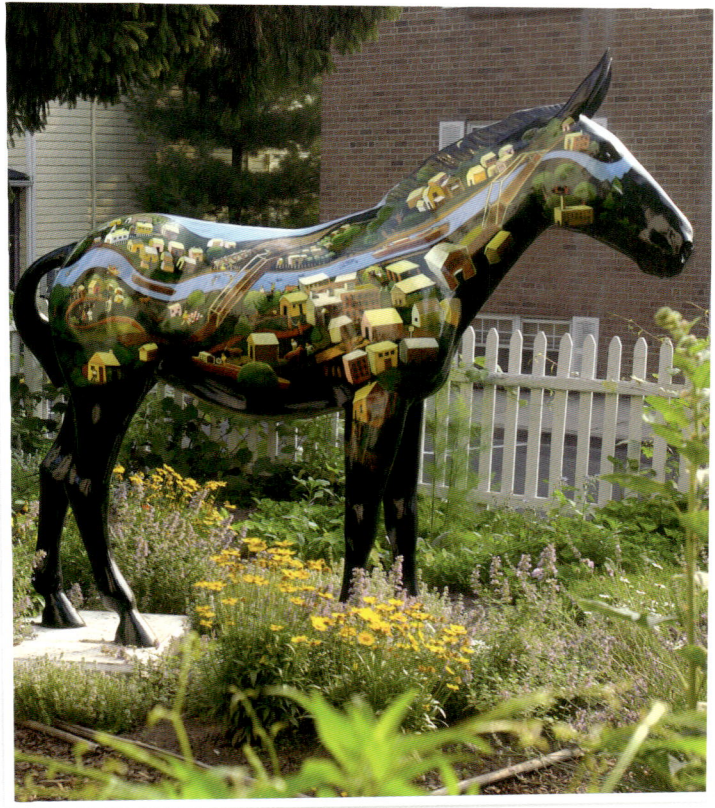

Artist: Didi Goldmark
Sponsor: Nine Lives Rescue, Inc., thanks to Odette's, Friends of the Artist with footwear by Be Adorned

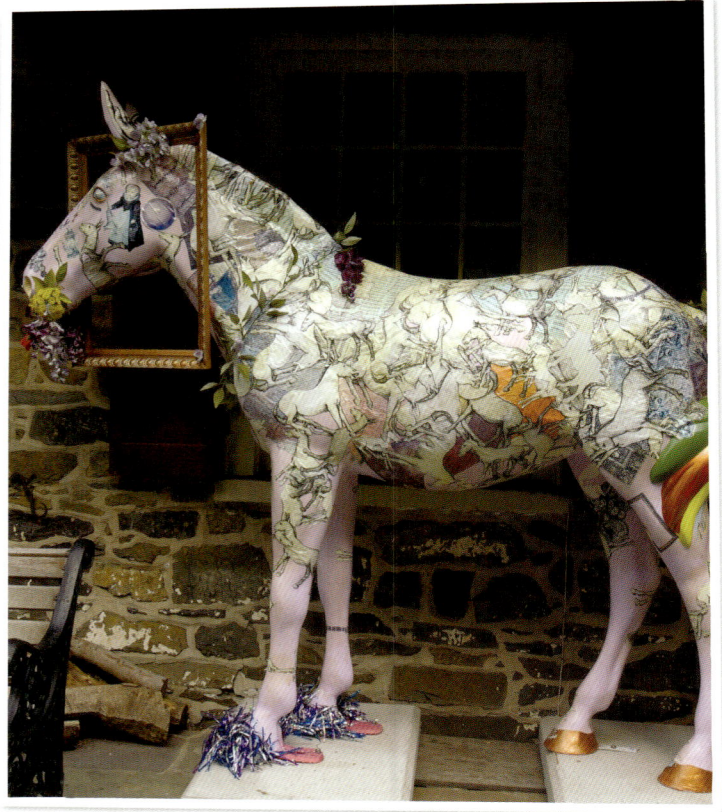

iLLUSTRATED CANAL MULE

NEW HOPE, PA

Rich in detail and color, Feehan's mule portrays the many diverse attributes, activities and pursuits the canal once engendered and supported.

ODETTE

NEW HOPE, PA

A collage artist and a fun-loving person, Goldmark created this mule to reflect her sense of whimsy, right down to the pink marabou "mules" on its front hooves.

Artist: Tristanne Davis
Sponsor: Solebury School, thanks to Havana Restaurant
and Penn's Grant Corp.

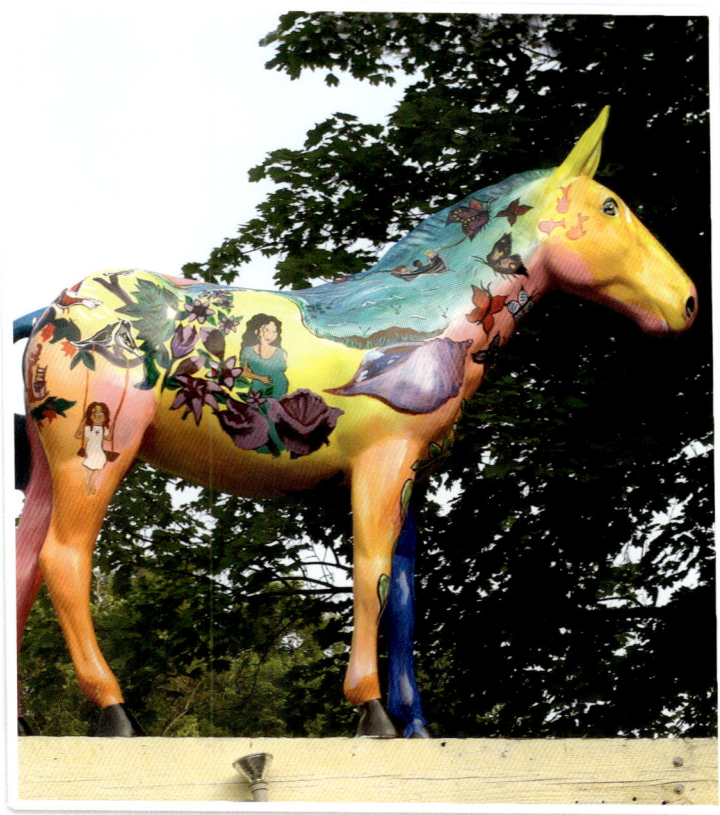

Artist: George and Betty Bramhall and Sue Eaton
Sponsor: New Hope Historical Society

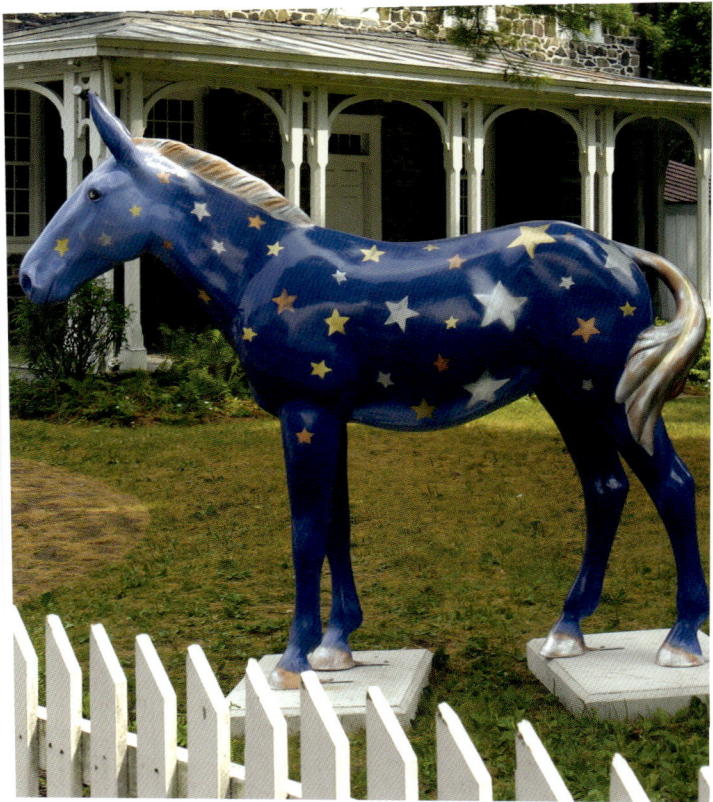

PUZZLED MULE

NEW HOPE, PA

Expresses the notion that all aspects of the world are connected in one way or another and all creatures are a part of the cycle, including mules!

FOUNTAINHEAD BEN

NEW HOPE, PA

A star-studded tribute to Benjamin Parry, who was a founding father of historic New Hope.

Artist: Judy Pearsall
Sponsor: Intercounty Newspapers/Journal Register Co.

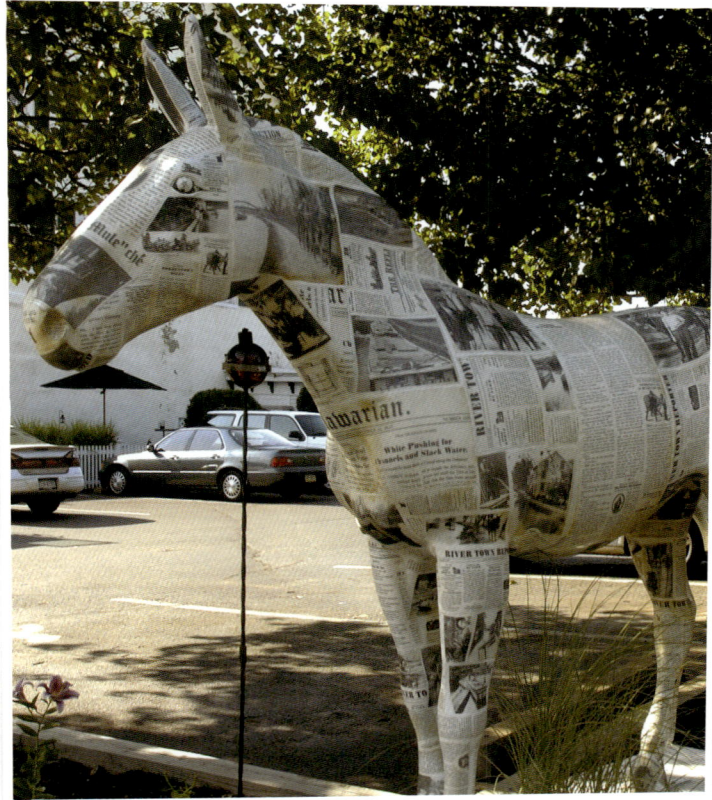

NEWSPAPIER-"MULE"CHÉ
NEWTOWN, PA

The artist found existing newspaper accounts of the canal region, transferred the text to fabric and dressed the mule in "prose clothes!"

Artist: Andrea L. Means
Sponsor: Rita's Ices, Cones, Shakes and Other Cool Stuff

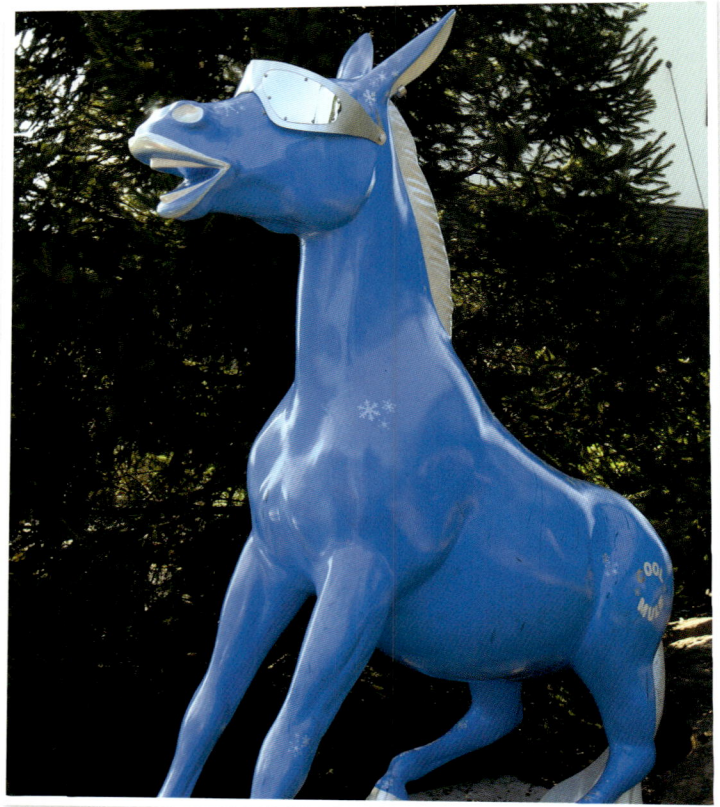

COOL MULE
NEWTOWN, PA

The artist indulged her sense of play with Cool Mule – a perfect match for its sponsor, makers of a popular summertime treat!

Artist: Judy Kieta LaTorre
Sponsor: Community Welfare Council of Newtown, Inc., thanks to
Stuckert & Yates, Attorneys

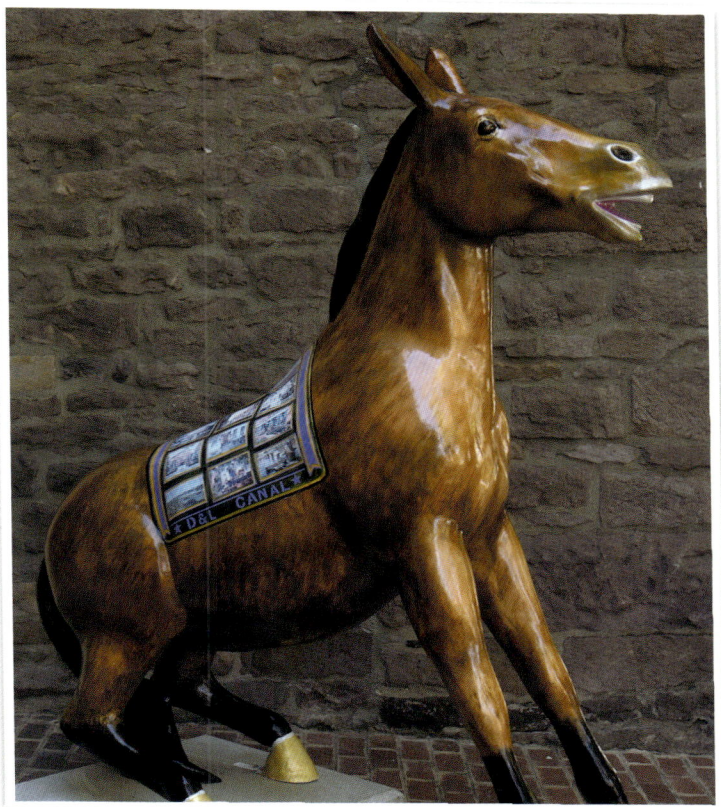

Artist: Glenn Harrington
Sponsor: Deep Run Partners

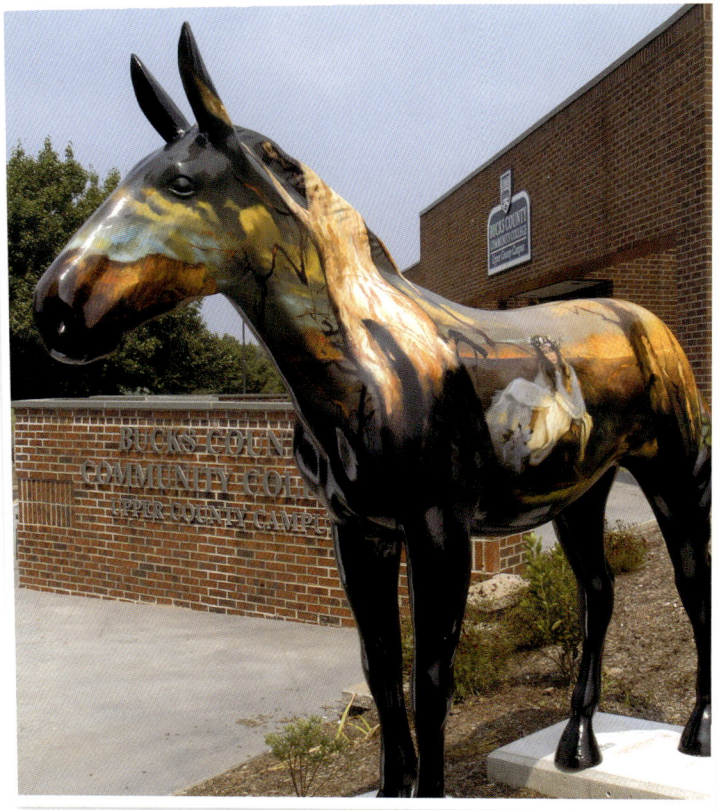

MARSHALL LAW

NEWTOWN, PA

Featuring images of the artist's paintings of Newtown, this mule
is a tribute to the historic town's character and charm.

BOTTOM, A MIDSUMMER NIGHT'S DREAM

PERKASIE, PA

Drawing on the rich heritage of the theater in Bucks County, the
artist painted diaphanous characters from the Shakespearean play
into existing scenes from today's canal.

Artist: Stephen C. Swayne
Sponsor: Hugh A. Marshall Landscape Contractor, Inc.

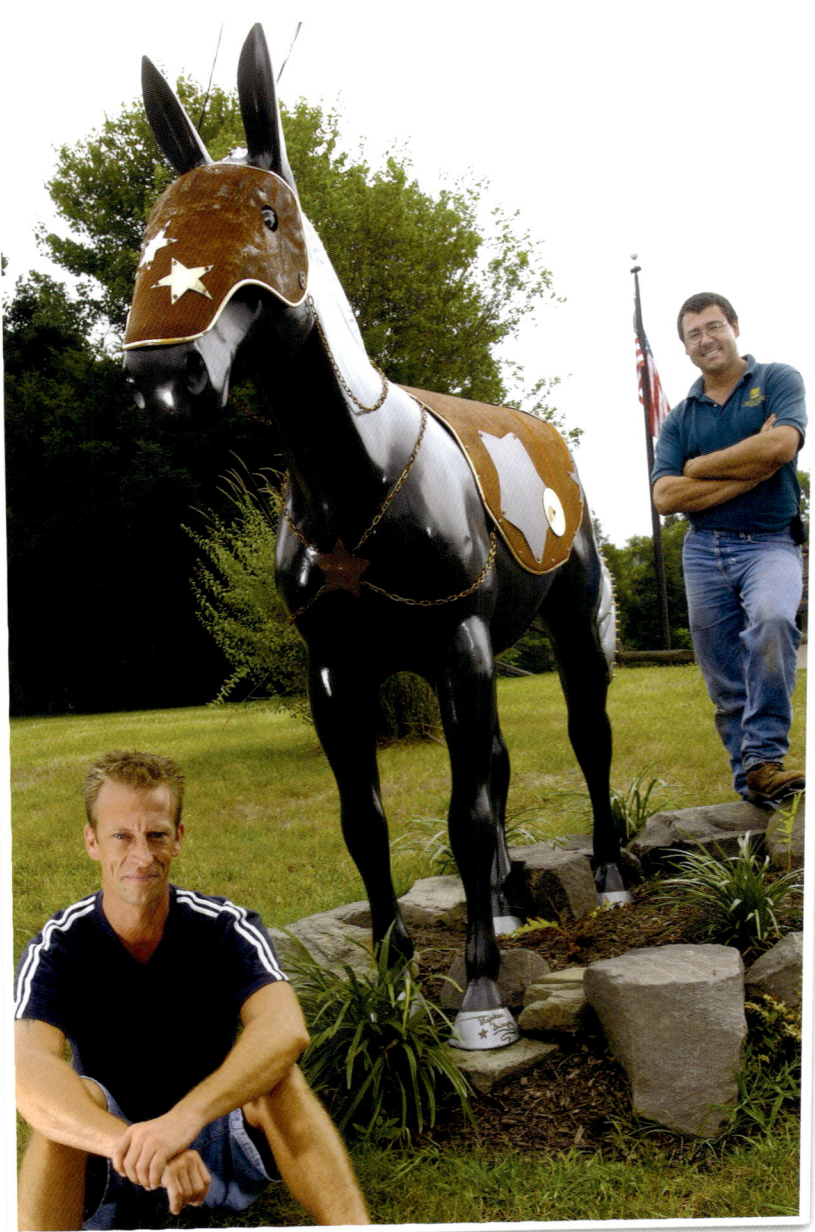

Artist: Stephen C. Swayne (foreground); Sponsor: Hugh A. Marshall

Sir Night
NEW HOPE, PA

This spring and summer, landscape contractor and long-time Michener Art Museum supporter Hugh A. Marshall volunteered his time and crew (which included artist Stephen C. Swayne) to install the 73 mules in the Southern Corral of the **Miles of Mules** project.

Several weeks into the work, one of the Museum's unpainted mules blew over in a wind storm. The fiberglass beast incurred severe damage and was thought to be unsalvageable. But Swayne, who does metal sculpture when he isn't land-scaping at Marshall's company, offered to fix the fallen mule and transform him into something powerful.

Marshall became the mule's sponsor and Swayne began the work. To conceal the cracks, Swayne created a helmet to cover the animal's face, then a steel sheath to cover its back. Stars and a moon were painted on the mule's dark body and it was dubbed *Sir Night*.

In addition to landscaping, an ambitious Swayne was installing mules and concrete bases in Bucks County by day and then returning to his studio at night to revitalize *Sir Night,* a task he amazingly completed in less than two weeks.

Marshall's contributions to the Museum are many: he maintains the grounds, is an active member of the Corporate Business Partner Advisory Board and creates spectacular lobby displays for special Museum events.

"...transform him into something powerful."

Artist: Glenna Lange Bye
Sponsor: Sigety Family Foundation

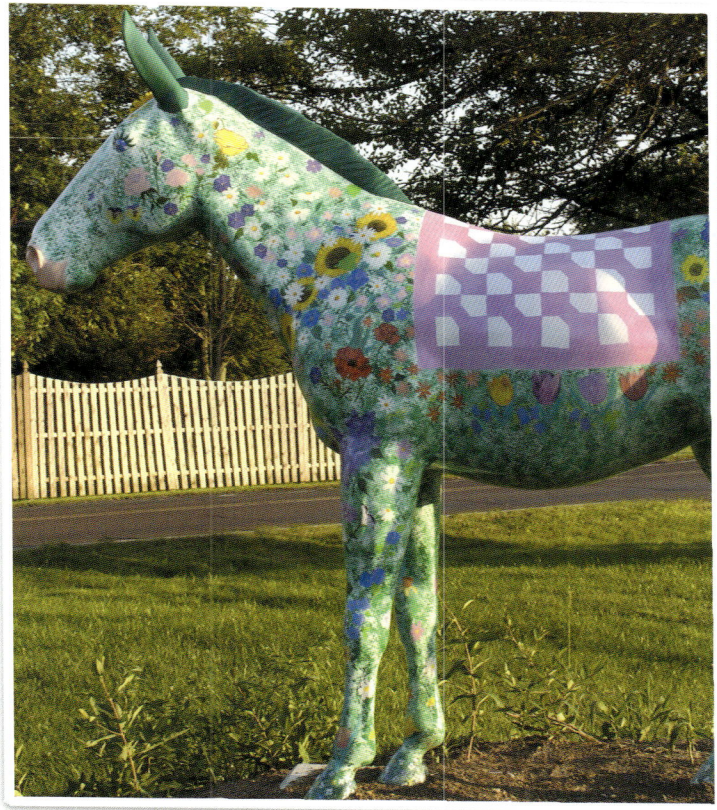

Artist: Plumstead Christian School Students
Sponsor: Plumstead Christian School, thanks to Millham Companies

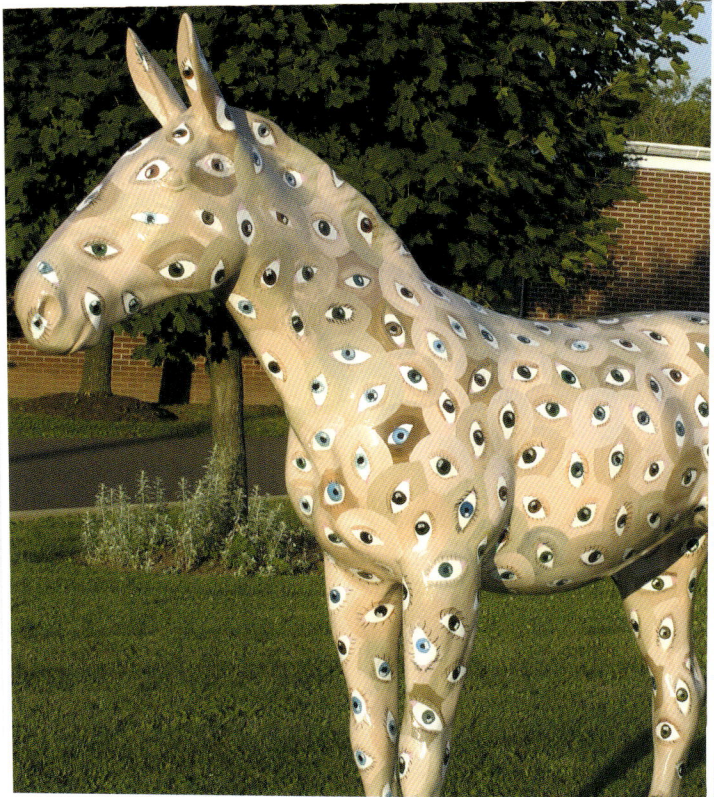

POSEY
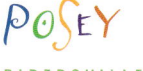

PIPERSVILLE, PA

Bucks County is known for beautiful landscapes and colorful country gardens and this mule is a delightful tribute to the region's flora, marked by abundant color and vivid detail.

EYE-ORE

PLUMSTEADVILLE, PA

The eyes are windows to the soul. Each eye is unique; together they reflect a multitude of perspectives.

Artist: Melinda Rizzo
Sponsor: Upper Bucks Chamber of Commerce, thanks to Red Lion Inn

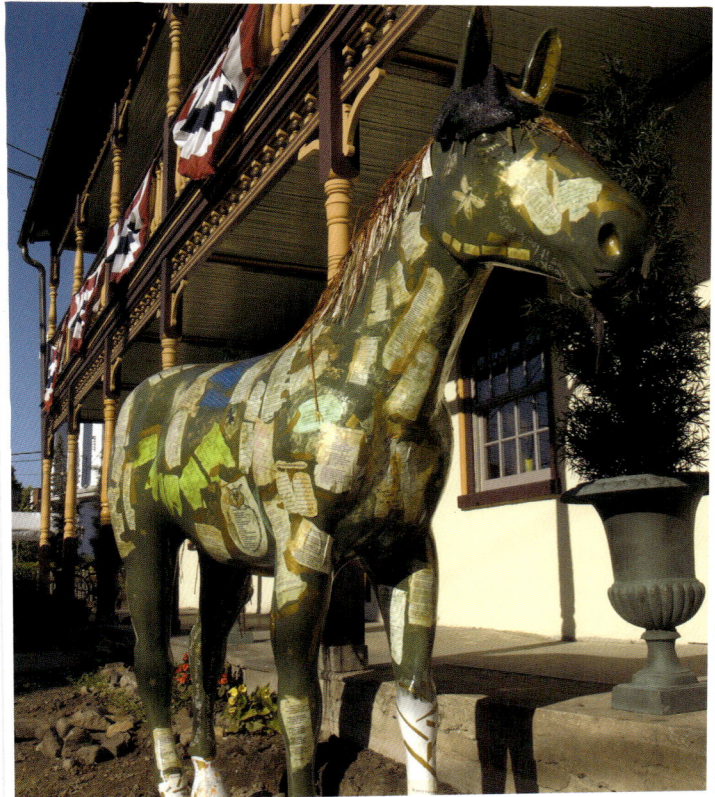

Artist: Quakertown Community High School Students
Sponsor: Main Street Theatre, thanks to Quakertown Art League

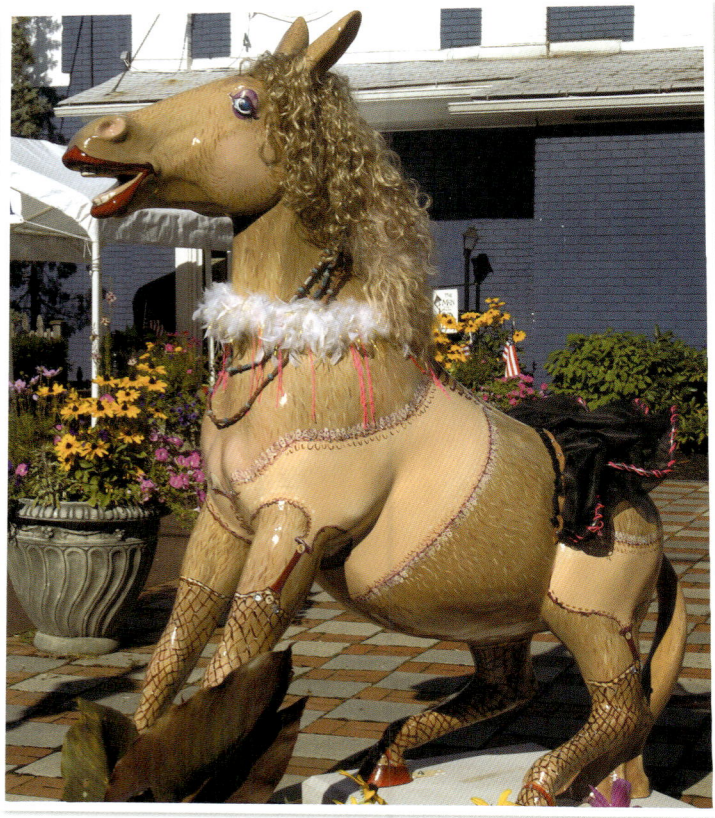

CLAUDE THEPOETRYCOOLMULE

QUAKERTOWN, PA

This is a visual expression of a poetic body of work, from the curve of its neck and mane to the actual letters on its body.

MULEON ROUGE

QUAKERTOWN, PA

Inspired by the Paris of Toulouse-Lautrec (and the movies!), this mule sports the trademark short skirt and fishnet stockings of the famed Parisian nightclub dancers.

Artist: Karen S. Sauter
Sponsor: Children's Developmental Program, thanks to Quaker Color

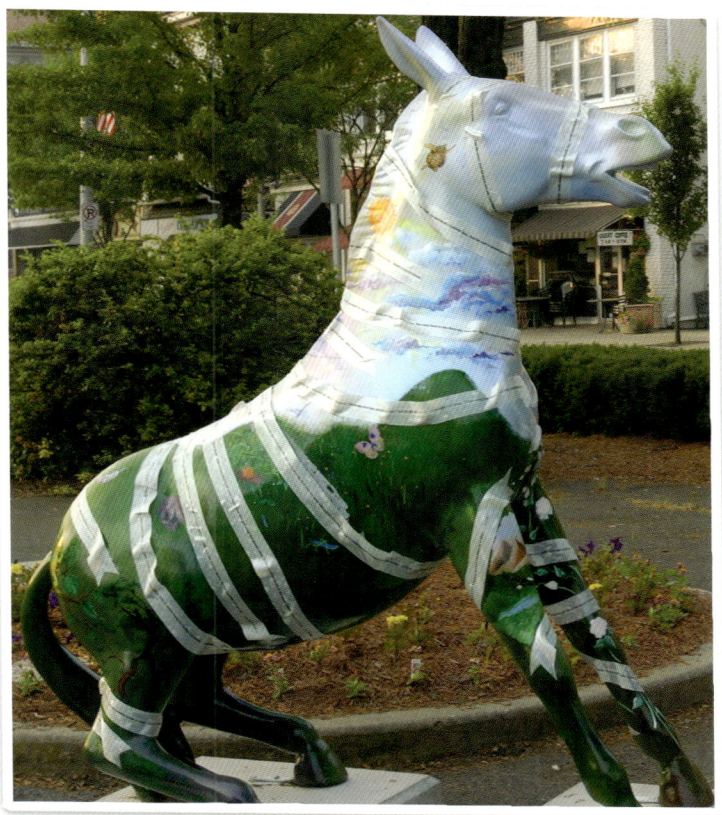

Artist: Quakertown Community High School Students
Sponsor: Quakertown Community High School, thanks to Quakertown National Bank

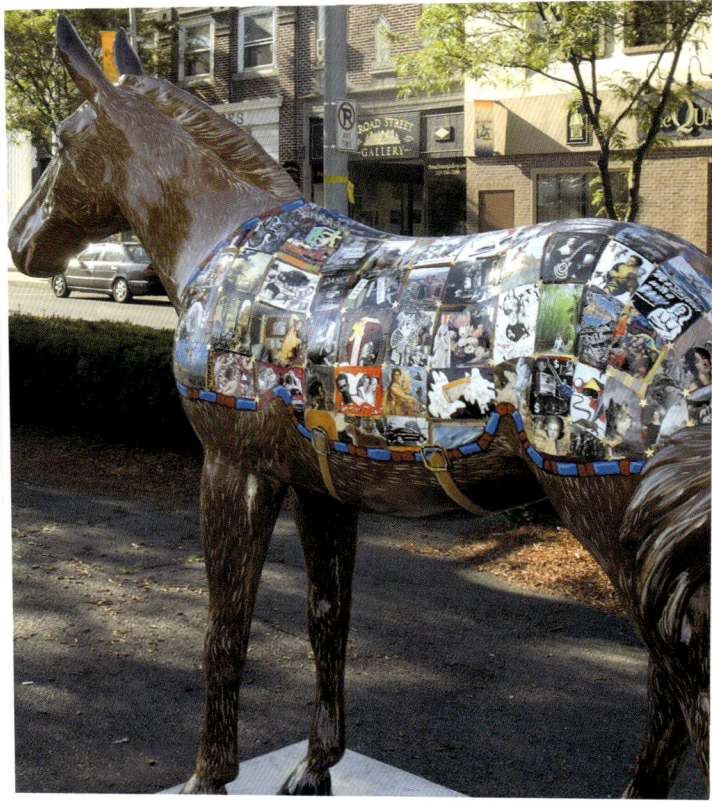

MY CHILD'S EYE
QUAKERTOWN, PA

Designed to be a storybook tour through the eyes of a child, the mule is painted with excerpts from Sauter's favorite children's stories on a background of magical landscapes.

THE HOPE MULESEUM
QUAKERTOWN, PA

Students were asked to combine a famous work of art with their individual hopes for the future in this concept created by art teacher Lynn Kraft.

Artist: Ginny Lee and Lavinia Louise
Sponsor: Penn-Jersey Educational Radio, thanks to WDVR

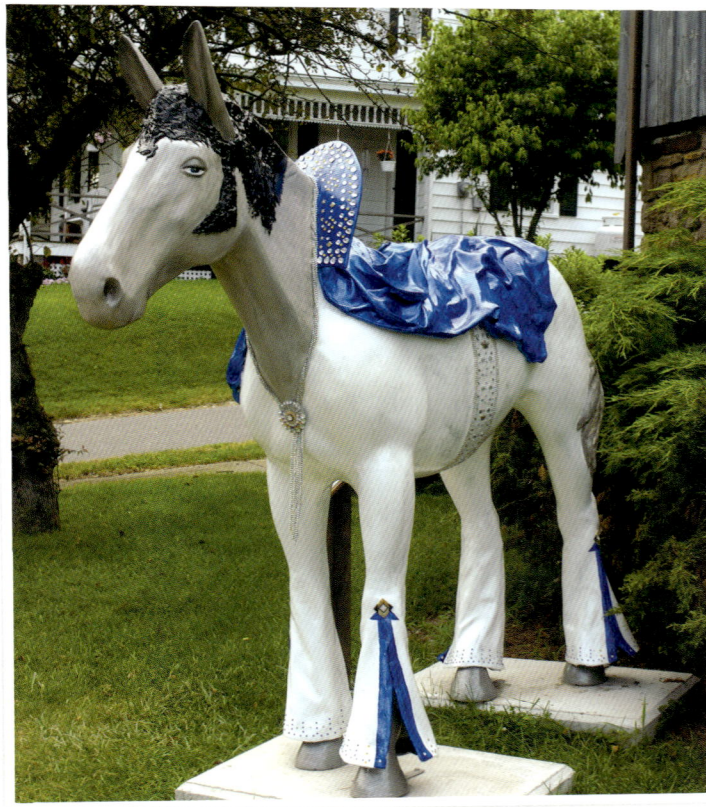

Artist: Jay Baldwin
Sponsor: Upper Makefield Township

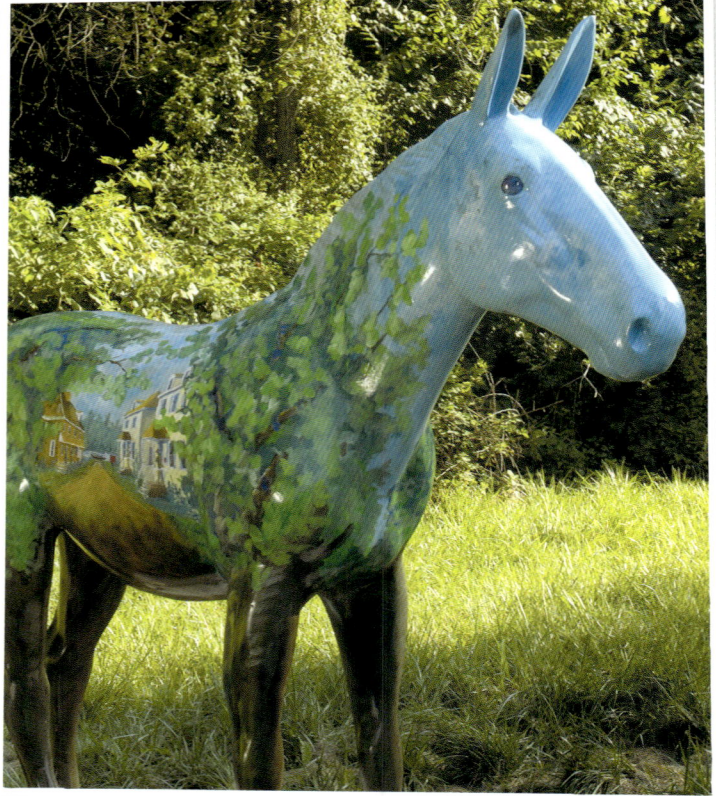

MULELVIS
SERGEANTSVILLE, NJ

Viva Las Mules! Fun-loving sisters who work at the unique community radio station WDVR in Sergeantsville designed this tongue-in-cheek tribute to the King of Rock n' Roll.

TAYLOR'S MULE
TAYLORSVILLE, PA

Standing sentry on Taylorsville Road, this mule reflects the history of Washington Crossing, where George Washington made his famous river crossing to battle the British in December 1776.

Artist: Amanda Penecale
Sponsor: Animal Rescue and Referral, Newtown/Richboro,
thanks to Friends and Family of the Artist

Artist: Quarry Hill Elementary Students
Sponsor: A gift to the Borough of Yardley from the
Yardley Business Association

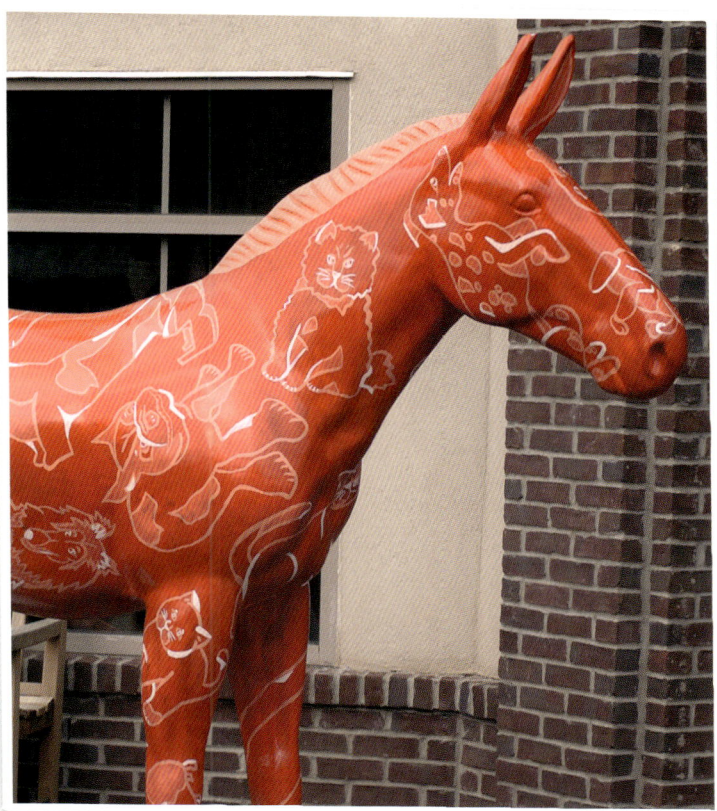

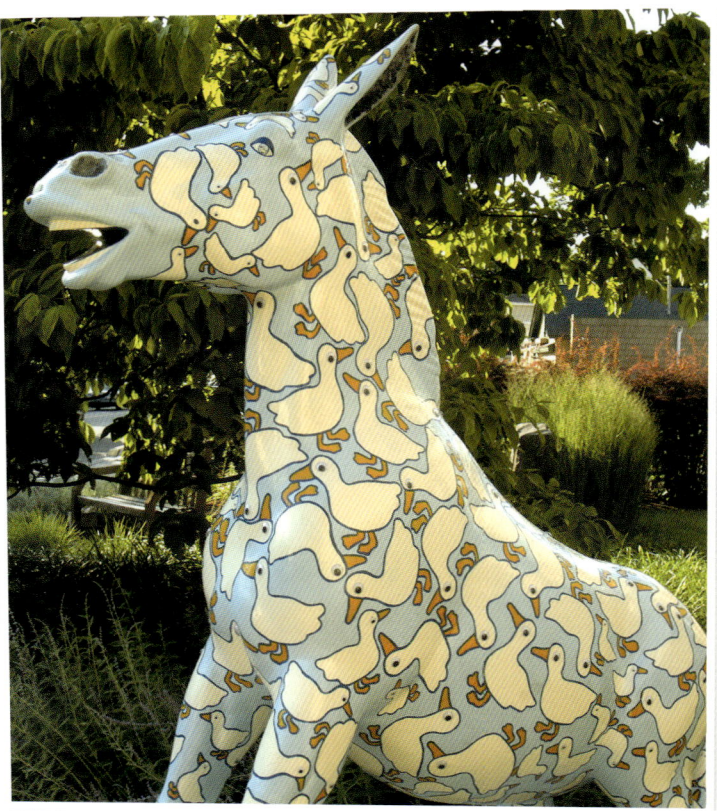

ANIMALS WITH HOPE

NEW HOPE, PA

The artist, a sophomore at the Rhode Island School of Design who works in many media, was motivated to create this whimsical design by her love of animals.

QUACKER JACK

YARDLEY, PA

Students from the third, fourth and fifth grades contributed to this creation, which celebrates the lively and often vociferous ducks on Lake Afton in Yardley.

Artist: Diane Keller
Sponsor: Russell Byers Charter School, thanks to Russell Byers,
Alexander M. Byers and Alison Byers

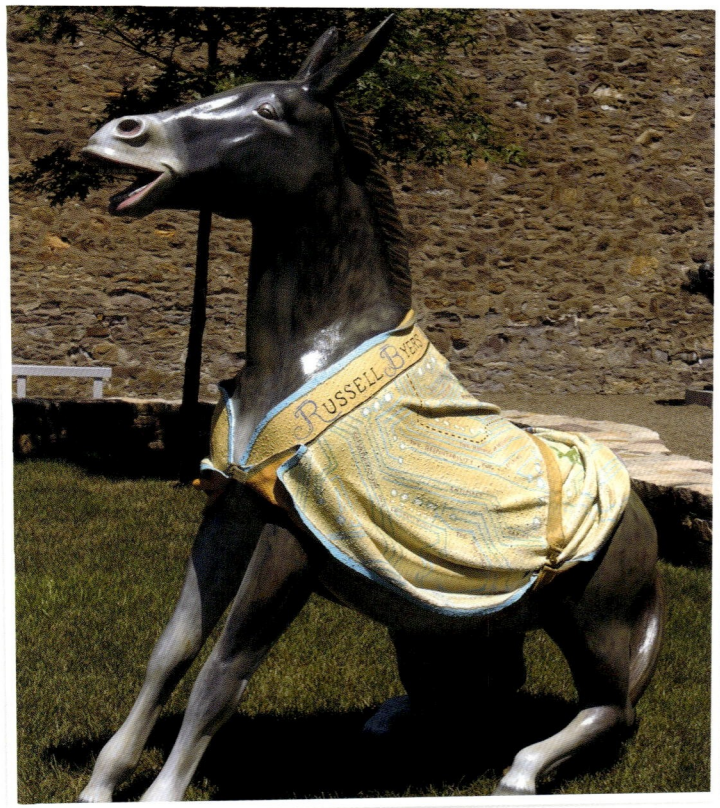

R U READY: EXPEDITION LEADER

WASHINGTON CROSSING, PA

The Russell Byers Charter School is based on expeditionary learning, so this concept incorporates a computer circuit board as a map that students can use to explore and find information.

Artist: R. Louisa Wismer
Sponsor: None Such Farm Market and the Yerkes Family

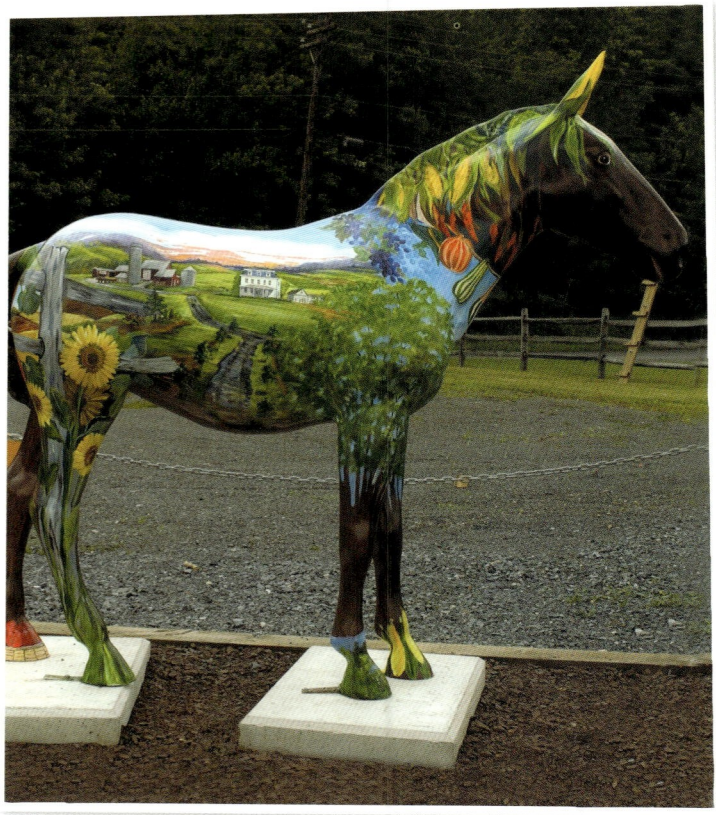

FARM PRESERVATION MULE

BUCKINGHAM, PA

Memories of her son tending a mule barge, her love of the Bucks County landscape and her passion to preserve open space inspired this artist's depiction of Bucks County farm life.

Artist: Pete and Jennifer Miller
Sponsor: Habitat for Humanity, Bucks County Chapter,
thanks to Stone House Furniture, Inc.

Artist: John McDowell Williams
Sponsor: Applebee's Neighborhood Grill & Bar

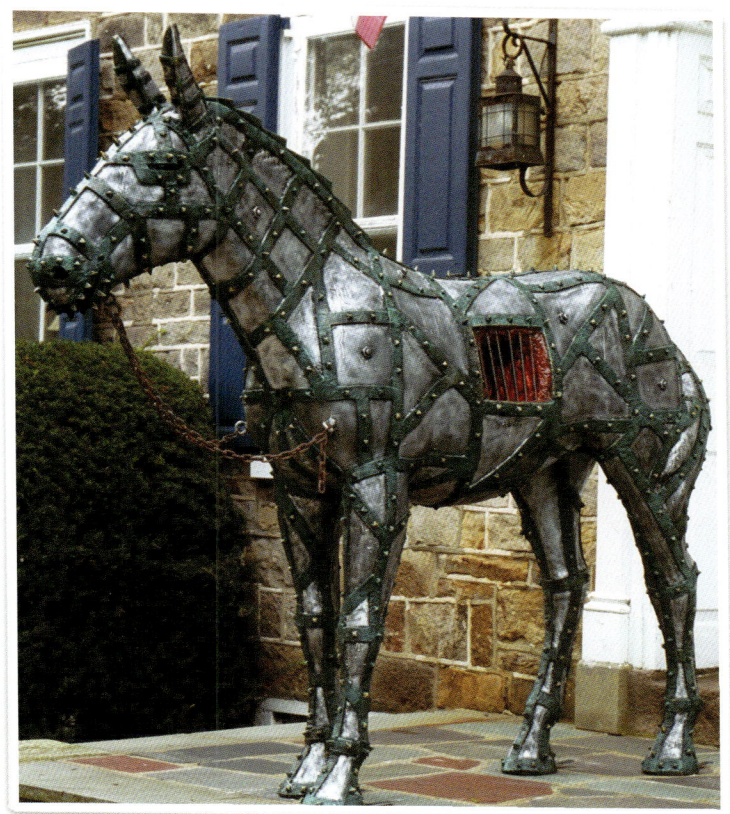

Photo by Jared Polin

SALVAGED
MECHANICSVILLE, PA

The product of a collaboration between husband and wife, this design consists of defensive metal hardware protecting a vulnerable, jeweled "heart of gold."

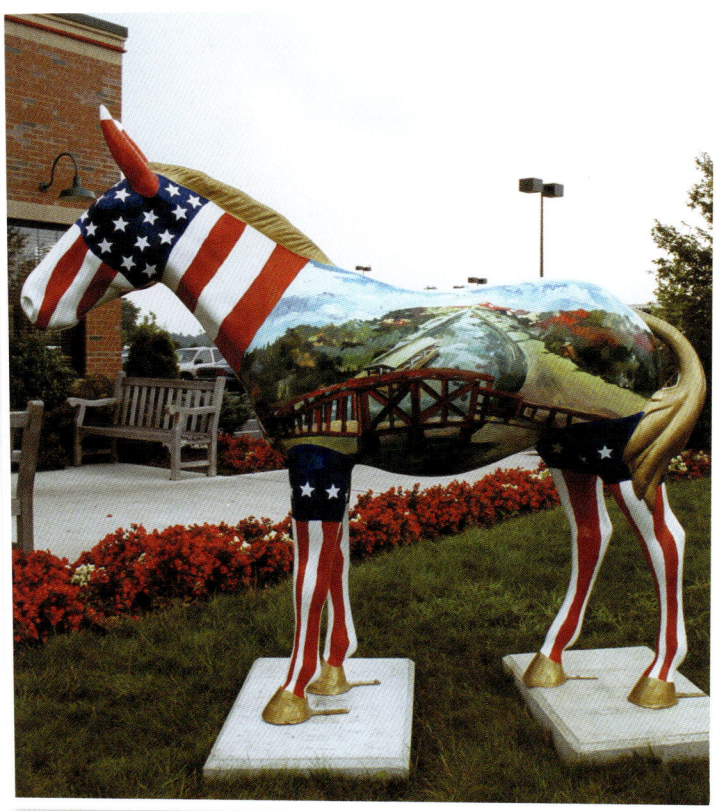

Photo by Jared Polin

THE AMERICAN MULE
NEWTOWN, PA

Inspired by the canal and its commerce, the artist painted scenes of canal life on the mule's body and included elements of Americana on the head and legs.

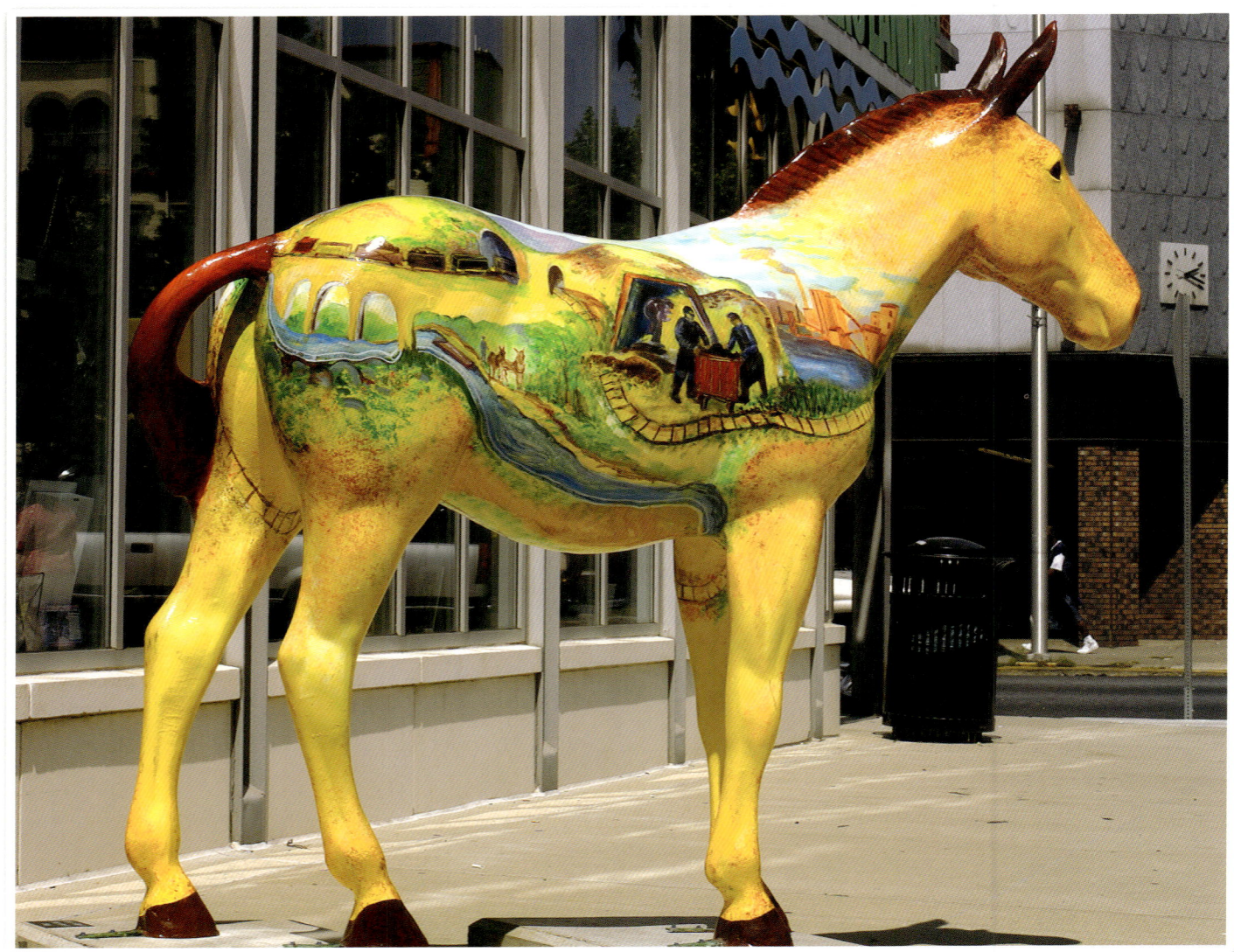

tHANKS A MULE-iOn

EASTON, PA

Artist: Kathy Bruce
Sponsor: Delaware & Lehigh National Heritage Corridor

Thanks a Mule-ion was the last art-decorated fiberglass mule produced, sponsored by the Delaware & Lehigh National Heritage Corridor. It is a symbol of appreciation to the many contributors and supporters of this public art project.

tHANKS A MULE-iON

A SPECIAL THANKS GOES TO:

The D & L staff, for their assistance and support; our art partners: the James A. Michener Art Museum, The Banana Factory, and the Cultural Council of Luzerne County for their help making this a spectacular public art exhibit; Pennsylvania Department of Conservation and Natural Resources for their vision and funding assistance; the sponsors of our 175 mules; the artists who gave the project life through their creative expressions; the D & L Mule Tenders, volunteers, residents and visitors of the Corridor; Oxford Communications in Lambertville, N.J., for public relations, website, brochure, book design and editing; Workhorse Design, Inc., in Lehighton, Pa., for the logo, sponsorship brochure and letterhead; and the Hugh Moore Historical Park and Museum archives in Easton, Pa., for the historical photographs.

Together, we really gave our communities a "Kick in the Arts."

C. Allen Sachse
Executive Director
Delaware & Lehigh NHC

Rayne R. Schnabel
Miles of Mules Coordinator
Delaware & Lehigh NHC

DET★ILS

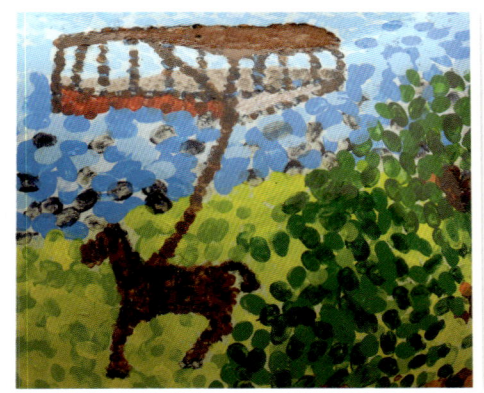
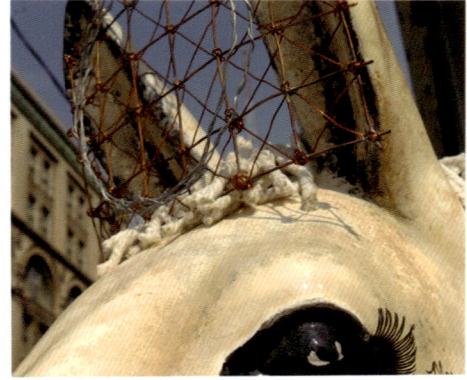
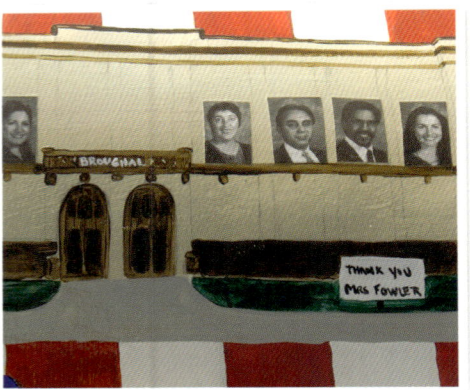
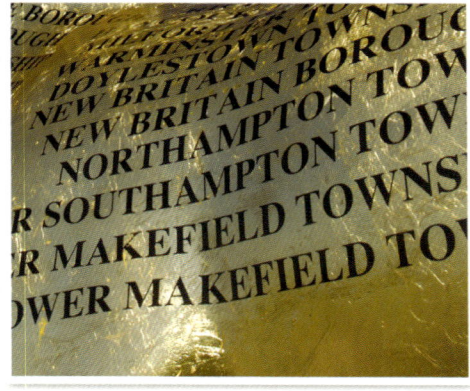
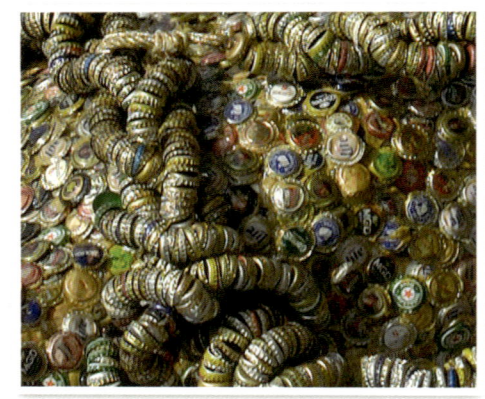
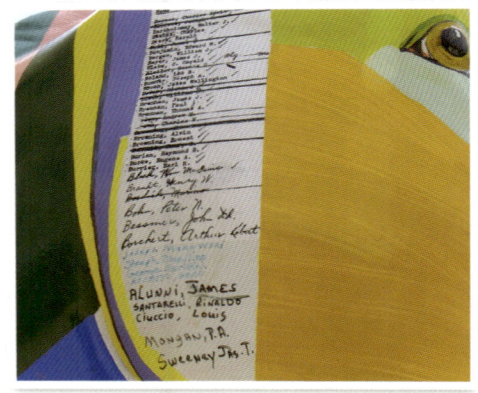
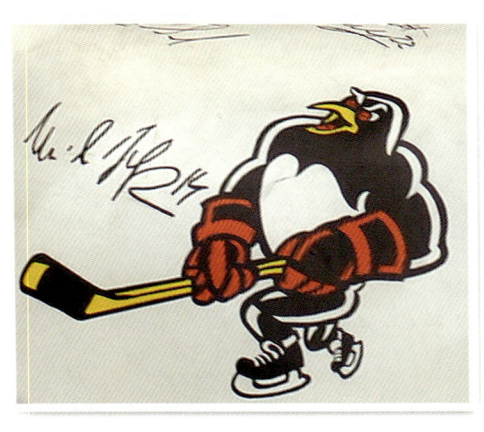
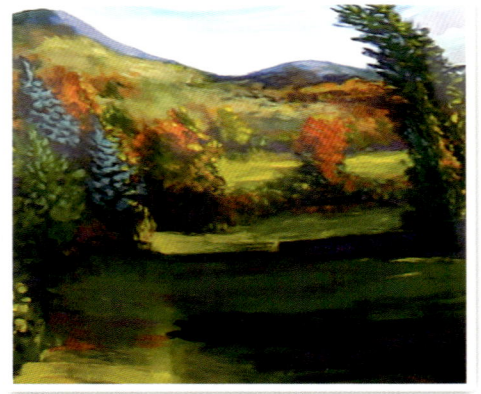
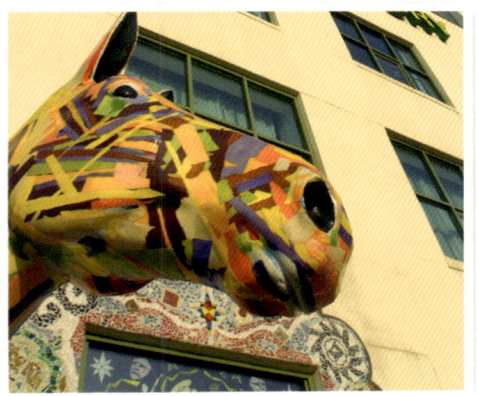